to

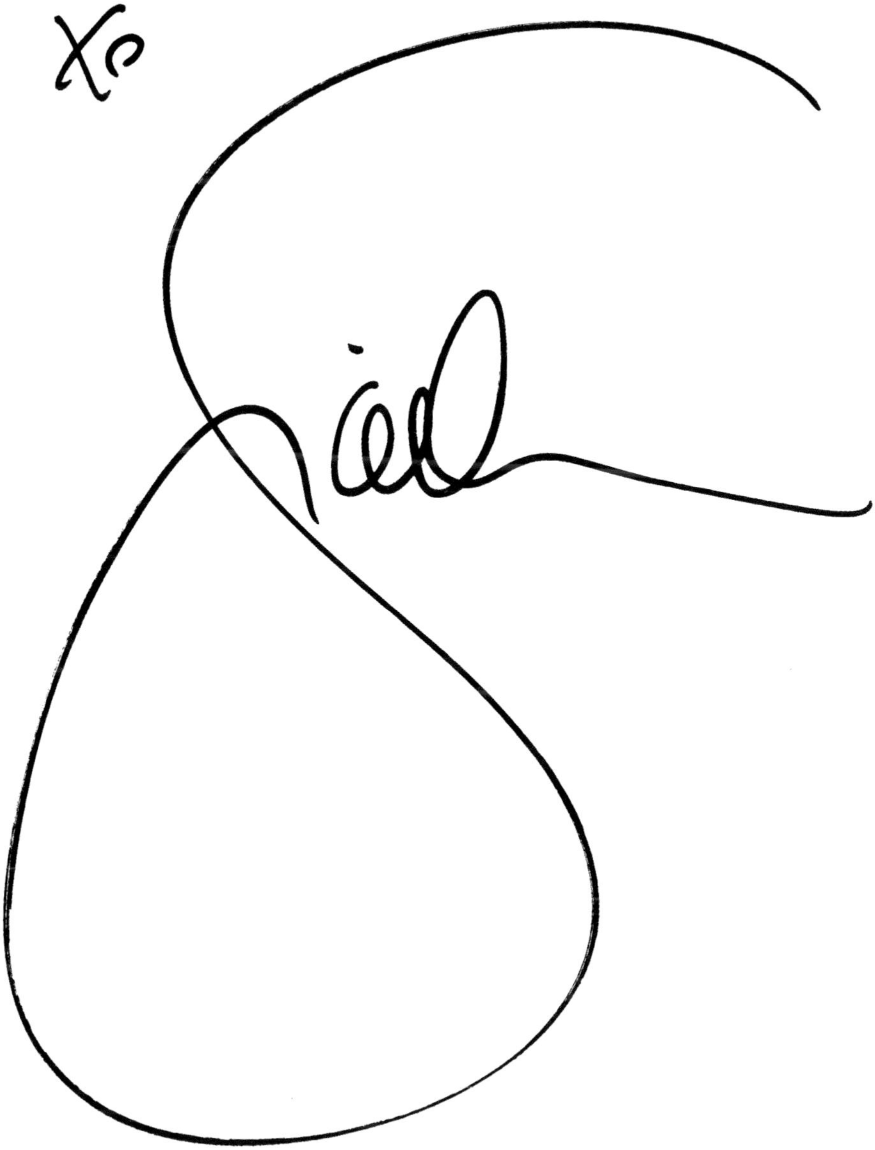

HAPPY cooking

Giada De Laurentiis

HAPPY cooking

Make Every Meal Count . . . Without Stressing Out

PAM KRAUSS BOOKS
NEW YORK

Published in the United States by Pam Krauss Books,
an imprint of the Crown Publishing Group,
a division of Penguin Random House LLC, New York.
www.crownpublishing.com

Portions of this work were previously published in *Giada*, the digital magazine,
between August 2013 and the present.

Library of Congress Cataloging-in-Publication Data
De Laurentiis, Giada.
Happy Cooking / Giada De Laurentiis. — First edition.
1. Cooking. I. Title.
TX714.D42325 2015
641.5—dc23 2015022028

ISBN 978-0-8041-8792-3
eBook ISBN 978-0-8041-8793-0

Printed in the United States of America

Book design by Amy Sly
Jacket design by Amy Sly
Front Jacket photography by Lauren Volo and Megan Fawn Schlow
A complete list of photography credits appears on page 302.

10 9 8 7 6 5 4 3 2 1

First Edition

For Jade, and all the
mommy-daughter
adventures yet to come.

Contents

Introduction

As I sat down to start compiling material for this, my eighth cookbook, I couldn't help thinking about all the significant milestones reflected in the pages of each book I've published, starting with *Everyday Italian*. Every few years my life takes a big turn—getting married, making my debut on Food Network, publishing my first cookbook, and, of course, becoming a mother to my amazing daughter, Jade—and all those changes and transitions inevitably impact the way I think about food, cooking, and entertaining. And it's reflected in the food that ends up between the covers of my books.

This one is no different. The past year has been a particularly big time of change for me, and on so many levels I'm starting a new chapter in my life, one that is exciting in some ways—and challenging in others. The sadness that comes with ending my marriage of more than twenty years is balanced by the joy I take in watching Jade come into her own as a strong and creative young lady and the adrenaline rush of launching my restaurant in Las Vegas as well as a digital magazine, a bold new venture that allows me to connect to my readers every week, in real time.

All of these factors have made me take another look at how I want to live and eat on a daily basis, and how the food I cook fits into an overall approach to wellness that works for me. I don't have all the answers, but the questions fascinate me, and I happen to think a lot of people are on the same journey that I am. These life passages have also encouraged me to take a good, hard look at what's important to me and how I want to spend my time, as well as what truly makes me happy. And eight cookbooks and countless episodes of television later I realized there is no place I feel more at ease, more grounded, and more completely myself than in the kitchen. It's where

I can express my creativity, make important memories (and share life skills) with my daughter, and quiet all the noise of the outside world as I lose myself in the pure pleasure of making something beautiful and delicious. I am, quite simply, happy cooking.

For me, cooking is also a way of being good to myself and the people I cook for. Of course this will mean different things to different people, or even different things on different days, and that's fine. For me, being good to myself means eating clean and healthy as often as I can, but making sure that I enjoy every bite. And when I do indulge in something that tips the scales in the other direction, then it had most definitely better be worth it. I'm not the first to say it, but eating well truly is about balance, not sacrifice. Living without the foods that I love, that make me happy, is not something I'm willing to do. That said, I've learned there are some foods that I love that just don't love me back. In those cases, eliminating those foods from my diet, as well as the bloating or discomfort that results when I eat them, is another way I'm good to myself. No doubt your daily menus won't look exactly like mine and that's okay. Life is not one size fits all; I'm here to give you options, all of them delicious. And speaking of size, being good to yourself is not about achieving some elusive "perfect" weight, and eating healthy for me is not, and never has been, about dropping pounds. It's about fueling my high-performance life efficiently and beautifully with meals that respect the traditions of my Italian heritage and the tried-and-true flavor combinations that I have learned people love. After all, food can be powerful medicine, but eating shouldn't be reduced to science.

As a single mom, I'm now also more focused than ever before on simplicity and convenience and finding ways to ensure as much of the time I spend with my daughter is filled with fun and happy memories. Sometimes that means planning ahead so there are leftovers ready to repurpose into virtually instant meals on busy weeknights; other times that means standing side by side at the kitchen counter as we make an over-the-top dessert. Either way, knowing that the food Jade is eating is home-cooked, wholesome, and gives her the fuel she needs to grow and thrive...well, nothing makes me happier than that.

It's my hope that this book, like *Giada Weekly*, my digital magazine (in which many of these recipes appeared originally), is more like a conversation, one that provides practical solutions for the everyday situations—or big events—that arise throughout the year and help you to navigate them with ease and without stress. Whether you're packing a lunch for yourself or a child, making a quiet dinner for one, looking to eat a bit cleaner to get your digestion back on track, or hosting a holiday gathering, you'll find ideas here to get you through without feeling like a short order cook. With luck you'll come across a new ingredient, technique, or shortcut that will expand your horizons and help you get more satisfaction out of the time you spend in the kitchen. I've also been fortunate to have many exceptional people in my life who have helped and influenced me over the years, from my dear aunt Raffy to fellow chefs and food purveyors, and I'm thrilled to have a way to shine a spotlight on some of them as well.

With nearly 200 recipes here to choose from and plenty of hard-won advice on entertaining and choosing ingredients that deliver flavor without fuss, this is my biggest book yet. And it's my hope that the recipes and information I've gathered will help make feeding yourself and your dear ones as pleasurable as possible. Happy cooking!

xo Giada

A NOTE ABOUT THE RECIPES IN THIS BOOK

Because I know many of my readers are dealing with food sensitivities and allergies—either their own or those of the people they cook for—I have indicated throughout the book which recipes are gluten-free (GF) as well as those that are vegetarian (V) or vegan (V). However, those on special diets should be especially careful to read labels on all packaged foods, as many contain unwanted ingredients, including gluten and animal products, where they are least expected. This applies to things such as oats, rice, wild rice, almond paste, soy sauce, and packaged broths, among others, so always shop with care and cook with whole, unprocessed foods as much as you can.

FIRST THINGS FIRST

#breakfast

Weekdays or weekends, it pays to devote a bit of extra attention to the first meal of the day. Not only does it set the nutritional tone for the day, but in the case of brunch or a lazy weekend breakfast, it's a way to start out on an upbeat note that will carry you through all day long. Not a bad payoff for spending just ten or fifteen more minutes in the kitchen than it takes to toast a frozen waffle. (Not that there's anything wrong with that—especially if it's one of my polenta waffles that you made ahead and stashed in the freezer.)

In this chapter, you'll find better, smarter alternatives to standard grab-and-go fare that will leave everyone feeling more satisfied and energized throughout the day. Think like a chef and do much of the prep work—chopping veggies and fruit, mixing batters—the night before so making breakfast is as easy as firing up the stove and looking like a star. You'll start the day with a smile on your face and with a happier metabolism, too.

Drink to Your Health

Where would we be without our blenders in the a.m.? The sweet, cold notes of smoothies and fresh juices are a refreshing way to start the day. They are also quick to make and easy to pack with wholesome, good-for-you, whole-food ingredients that leave processed drinks in the dust. And then there's the color factor. Deep, bright fruit and vegetable colors give these drinks not only their tempting looks but also a giant nutritional boost. Bonus: The water and fiber help fill you up and may help you ward off the temptation of other less virtuous snacks. Make it easy on yourself by cutting fresh fruits in chunks and freezing them so all you need to do in the morning is fill your blender and push puree!

Pineapple-Ginger Smoothie

V V GF

SERVES 4

The next time you buy fresh pineapple, store any leftovers in the freezer. To partially thaw the pineapple chunks, microwave them on high for twenty to thirty seconds.

2 cups frozen unsweetened pineapple chunks, partially thawed
1 orange, peeled, seeded, and quartered
1 (1-inch) piece of fresh ginger, peeled and chopped
3 tablespoons fresh lemon juice (from 2 lemons)
Dash of cayenne pepper (optional)

Put the pineapple, orange quarters, ginger, and lemon juice in a blender. Add ½ cup ice, 1 cup cold water, and the cayenne, if using. Puree until smooth and serve immediately.

Pineapple-Ginger Smoothie

Orange Is the New Healthy

Orange Is the New Healthy

V V GF

SERVES 2

Fresh ginger and turmeric give this orange-carrot blend a slight kick. Turmeric gives Indian food its orange-yellow color, and it's also packed with antioxidant and anti-inflammatory properties.

1 cup fresh carrot juice
¾ cup freshly squeezed orange juice
2 teaspoons fresh ginger juice (see Cook's Note)
⅛ teaspoon ground turmeric

In a small pitcher, stir together the carrot juice, orange juice, ginger juice, and turmeric. Pour half of the mixture into a shaker filled with ice and shake for 30 seconds. Strain into a large glass. Repeat with the remaining juice.

Cook's Note: **To make ginger juice, use a Microplane grater to grate peeled fresh ginger into a fine-mesh strainer set over a bowl. Press on the ginger to squeeze the juice through the strainer. Discard the pulp.**

Cool Green Smoothie

V V GF

SERVES 1

Ginger lends a bit of zing to this energizing drink, which can be served as is, like a smoothie, or strained for a more juice-like beverage.

1 (1½-inch) piece of fresh ginger, peeled and chopped
1 Bartlett pear, cored and chopped
2 cups baby spinach
2 tablespoons fresh mint leaves
2 tablespoons fresh lemon juice (from 1 lemon)
1 cup coconut water
½ cup ice
⅛ teaspoon kosher salt

To the pitcher of a blender add the ginger, pear, spinach, mint, lemon juice, coconut water, ice, and salt. Puree on high for 2 minutes, scraping down the sides of the blender as needed.

Cool Green Smoothie

BPA FREE
LTRS
MAX
CUPS

BPA FREE
CUPS

Aw, Nuts

There are plenty of good reasons to swap in alternative milks for the good old dairy milk we all grew up drinking. Sensitivities to dairy products are a reality for many people, and environmental issues, as well as the movement to treat farm animals ethically, have persuaded lots of us to look for more sustainable alternatives to animal products, including dairy foods. And plenty of people simply prefer the flavor of alt milks on their cereal or in their coffee.

You'll find a huge variety of nondairy milks to choose from in even the most mainstream grocery stores these days. Soy and almond milks are the most common, but you'll also find milks made from oats, rice, coconut, or hemp. Personally, I've never been able to warm up to the flavor of hemp milk despite the fact that it packs a decent punch of omega-3s; I've always gravitated to the nut milks for their subtle flavor and because they are lower in carbs and more nutritious than options like rice milk.

Before you start loading up your cart, though, one caveat: Alt milks that you buy at the store should really be considered a processed food. Take a look at the label; chances are you will see ingredients that you don't recognize or necessarily want in your diet, like gums, added sugars, and that suspicious catchall, "natural flavors." If you haven't tried making nut milk at home, though, I bet you'll be surprised by how easy it is. Just soak 1 cup of nuts—almonds, hazelnuts, cashews—overnight, then drain and puree with 3 cups of water. Strain and chill. The ground nuts can be dried and toasted to use in baking, granola, or salads, too!

"Nutella" Milk

"Nutella" Milk

V V GF

MAKES ABOUT 3 CUPS

This tastes like a treat but is only lightly sweetened.

1 cup unpeeled hazelnuts
2 tablespoons unsweetened cocoa powder
2 tablespoons agave syrup
¼ teaspoon kosher salt
¼ teaspoon pure vanilla extract

Place the hazelnuts in a bowl and add enough filtered water to cover the nuts by 1 inch. Soak the hazelnuts overnight or for at least 12 hours.

Drain the nuts and rinse well under cold water. Transfer the nuts to a blender and add 3 cups filtered water. Puree on high for 2 minutes. Add the cocoa powder, agave, salt, and vanilla and puree for about 1 minute longer or until smooth.

Strain the mixture through a fine-mesh strainer lined with cheesecloth. Serve immediately or refrigerate for up to 3 days.

Raffy's Healthy Granola

MAKES ABOUT 8 CUPS

A favorite breakfast treat in my family, this granola is made with agave for just a touch of sweetness. Add a few spoonfuls of granola to yogurt. Sprinkle some on top of muffin batter before baking them. Put some broken pieces into waffle or pancake batter.

1 teaspoon safflower or flaxseed oil
3 cups rolled oats
1 cup dried cranberries, chopped
¾ cup raw almonds, coarsely chopped
¾ cup hazelnuts, coarsely chopped
¾ cup sunflower seeds
¾ cup pepitas (pumpkin seeds)
¾ cup flaxseeds
1½ teaspoons kosher salt
1½ teaspoons ground cinnamon
¾ cup agave syrup

Place 2 racks in the upper and middle thirds of the oven and preheat the oven to 400°F. Lightly grease 2 rimmed baking sheets with the oil.

In a large bowl, combine the oats, cranberries, almonds, hazelnuts, sunflower seeds, pepitas, flaxseeds, salt, and cinnamon. Add the agave and ¾ cup water and toss well to moisten the dry ingredients evenly. Divide the mixture between the baking sheets and use the back of a spoon or a spatula to press the granola into an even layer about ½ inch thick.

Bake until golden, about 30 minutes, rotating the baking sheets halfway through.

Remove the baking sheets from the oven and use a spoon or spatula to lift and toss the granola on each one. Turn the heat off and return the baking sheets to the oven for about 2 hours to dry out the granola. Transfer the granola to airtight containers and store for up to a month.

Overnight Oats

SERVES 2

This porridge-like blend requires no cooking. It's easy to stir up before you go to bed; the next morning you can spoon some into a pack-along container, top with fruit and nuts, and be out the door in minutes.

1 cup rolled oats (not quick-cooking or instant)
1 tablespoon chia seeds
1¼ cups unsweetened almond milk
½ teaspoon pure vanilla extract
¼ teaspoon ground cinnamon
1 tablespoon pure maple syrup, grade B preferred
1 cup mixed berries or chopped stone fruit
¼ cup chopped raw almonds

In a medium bowl combine the oats, chia seeds, almond milk, vanilla, cinnamon, and maple syrup. Stir together with a rubber spatula. Cover and refrigerate overnight.

To serve, spoon into 2 bowls and top with the fruit and nuts.

Overnight Oats

Oatmeal with Olive Oil and Oranges

Oatmeal with Olive Oil and Oranges

(V) (V)

SERVES 4

A twist on traditional sweet oats, this savory variation uses extra-virgin olive oil and oranges in lieu of brown sugar. Olive oil is packed with heart-healthy monounsaturated fats to help stabilize blood sugar and control cravings throughout the day.

½ teaspoon fine salt
2 cups rolled oats
Grated zest of ½ lemon, or more to taste
1 teaspoon fresh thyme leaves, or more to taste, chopped
4 teaspoons extra-virgin olive oil
1 orange, peeled, seeded, and cut into segments (see Cook's Note, page 149)
¼ cup raw almonds, chopped

In a medium saucepan, bring 3½ cups water and the salt to a boil over medium heat. Add the oats and cook, stirring frequently, until creamy, 6 to 7 minutes. For a thicker consistency, cook for 1 to 2 minutes longer.

Stir in the lemon zest and thyme. Spoon the oatmeal into 4 bowls. Drizzle with the olive oil and top with the orange segments and almonds.

Pressure Cooker Oat, Barley, and Coconut Porridge

(V) (V)

SERVES 4 TO 6

Steel-cut oats are satisfyingly chewy, but they take too long to cook on a busy morning . . . unless you take a shortcut. My pals Bruce Weinstein and Mark Scarbrough are whizzes with a pressure cooker and shared their secret for making a satisfying hot cereal in less than twenty minutes. Be sure to use only steel-cut oats and pearled barley here, and add some sliced banana or mango to each bowl if you like.

1 cup pearled barley
1 cup steel-cut oats
⅔ cup unsweetened shredded coconut
⅔ cup (packed) light brown sugar
1 teaspoon ground ginger
½ teaspoon ground cardamom
½ teaspoon kosher salt

In a 6-quart pressure cooker, stir together the barley, oats, coconut, brown sugar, ginger, cardamom, and salt. Add 6 cups water and stir until the sugar dissolves. Lock the lid onto the pot and set over high heat. Bring the pot to high pressure (15 psi). Once this pressure is reached, reduce the heat as much as possible while keeping the pressure constant. Cook for 14 minutes.

Reduce the pressure. Remove the pot from the heat and let it sit for about 10 minutes or until its pressure falls to normal. If the pressure hasn't returned to normal within 12 minutes, use the quick-release method (check the manual that came with your appliance) to bring it back to normal. Unlock and open the lid; stir the porridge before serving.

Pressure Cooker Oat, Barley, and Coconut Porridge

Go with the Grains

To be at my best in the morning I keep my breakfast savory and full of healthy, slow-digesting whole grains. My go-to is good old oatmeal, but recently I've become partial to brown rice. The trick is to be smart about the toppings. Forget brown sugar, maple syrup, or even dried fruit. I often give mine a drizzle of olive oil and a sprinkle of salt. Or maybe some chopped nuts, fresh herbs, and a bit of fresh fruit—even a touch of pesto! These may sound weird at first, but once you've tried them you'll be hooked, and you'll love the way those sugar highs and lows disappear for good.

Here's a secret: Both brown rice and oatmeal reheat brilliantly and keep in the refrigerator for at least four or five days. So on the weekend, cook up a double or triple batch of plain oatmeal or rice, let it cool, and portion it out into covered containers. Stack 'em up in the fridge so you can grab one on your way out the door to reheat in the microwave. Keep a bottle of olive oil at your desk to add a tablespoon or bring a separate bag of savory toppings to sprinkle on each serving. To reheat the oatmeal, microwave it with an extra half cup or cup of water; it may seem too loose, but it will thicken up as it cools.

American Breakfast Rice Bowl

MAKES 1 BOWL

¾ scant cup cooked brown rice
1 recipe Maple Mustard Dressing (below)
½ cup cleaned and chopped escarole
1 recipe Bacon and Shallot mixture (below)
1 sunny-side up egg, seasoned with a pinch of kosher salt
Freshly ground black pepper
½ orange segmented (optional)

MAPLE MUSTARD DRESSING

½ teaspoon spicy mustard
2 teaspoons apple cider vinegar
2 teaspoons pure maple syrup, grade B preferred
1 tablespoon extra-virgin olive oil
⅛ teaspoon kosher salt

BACON AND SHALLOT

2 slices of applewood smoked bacon, cut into ½-inch pieces
1 shallot, diced

Place the brown rice in the bottom of a bowl. Drizzle with half of the dressing. Place the escarole in one corner of the bowl, on top of the rice. Drizzle with the other half of the dressing. Put the bacon and shallot mixture next to the escarole, and the cooked egg in the area that should be open. Top with a few cracks of black pepper and scatter the orange segments around, if using.

For Maple Mustard Dressing: In a medium bowl, whisk together the mustard, vinegar, maple syrup, olive oil, and salt.

For Bacon and Shallot mixture: Place the chopped bacon in a small skillet. Place the skillet over medium heat and cook the bacon, stirring often, for about 8 minutes or until most of the fat is rendered and the bacon is almost completely crisp. Add the shallot and stir with a wooden spoon. Continue to cook for an additional 3 minutes or until the bacon is completely crisp and the shallots are soft and beginning to brown. Drain on a paper towel.

American Breakfast Rice Bowl

Greens, Eggs, and Ham Wrap

Greens, Eggs, and Ham Wrap

SERVES 4

Better in both taste and in nutrition than anything you'll get at the drive-through window, this tasty breakfast sandwich will keep you going strong all morning long.

6 eggs
3 tablespoons mayonnaise
1 tablespoon chopped fresh dill
1 teaspoon Dijon mustard
4 whole-wheat wraps
4 thin slices ham, preferably Black Forest ham, dried well
2 cups baby arugula

Place the eggs in a medium saucepan and cover with cold water. Bring to a rapid boil over high heat, then turn off the heat and cover the pot with a lid. Let the eggs sit for 9 minutes to set hard. Drain well and place in a bowl of ice water to cool. Peel the eggs and roughly chop. Add them to a medium bowl along with the mayonnaise, dill, and mustard. Fold together with a rubber spatula to combine.

Lay the four wraps on your work surface. Lay a slice of ham in the middle of each, keeping it closer to one end. Top with some of the arugula, then place a portion of the egg salad on each. Roll each wrap as you would a burrito, pulling half of the wrap over the egg salad, bringing the bottom of the wrap up, and then continuing to roll so that you have one end open and one end closed to keep everything in. Wrap tightly in plastic wrap and refrigerate until ready to serve, up to an hour or two.

Breakfast Tofu Scramble

V V GF

SERVES 4

Even people who claim not to love tofu seem to find it irresistible when it's scrambled up with veggies and served hot for breakfast. Serve with warm corn tortillas.

2 tablespoons extra-virgin olive oil
1 red bell pepper, cored, seeded, and cut into ⅓-inch dice
2 shallots, sliced into rings
1 serrano chile, diced small
1 garlic clove, minced
1 (12-ounce) container extra-firm tofu, drained and dried well with paper towels
1¼ teaspoons ground cumin
1 teaspoon kosher salt
½ teaspoon ground turmeric
¼ teaspoon ground coriander
⅛ teaspoon cayenne pepper
1 (15-ounce) can black beans, drained and rinsed
¼ cup coarsely chopped fresh cilantro

Heat a medium sauté pan over medium-high heat. When hot, pour the oil in the pan and add the bell pepper, shallots, and chile. Sauté for 2 to 3 minutes or until the bell pepper begins to soften. Add the garlic and cook for 1 minute longer.

Crumble the tofu into the pan and mix with a rubber spatula to combine. Add the cumin, salt, turmeric, coriander, and cayenne and cook for an additional 4 minutes, stirring often to distribute the spices evenly. Stir in the black beans and cook for another 2 minutes or until the beans are heated through. Sprinkle with the cilantro and serve.

Breakfast Tofu Scramble

Eggs Cacio e Pepe

A Toast to Breakfast

We've come a long way since Adam and Eve on a raft (two eggs on toast) was the standard breakfast order. Most of us have upgraded from squishy white-bread toast to a more nutritious slice made with whole grains and seeds, and passed up sugary jelly or jam for something with energy-stoking protein. It's a sustaining and simple way to make breakfast; but any of these gussied-up toasts would be a perfect light lunch or anytime snack, too. Keep a loaf of hearty whole-grain bread in the freezer (unlike preservative-laden supermarket loaves, whole-grain breads won't last long at room temperature, and storing bread in the fridge can cause it to become dried out and stale) and pull out a slice or two as needed. Just toast and top, and breakfast is done. Try one of these recipes, or simply top your toast with natural nut butter and a drizzle of honey; Greek yogurt and citrus segments; or sliced tofu, tomato, and flaked sea salt. And I'm just getting started. . . .

Eggs Cacio e Pepe

V GF (IF SERVED WITHOUT BREAD)

SERVES 3

Cacio e pepe is a Roman pasta dish made with salty Pecorino-Romano cheese and lots of black pepper. The same flavor combination is delicious with soft scrambled eggs; a tablespoon of yogurt makes the eggs even creamier.

6 large eggs
⅔ cup grated Pecorino Romano cheese
2 teaspoons freshly ground black pepper
1 tablespoon nonfat plain Greek yogurt
3 tablespoons unsalted butter
Toasted or grilled bread (optional)

In a large bowl, whisk together the eggs, cheese, pepper, and yogurt. In a 10-inch nonstick pan, melt the butter over medium heat. Pour the eggs into the warm pan and immediately start stirring the egg mixture using a rubber spatula. Stir the eggs constantly and cook until small soft curds form and the eggs begin to set but are still creamy. Remove the eggs from the heat and serve immediately with toasted or grilled bread if desired.

Ricotta Toast with Strawberries

V

SERVES 4

No strawberries? Sliced peaches, mango, or cantaloupe also make delicious toppings for ricotta-spread pieces of toast. Think of this as breakfast crostini, a better way to have your morning toast.

¼ cup sugar
⅓ teaspoon ground cinnamon
1¼ cups whole-milk ricotta cheese
½ teaspoon grated orange zest
¼ teaspoon kosher salt
4 thick slices rustic bread
3 tablespoons extra-virgin olive oil
12 strawberries, hulled and sliced thin

Preheat the broiler to high. In a small bowl, mix together the sugar and cinnamon. In a separate bowl, mix together the ricotta, orange zest, and salt. Brush both sides of each slice of bread with the olive oil. Sprinkle the tops of the slices evenly with half of the sugar mixture. Place on a rimmed baking sheet, sugar side up, and broil on high for 3 minutes.

Flip the slices, sprinkle evenly with another quarter of the sugar mixture, and continue to toast until golden brown and caramelized on both sides. Remove from the oven and spread the ricotta mixture evenly over the tops. Arrange the sliced berries decoratively over the ricotta. Sprinkle with the remaining sugar mixture and serve.

Ricotta Toast with Strawberries

Sweet Pea and Avocado Toast

Sweet Pea and Avocado Toast

V

SERVES 4

Avocado toast has become something of an obsession for a lot of people these days—maybe because the textures and colors are so appealing together. Add a runny poached egg and minty peas and a good thing gets a whole lot better.

¾ cup frozen petite peas, thawed
⅓ cup fresh mint leaves, chopped
1 teaspoon grated lime zest
1 teaspoon fresh lime juice (from 1 lime)
½ teaspoon kosher salt
1 tablespoon extra-virgin olive oil
1 avocado, halved, pitted, and diced in the skin
1 tablespoon white vinegar
4 eggs
4 (¾-inch) slices of a bâtard loaf or other small rustic bread loaf, toasted
Dried pequin chiles or crushed red pepper flakes (optional)
Flaked salt, such as Maldon (optional)

In a food processor, combine the peas, mint, lime zest and juice, salt, and olive oil. Pulse until the peas are coarsely chopped. Spoon out and add the avocado and pulse to combine and form a coarse spread. Set aside.

In a shallow medium saucepan, combine 4 cups water with the vinegar. Bring to a simmer over medium heat. Adjust the heat to maintain the gentle simmer (don't allow it to boil). One at a time, break each egg into a small bowl; swirl the water with a spoon, creating a vortex, and gently slide the egg into the simmering water. Use a slotted spoon to gently coax the egg white up and around the yolk.

Repeat with the remaining eggs (depending on the size of your pan, it may be easier to do just 2 eggs at a time so you can keep an eye on them and not crowd the pan). Cook the eggs for 3 to 4 minutes or until the whites are set but the yolk is still soft when touched. Remove the eggs with a slotted spoon and drain well on a paper towel–lined plate.

Spread a good amount of the pea puree on each piece of toast. Top with a poached egg. If using, crush 2 pequin chiles on the top of each egg and crunch a small pinch of flaked salt over the top.

Eggs: All They Are Cracked Up to Be

Eggs have a lot going for them: They are an inexpensive, readily available, and endlessly versatile source of protein that can hang out in the fridge for weeks, ready when you are—they even come in their own nifty, airtight packaging. And now that we know that the dietary cholesterol in eggs does not translate to high blood-cholesterol levels, there is no reason not to eat them as often as we like. For me, that means a few times a week.

When I was a child, my mother served eggs frequently, and not only for breakfast. Frittatas were a staple, and we even ate them in sandwiches for lunch. For dinner, she would make a stack of thin, crepe-like omelets that she filled with mozzarella and baked in a casserole topped with marinara sauce and a bit more cheese. I loved it then and still do today. Any of these recipes would make a great Breakfast for Dinner candidate, and leftovers are perfect to pack along for lunch. All good reasons to get cracking!

Caprese Frittata

Caprese Frittata

V GF

SERVES 4

A classic summertime combination—tomatoes, mozzarella, and basil—becomes a simple brunch, lunch, or dinner dish when eggs are added. You can even serve small wedges with cocktails. Bring the eggs, cream, and mozzarella to room temperature for even results.

2 tablespoons extra-virgin olive oil
1 cup cherry tomatoes, sliced into rounds
½ teaspoon kosher salt
7 large eggs, at room temperature
¼ cup heavy cream, at room temperature
½ cup coarsely chopped fresh basil leaves
½ cup diced mozzarella, at room temperature

Place the oven rack in the middle of the oven. Preheat the broiler to high.

Heat an 8-inch ovenproof nonstick skillet over medium heat. Put the olive oil and tomatoes in the pan. Season the tomatoes with ¼ teaspoon of the salt and cook for about 4 minutes or until they are soft and beginning to fall apart.

Meanwhile, in a large bowl, whisk the eggs with the cream, basil, and remaining ¼ teaspoon salt until light. Pour the egg mixture over the tomatoes, sprinkle with the mozzarella, and cook for 2 minutes without stirring. Using a rubber spatula, loosen the cooked eggs from the sides and bottom of the pan and tilt the pan to allow the raw egg to run underneath. Cook for 1 minute longer and repeat.

Put the skillet under the broiler for 5 to 6 minutes or until the eggs are just set. Slide the frittata onto a board, slice, and serve.

Smoked Trout Frittata

V GF

SERVES 4

Smoked salmon and eggs is a classic combo, but I find smoked trout retains a nicer texture when cooked than salmon, and it's well priced, too. Four-ounce packages of smoked trout fillets are available in most supermarkets.

8 large eggs, at room temperature
½ cup heavy cream, at room temperature
3 tablespoons extra-virgin olive oil
1 fennel bulb, cored and chopped fine
1 shallot, chopped fine
½ teaspoon kosher salt
7 cherry tomatoes, quartered
1 (4-ounce) smoked trout fillet, skin and bones removed, flaked
¼ cup torn fresh basil leaves
2 ounces fresh goat cheese

Preheat the broiler to high. In a large bowl, whisk together the eggs and cream until completely smooth. Set aside.

Heat an 8-inch ovenproof nonstick skillet over medium-high heat. Pour the oil into the pan and heat for a few more seconds. Add the fennel and shallot and cook for 3 minutes or until the fennel softens. Season with the salt and add the tomatoes and trout. Cook for 1 minute longer. Pour the egg mixture over the trout mixture and let the eggs cook for 1 minute.

Using a rubber spatula, lightly scrape the bottom of the pan to bring up some of the cooked egg mixture. Repeat this 3 times and evenly spread the mixture in the pan. The top will still be liquid. Dot the top with the basil and goat cheese and put under the broiler for 3 to 4 minutes or until cooked through and lightly browned on top. Allow the frittata to cool slightly before sliding from the pan, slicing, and serving.

Smoked Trout Frittata

Sausage, Spinach, and Apple Strata

Breakfast Strata

When it comes to a one-dish make-ahead brunch or breakfast, strata is my go-to. It's perfect when I have overnight guests or the family is coming for Mother's Day or Christmas morning. Even if it's just Jade and me, I like to serve something comforting and warm that will keep us sustained well into the afternoon. A sweet or savory strata, bursting with good things like sausage, green veggies, or fresh (or frozen) fruit solves the problem beautifully. It's the ideal make-ahead dish because it is even better when it's assembled the night before and refrigerated. The overnight stay in the fridge allows the bread to soak up the egg mixture completely, making for a more luscious, custardy bread pudding. The next morning just pop it in the oven (let it come to room temperature if possible, for more even cooking, but if not, no worries) and let it bake while you read the paper, take a power walk, or catch up on e-mails. It will fill the house with delicious aromas, and the beautiful, crusty surface and tender, eggy interior are completely satisfying.

Sausage, Spinach, and Apple Strata

SERVES 6

While the sausage in this sweet-savory combo does add a lot of flavor, you can certainly leave it out to make this a vegetarian dish, and it will still be incredibly tasty.

2 tablespoons extra-virgin olive oil
1 pound breakfast sausage, casings removed
2 shallots, chopped
1 apple, such as Honeycrisp, cored and chopped into ⅓-inch pieces
1 (10-ounce) box frozen chopped spinach, thawed and squeezed dry
Butter for the baking dish
8 cups cubed Italian bread (1-pound loaf)
1 cup shredded mozzarella cheese
3 cups whole milk
1 cup heavy cream
6 large eggs
1 teaspoon kosher salt
½ teaspoon freshly ground black pepper
¼ cup finely grated Parmesan cheese

Heat the oil in a large heavy skillet over medium heat. Add the sausage and cook for about 5 minutes, breaking it into small pieces with a wooden spoon. Add the shallots and sauté for about 3 minutes or until translucent. Add the apple and the spinach and sauté over medium-low heat for another 2 minutes. Set aside to cool slightly.

Generously butter a 3-quart baking dish. Place half of the bread cubes in the dish. Sprinkle half of the mozzarella over the bread and then top with half of the sausage mixture. Repeat layering.

Whisk the milk, cream, eggs, salt, and pepper in a large bowl and pour evenly over the strata. Top with the Parmesan cheese. Refrigerate the strata, covered with plastic wrap, for at least 2 hours and up to 12 hours.

Remove the strata from the refrigerator about 30 minutes before baking to allow it to come to room temperature. Preheat the oven to 350°F.

Bake the strata, uncovered, for about 50 minutes or until puffed, golden brown, and cooked through. A thin knife inserted in the middle of the strata should come out clean. If the top browns too quickly, cover with a sheet of aluminum foil. Let the strata stand for 5 minutes before serving.

Green Strata

V

SERVES 6

If you're looking for a way to get your quota of greens early in the day, you won't do better than this brilliantly verdant brunch dish.

- 2 tablespoons unsalted butter, plus 1 teaspoon for the pan
- 4 leeks, cleaned and chopped
- 1 (5-ounce) container fresh baby spinach, chopped
- 1½ teaspoons kosher salt
- ½ teaspoon crushed red pepper flakes
- 1 bunch of asparagus, trimmed and chopped
- 7 large eggs, at room temperature
- 1¼ cups grated Pecorino Romano cheese
- 2½ cups whole milk, at room temperature
- 8 cups cubed Italian bread (1-pound loaf)

In a large skillet, melt the 2 tablespoons of butter over medium heat. Add the leeks and cook for about 8 minutes, stirring often, until soft and beginning to brown slightly. Add the chopped spinach and cook for 2 minutes longer until the spinach is wilted.

Transfer the mixture to a colander to drain any excess liquid. Place in a bowl and add 1 teaspoon of the salt, the red pepper flakes, and the asparagus and stir to combine.

Preheat the oven to 375°F. Butter a 9 x 13-inch baking dish with the remaining teaspoon of butter.

In a large bowl, whisk the eggs to break up the yolks. Add ¾ cup of the cheese, the milk, and the remaining ½ teaspoon salt and whisk until smooth. Add the bread and spinach mixture and mix well.

Pour the mixture into the prepared baking dish and sprinkle with the remaining ½ cup of cheese. Cover tightly with aluminum foil and bake for 15 minutes. Uncover the dish and continue to bake for about 20 minutes longer or until the custard is set, the top is golden brown, and a toothpick inserted in the middle of the dish comes out clean. Let the strata rest for 10 minutes before cutting into squares and serving warm.

Green Strata

Savory Breakfast Crepes

Savory Breakfast Crepes

V

SERVES 4

Crepes are very versatile and can be made ahead and stored in the fridge or even frozen. Just defrost them overnight in the fridge and fill, roll, and bake as few or as many as you need.

1 cup (8 ounces) part-skim ricotta cheese
4 ounces black forest ham, diced
½ teaspoon kosher salt
2 tablespoons olive oil
2 large shallots, diced
¼ teaspoon crushed red pepper flakes
4 cups baby spinach, thoroughly washed and dried
1 teaspoon lemon zest (from 1 lemon)
½ cup pancake mix, such as Nature's Path
1 egg, at room temperature

Nonstick cooking spray
3/4 cup grated Parmesan cheese

In a medium bowl, use a rubber spatula to combine the ricotta, ham, and ¼ teaspoon salt. Heat a medium skillet over medium-high heat. Add the olive oil and when hot, add the shallots, red pepper flakes, and remaining ¼ teaspoon salt.

Cook, stirring often with a wooden spoon, for 3 minutes or until fragrant and the shallots are softened. Add the spinach and cook another 2 minutes or until just barely wilted. Stir in the lemon zest. Remove the spinach from the heat and use the back of a spoon to press out as much liquid as possible. Transfer the spinach to a cutting board and chop coarsely. Fold the spinach into the ricotta mix. Set aside.

In another medium bowl, whisk together the pancake mix, ¾ cup of water, and the egg, mixing just until smooth. Heat an 8-inch nonstick skillet over medium heat. When the pan is hot, spray with nonstick cooking spray. Using a ladle or measuring cup, add approximately ¼ cup batter to the pan, immediately swirling the pan to coat the bottom with a thin layer of batter. Cook for 1 minute on the first side or until the middle is just set and the edges are dry and beginning to brown. Gently flip the crepe using a rubber spatula or your fingers. Cook the other side for 30 seconds, then remove the crepe to a plate. Continue with the remaining batter. Stack the crepes with a piece of parchment paper in between each crepe.

Preheat the oven to 350°F. Spray a 9 x 13-inch glass baking dish with nonstick cooking spray. Place a crepe on your work surface and spoon some of filling down the center. Roll the crepe like a cigar and place it in the pan. Roll and fill the remaining crepes. Sprinkle with the Parmesan and bake for approximately 10 minutes, or until the filling is warmed through and the Parmesan is melted.

Fruit in Spiced White Wine

V V GF (IF SERVED WITHOUT SHIPPED CREAM)

SERVES 6

A warm syrup of white wine, sugar, and spices is poured over a mix of fruits for a grown-up fruit salad.

1¼ cups dry white wine, such as pinot grigio
⅓ cup sugar
⅛ teaspoon ground cardamom
1 vanilla bean, split lengthwise and seeds scraped out
2 ripe persimmons, cut into 1-inch pieces
8 ounces strawberries, hulled and quartered
1 cup green grapes, halved
2 tablespoons chopped fresh mint leaves
Freshly whipped cream (optional)

Add the white wine, sugar, cardamom, and vanilla bean and seeds to a small saucepan. Place it over medium heat and bring to a simmer. Stir to dissolve the sugar. Place the persimmons, strawberries, grapes, and mint in a heat-proof medium bowl. While the wine mixture is still hot, pour it into the bowl of fruit and toss gently with a rubber spatula.

Cover the bowl with plastic wrap and place in the refrigerator for at least 2 hours or up to 4 hours, tossing every hour. Bring to room temperature before serving. Serve dolloped with whipped cream if desired.

Fruit in Spiced White Wine

Polenta Waffles

Open Your House

So many people find entertaining intimidating, but to me, cooking for others is one of the great joys in life. Watching people taste food I've prepared and seeing that look of bliss on their faces makes all the planning and shopping and cleaning and prepping worthwhile! If the idea of hosting a formal dinner party is what's hanging you up, consider a more laid-back option: a brunch open house. It's a great way to connect and entertain without the pressure of a tightly scripted event. And because your guests don't all arrive at once, you'll have a chance to spend a little quality time with everyone before they move on. Babies and kids? Would love to see them. Relatives visiting from out of town? Sure, the more the merrier. The women you only have time to nod to before and after yoga class? Let's get to know each other a little bit better.

Because an open house is a more fluid kind of event, I always plan a flexible, casual menu. I like to include some straight-up breakfast foods, like bagels, cream cheese, fruit salad, and bowls of yogurt with granola. A make-your-own waffle bar with toppings is always a huge hit with kids of all ages, and a pitcher of Bloody Marys or another low-alcohol cocktail is a good addition to the standard juice-and-coffee lineup. As the day moves on, I bring out heartier fare, like a couple of room-temperature frittatas and an antipasto platter. The most important thing is to have replenishments so the table never looks picked over or bedraggled. Have backup platters assembled and ready to swap in for the decimated ones, put out fresh cream cheese and condiments rather than refilling the bowls, and make sure there are plenty of clean plates, napkins, and silverware at hand.

Polenta Waffles with All the Fixings

V (IF SERVED WITHOUT BACON OR PANCETTA)

SERVES 6 TO 8

If you can't decide whether to go sweet or savory for your brunch centerpiece, this is a great option; the array of toppings lets your guests customize their own plates.

WAFFLES

1 cup all-purpose flour
1 cup medium-grind cornmeal
1 tablespoon sugar
1 teaspoon baking powder
1 teaspoon baking soda
½ teaspoon kosher salt
¼ teaspoon ground cinnamon
2 large eggs, separated, at room temperature
¾ cup buttermilk, at room temperature
¾ cup low-fat milk, at room temperature
½ cup vegetable oil
1 teaspoon pure vanilla extract
Vegetable oil cooking spray, for the waffle iron

FIXINGS

Bacon or pancetta, cooked and crumbled
Strawberries, raspberries, and blueberries
Grated Cheddar or crumbled feta cheese
Chopped fresh herbs
Dark chocolate chips
Chopped toasted walnuts, pecans, and almonds
Chocolate-hazelnut spread, such as Nutella
Maple syrup

Preheat the oven to 200°F. Heat a waffle iron. In a large bowl, whisk together the flour, cornmeal, sugar, baking powder, baking soda, salt, and cinnamon.

In a separate bowl, whisk or beat the egg whites until soft peaks form. If you prefer, beat the eggs in the bowl of an electric mixer fitted with the whisk attachment until soft peaks form.

Form a well in the dry ingredients and add the egg yolks, buttermilk, milk, oil, and vanilla. Whisk until combined, being careful not to overmix. A few lumps are fine. With a large rubber spatula, gently fold the whites into the mixture until just barely combined, taking care to maintain the airy texture.

Lightly spray the heated waffle iron with vegetable oil spray. Ladle the batter onto the waffle iron and cook until the waffles are lightly browned and steam is no longer emerging from the sides of the waffle maker. Keep them warm in the oven while you cook the remaining batter.

Arrange the waffles on a platter and surround them with small bowls of toppings.

Fluffy Lemon Buttermilk and Mascarpone Pancakes

V

SERVES 2 TO 4

When I make pancakes on the weekend I like to use up all the batter and freeze the extras. That way I can defrost a few in the toaster oven on weekday mornings so Jade can have a hot breakfast without my having a lot of kitchen cleanup. These pancakes are not sweetened (look at your box mix if you don't think of pancakes as a sweetened food!) so do indulge in a drizzle of syrup.

2 teaspoons vegetable oil
1 cup all-purpose flour
1 teaspoon baking powder
½ teaspoon baking soda
⅛ teaspoon kosher salt
½ cup buttermilk, at room temperature
½ cup mascarpone cheese, at room temperature
1 teaspoon pure vanilla extract
1 teaspoon grated lemon zest (from 1 lemon)
3 eggs, separated, at room temperature
1 cup berries, such as blueberries, raspberries, or hulled and sliced strawberries (optional)
Pure maple syrup, for serving

Preheat a griddle or large skillet over medium-low heat. Use a paper towel to coat lightly with vegetable oil.

In a large bowl, whisk together the flour, baking powder, baking soda, and salt. Set aside.

In a liquid measuring cup, combine the buttermilk, mascarpone, vanilla, lemon zest, and egg yolks. Stir together with a fork. In a separate medium bowl, whisk the egg whites until soft peaks form, about 3 minutes. You can use a handheld mixer for this as well.

Add the buttermilk mixture to the flour mixture and gently stir together with a rubber spatula until nearly but not completely incorporated. Some of the flour will still be visible. Now gently fold in the egg whites, being careful not to deflate the whites, until the mixture is just barely combined.

Raise the heat under the griddle or skillet to medium and ladle the batter by ½ cupfuls. Cook until bubbles start to form on the surface of the first side, about 2 minutes. Flip the pancakes and cook for an additional minute or until cooked through. Remove to a plate and keep warm in a low oven until all of the batter is used and you are ready to serve. Wipe the griddle with more oil between batches if needed. Serve with berries, if desired, and maple syrup.

Carrot and Apple Muffins

Carrot and Apple Muffins

V

MAKES ABOUT 12 MUFFINS

Mix up the batter for these wholesome muffins before you go to bed, then scoop and bake it the next morning to fill the house with a wonderful aroma. Goji berries are nutritional powerhouses that give these a little extra oomph, but you can substitute raisins or cranberries if you prefer.

½ cup all-purpose flour
¾ cup whole-wheat flour
2 tablespoons ground flax meal
1½ teaspoons baking powder
1 teaspoon ground cinnamon
½ teaspoon fine salt
⅛ teaspoon ground allspice
6 tablespoons (¾ stick) unsalted butter, at room temperature
1 cup (packed) dark brown sugar
2 large eggs, at room temperature
¼ cup unsweetened applesauce
¼ cup fresh unfiltered apple juice
1 small carrot, peeled and finely grated (½ to ⅔ cup)
¼ cup dried goji berries

Position a rack in the center of the oven and preheat the oven to 350°F. Line a 12-cup muffin tin with paper liners.

In a medium bowl, whisk the flours, flax meal, baking powder, cinnamon, salt, and allspice to blend. Using a handheld electric mixer or a stand mixer with the paddle attachment, beat the butter and brown sugar in a large bowl until fluffy, about 2 minutes. Beat in the eggs, one at a time. Beat in half the flour mixture, then add the applesauce and apple juice. Beat in the remaining flour mixture just until combined. Use a spatula or wooden spoon to fold in the grated carrot and goji berries.

Drop 2 well-rounded tablespoons of batter into each paper liner. Bake until a toothpick inserted into the center (not the edge) of a muffin comes out clean, about 18 minutes. Cool the muffins in the pan for 5 minutes, then gently transfer them to a rack to cool completely.

Snacks & Small Plates

I admit it: I like to snack. But I'm not talking about noshing on chips and cookies. To me, snacking means eating small healthy meals over the course of the day. It keeps my metabolism humming along and helps me avoid feeling starved—and overeating when it's mealtime.

I love the concept of small plates—just a few bites that I can enjoy on my own or share with others at my table—that's popular in so many restaurants. It's more fun to sample a lot of different flavors, and I don't end up feeling overstuffed the way I do with many entrées.

Many of these recipes can be prepped and made ahead, and would make a perfectly lovely and elegant first course for a more formal seated dinner.

In this chapter you'll find lots of ways to stave off the afternoon (or anytime) munchies while avoiding the snack aisle altogether. You'll find lots of fun and easy ways to fit more vegetables, healthy grains, and legumes into your diet. I've even put my own spin on jerky, and movie night is made for my spiced-up popcorns.

G's Pico de Gallo

V V GF

SERVES 4

I like guacamole but I LOVE pico de gallo. It's practically fat-free, makes everything from fish and seafood to beans and grains of all kinds taste amazing, and is a guilt-free topping for tacos and dip for chips. You can reduce or increase the amount of chile to taste.

2 cups diced ripe tomatoes (about 2 large tomatoes)
1 serrano chile, minced
1 small shallot, minced
1 cup grated carrot (about 1 large carrot)
¼ teaspoon ground coriander
1 tablespoon chopped fresh basil leaves
1 tablespoon white balsamic vinegar
2 teaspoons extra-virgin olive oil
¾ teaspoon kosher salt

In a medium bowl, combine the tomatoes, chile, shallot, grated carrot, coriander, basil, vinegar, olive oil, and salt. Toss gently to combine.

G's Pico de Gallo

Dips and Dunkers

As snack foods go, you could do a whole lot worse than a container of hummus and fresh vegetables. On the other hand, you could do a whole lot better with any of the dips and spreads included here! Not only are they more flavorful, they are much more versatile than you might think.

My "only bean dip you'll ever need" and the fennel puree, for example, can wear many different hats. For entertaining, serve them with pita chips or crudités. Smear the spreads on toasted baguette slices, drizzle with olive oil, sprinkle with a bit of parsley, and voilà!—you've got healthy vegetarian crostini. Use them as a side dish or as a bed for grilled fish, or spread some on whole-grain toast and pile on the veggies for a healthy lunch. You can even thin them out with a bit of water or chicken broth for a suave pureed soup; garnish with a bit of crispy pancetta or a swirl of pureed roasted red pepper. These are pretty compelling reasons to keep one of these multitasking dips on hand at all times.

The Only Bean Dip You'll Ever Need

V GF

SERVES 6 TO 8

Serve this whenever you might reach for hummus. The flavor is a bit more nuanced, and the mascarpone makes it smooth and rich tasting without being heavy.

½ cup extra-virgin olive oil
3 garlic cloves, smashed and peeled
1 (15-ounce) can cannellini beans, rinsed and drained
¼ cup mascarpone cheese, at room temperature
2 teaspoons grated lemon zest
⅓ cup fresh lemon juice (from 2 lemons)
1¼ teaspoons kosher salt
1 (15-ounce) can chickpeas, rinsed and drained

In a small saucepan, warm the olive oil and garlic cloves over medium-low heat for about 10 minutes or until the garlic is golden brown and soft all the way through. Set aside to cool slightly.

Put the cannellini beans in the bowl of a food processor fitted with the metal blade. Add the mascarpone, lemon zest and juice, and salt. Pulse to combine. Add the cooled oil and garlic mixture and process until smooth.

Add the drained chickpeas and process until the dip is mixed but still has a bit of texture. Serve immediately or refrigerate until ready to use.

Fennel and Yogurt Puree

V GF

SERVES 4 TO 6

Enjoy this warm as a side dish or chilled as a snack with crudités, such as carrots, cucumbers, and peppers, and with pita chips, for dipping.

1 pound fennel, cored and cut into 1-inch pieces (1 large or 2 small bulbs)
1 tablespoon plus ¼ teaspoon kosher salt
3 tablespoons extra-virgin olive oil
1½ tablespoons nonfat plain Greek yogurt

In a medium saucepan, cover the fennel with cold water and sprinkle with 1 tablespoon of the salt. Bring to a boil over high heat, reduce the heat, and simmer the fennel for about 10 minutes or until very tender.

Drain the fennel well and transfer to the bowl of a food processor fitted with the metal blade. Add the oil, yogurt, and remaining ¼ teaspoon salt and process until smooth. Scrape down the sides of the processor as needed.

Serve warm, at room temp, or chilled.

Crudités with Walnut Butter

Crudités with Walnut Butter

V

SERVES 6 TO 8

Crudités—raw vegetables—are a staple in my house. Keep cut vegetables in the fridge for quick snacking. Plus, the leftover walnut butter is fabulous over chicken, steak, or fish, or tossed with pasta.

CRUDITÉS

1 fennel bulb, cored and cut into 8 thin wedges
8 red or breakfast radishes, halved
4 thin carrots, peeled and cut in half lengthwise
1 heart of romaine, leaves pulled apart
1 yellow bell pepper, cored, seeded, and cut into 8 wedges
1 pint cherry tomatoes
4 celery stalks, cut in half on the diagonal
1 baguette, sliced ½ inch thick on the diagonal

WALNUT BUTTER

½ cup toasted walnut halves and pieces (see Cook's Note, page 75)
1 teaspoon chopped fresh thyme leaves
8 tablespoons (1 stick) unsalted butter, at room temperature
½ teaspoon kosher salt
⅛ teaspoon freshly ground black pepper

For the crudités: Arrange all of the vegetables and the baguette slices on a platter or board or in a basket.

For the walnut butter: Place the walnuts and thyme in the bowl of a food processor fitted with the metal blade. Pulse until the nuts are finely chopped. Add the butter, salt, and black pepper and puree until smooth. Scrape down the sides of the bowl as needed.

Serve the butter at room temperature alongside the crudités and bread.

Roasted Eggplant and Almond Dip

V

SERVES 4

Even avowed eggplant-phobes will scarf up this velvety-smooth mixture. A bit of almond butter gives it depth and body.

1 (1½-pound) globe eggplant
1 head garlic
1 tablespoon extra-virgin olive oil
¾ teaspoon kosher salt, divided
2 tablespoons unsweetened almond butter
1 teaspoon grated lemon zest
1 teaspoon lemon juice
1 tablespoon chopped Italian parsley

Pita chips or crudités, for dipping

Preheat the oven to 350°F.

Pierce the eggplant all over with the tip of a paring knife and place on a rimmed baking sheet. Cut off the top third of the head of garlic and place on a sheet of aluminum foil large enough to enclose it. Drizzle the garlic with the olive oil and sprinkle with ¼ of the teaspoon salt. Bring the foil up and around the garlic and crimp to seal. Place the package on the baking sheet with the eggplant and bake for 45 minutes. After 45 minutes, remove the garlic from the oven and bake the eggplant an additional 30 minutes or until very soft and slightly deflated. Allow the eggplant to cool slightly.

Squeeze the roasted garlic into the bowl of a food processor. Cut the eggplant in half and use a large spoon to scrape out all of the flesh, leaving the skin behind. Add the flesh to the food processor along with the almond butter, lemon zest, lemon juice, and remaining salt. Puree on high for 2 minutes or until the mixture is smooth and silky. Place in an airtight container and chill completely. Serve cold, sprinkled with the parsley, with the pita chips or crudités for dipping.

Roasted Eggplant and Almond Dip

Fresh Fruit Leather

Fresh Fruit Leather

V V GF

MAKES 4 TO 6 SERVINGS

What kid wouldn't love to find some animal- or star-shaped fruit roll-ups in their lunch box? You can use other types of fruit, such as raspberries and peaches. To use frozen fruit, thaw first, and then drain off any juices before blending.

1 pint strawberries, hulled and quartered
1 tablespoon fresh lemon juice
1 tablespoon agave syrup

Place an oven rack in the center of the oven and preheat the oven to 170°F or the lowest setting. Line a heavy rimmed baking sheet with a silicone baking mat.

Put the strawberries, lemon juice, and agave in a blender and blend until smooth. Pour the puree onto the prepared baking sheet and spread evenly with a spatula, leaving a 1-inch border on all sides.

Bake for 6 to 7 hours or until the center of the puree has set and is not sticky when touched. Allow to cool completely.

Using scissors, cut the baked puree into 1-inch-wide strips. The baked puree can also be cut into shapes using decorative-edged scissors or cookie cutters. Store in an airtight container with wax paper between the layers.

Soy Citrus Turkey Jerky

MAKES ABOUT 8 OUNCES OF JERKY

Spicy, sweet, tangy, and satisfying, this is a snack food you can feel good about munching.

½ boneless, skinless turkey breast, about 2 to 3 pounds
⅔ cup tamari
3 tablespoons agave syrup
1 teaspoon crushed red pepper flakes
1 teaspoon grated lemon zest
¼ teaspoon garlic powder

Trim any excess fat from the turkey breast and remove the tenderloin. Place the tenderloin and breast on a rimmed baking sheet and put it in the freezer for 1 to 2 hours or until partially frozen but not frozen solid. Then slice both pieces lengthwise into ¼-inch strips, making them as even as possible.

Place the turkey strips in a resealable plastic bag. To the bag add the tamari, agave, red pepper flakes, lemon zest, garlic powder, and ⅓ cup water. Seal the bag tightly and mix everything together to coat the strips. Marinate in the refrigerator for at least 6 hours or overnight.

Soy Citrus Turkey Jerky

Remove the turkey strips from the marinade and drain well on paper towels. Lay the slices in a single layer on the racks of a dehydrator, being sure not to overlap them. Set the dehydrator to 160°F and dry the jerky for 4 to 5 hours, depending on the thickness of the strips and how dry you prefer your jerky.

Remove the jerky to a paper towel–lined platter and allow to cool completely. Store in an airtight container for up to 3 weeks.

Happy Trails Mix

Because I travel a lot, often with a child in tow, I've learned that the best way to avoid airport junk food is to be armed with my own healthier alternatives. Once every couple of weeks or so I make a batch of homemade trail mix with almonds, walnuts, carob chips, and dried cranberries, strawberries, apricots, or other dried fruit. I store it all in a large glass jar to keep the mix from getting soggy and scoop some into snack-size plastic bags as needed.

HEALTHIES (4 PARTS OF THESE)

Nuts: These give you lots of protein for sustained energy. Go for the ones with the most nutrients—almonds, cashews, and walnuts—and opt for raw when possible and always unsalted.

Seeds: Another source of protein and antioxidants, these bring crunch to the mix. Think pumpkin, chia, and sunflower.

Grains: Add filling fiber with a bit of granola, popcorn, corn nuts, sesame sticks, or whole-grain cereal. Avoid processed foods that have a lot of carbs (I'm talking about you, sugary cereals and white-flour pretzels).

Like anything else in life, trail mix is about balance—and moderation. Don't eat too much at a time; a portion should be less than what you can fit in your cupped hand. Avoid loading up on the sweet and starchy ingredients like sesame sticks, corn nuts, even M&M's or marshmallows. The key is to maintain the right proportion of wholesome, nutritious ingredients to indulgent ones. You can mix and match from the list below, aiming for a four-to-one ratio of healthy foods to goodies.

GOODIES (1 PART OF THESE)

Dried Fruit: These add color, chewiness, and sweetness. While they come from natural-food sources, be careful about adding too much of them, as they bring sugar and calories, too. I like dried berries best; they're small so they spread around the mix well, and they have plenty of fiber and antioxidants.

Sweets: Here's where you get to have a little fun. Add bits of chocolate candies or yogurt-covered raisins, but not too much! Remember you want these treats to be the smallest part of your 4-to-1 ratio. And if you're feeling extra nutrition-conscious, go for dark chocolate: it has heart-healthy antioxidants.

New, Improved "Puppy" Chow

New, Improved "Puppy" Chow

V V

MAKES ABOUT 6 CUPS

This Midwestern fave, an addictive blend of peanuts, pretzels, and cereal coated with melted chocolate and peanut butter, then tossed in confectioners' sugar to create individual "kibbles," is something like party mix on steroids. To up the fiber, omega-3s, and antioxidant power, I've replaced the milk chocolate chips with dark chocolate and a handful of cocoa nibs, and subbed golden flaxseed meal and powdered chia for some of the confectioners' sugar.

3 cups whole-grain cereal, such as Chex or Heritage Bites
1 cup unsalted peanuts
1 cup pretzel nuggets or broken pretzel rods
⅓ cup bittersweet or semisweet chocolate chips
⅓ cup natural peanut butter
1 cup confectioners' sugar
⅓ cup golden flaxseed meal
⅓ cup chia powder
¼ cup cocoa nibs

Combine the cereal, peanuts, and pretzels in a large bowl. Set aside.

In a heat-proof measuring cup or bowl, combine the chocolate chips and peanut butter. Microwave on 50% power for 1 minute. Stir and return to the microwave, continuing to heat and stir in 30-second increments until the mixture is completely melted and smooth.

Drizzle the chocolate mixture over the cereal mixture and toss very well, coating everything thoroughly.

Sift the confectioners' sugar into a bowl or onto a piece of wax paper. Add the flaxseed meal and chia powder and stir to combine.

Sprinkle the sugar mixture over the coated cereal mixture, tossing frequently to ensure every "kibble" is dusted with sugar and the pieces are separate and dry. Add the cocoa nibs and toss again. Store for up to a week in an airtight container.

Warm and Spicy Popcorn

Top Pops

For movie night, rainy afternoons, or any time hunger pangs rear their ugly heads, popcorn is my hands-down favorite snack food. I love how economical it is—a half cup of kernels costs less than a dollar and makes seven to eight cups of popped corn—as well as how unadulterated it is, especially if you pop your own. You can make it on the stovetop in a large heavy pan with a little oil, but recently I've been using a glass microwave air popper that lets me pop my corn without any oil at all. They are not expensive, and if you buy a lot of pre-packaged microwave popcorn, it will pay for itself quickly (and keep all that extra packaging out of the landfill!).

Warm and Spicy Popcorn

V V GF

SERVES 4

The flavors of the Middle East meet corn from the Midwest.

1 teaspoon ground cumin
1 tablespoon chopped fresh flat-leaf parsley leaves
¼ teaspoon ground coriander
¼ teaspoon cayenne pepper
¼ teaspoon kosher salt
7 cups popped popcorn (from ½ cup of kernels)
2 tablespoons extra-virgin olive oil

In a small bowl, stir together the cumin, parsley, coriander, cayenne, and salt. Put the popped popcorn in a large bowl and drizzle with the olive oil. Toss thoroughly to distribute. Sprinkle with the spice blend and toss again to coat the popcorn with the seasonings.

Pumpkin Spice Latte Popcorn

V GF

SERVES 4

When autumn rolls around, these are nice flavors to add to popcorn.

7 cups popped popcorn (from ½ cup of kernels)
3 tablespoons unsalted butter, melted
1 tablespoon (packed) light brown sugar
1 teaspoon pumpkin pie spice
1 teaspoon instant espresso powder

Put the popped popcorn in a large bowl.

In a small bowl, stir together the butter, brown sugar, pumpkin pie spice, and espresso powder. Drizzle over the popcorn and toss gently until combined.

Serve immediately or store in an airtight container for up to 1 day.

Parisian Sweet and Salty Popcorn

V V GF

SERVES 4

In Parisian movie theaters you can order sweet or salty popcorn—or the best of both worlds, a mixture. This is my nod to that tradition. Be sure to shake the pot continuously as the corn pops or the sugar will burn.

¼ cup canola oil
½ cup popcorn kernels
3 tablespoons sugar, preferably turbinado sugar
2 tablespoons fleur de sel (flaked sea salt)

Heat the oil in a heavy pot with a lid over medium-high heat. When hot, add the popcorn and sugar, swirl to distribute the sugar, and cover. Cook, shaking the pan continuously, for about 2 minutes or until the popping begins to slow.

Remove from the heat and set aside, covered, for 1 to 2 minutes. The residual heat will pop most of the remaining kernels.

Immediately turn the popcorn into a bowl and sprinkle with 2 tablespoons of the flaked salt or to taste. Use tongs to toss as the molten sugar is very hot.

Lemon Popcorn with a Kick

V GF

SERVES 4

Zesty lemony popcorn with a little extra pop.

2 tablespoons (¼ stick) unsalted butter
Grated zest of 1 lemon
⅛ teaspoon cayenne pepper
7 cups popped popcorn (from ½ cup of kernels)
½ teaspoon kosher salt

In a small sauté pan, melt the butter over medium heat. Add the lemon zest and cayenne and swirl to let the flavors mingle. Pour the butter over the popcorn in a large bowl and toss gently to coat. Season with the salt and serve.

Lemon Popcorn with a Kick

Drink Up!

Often when we think we're hungry, we're just thirsty. Especially when the temperatures climb, we'd all do well to remember this. While your body is pretty good at maintaining its temperature, it needs plenty of water to do the job. There are lots of ways to hydrate that go way beyond a plain glass of water. Give one of these ideas a swig!

Flavored Sparklers: I love juices and even some sodas, but you don't always want all that sugar or flavor when you're thirsty. I often dilute orange juice or ginger ale with sparkling water—one part juice to three parts water, or even more—and drink up without feeling weighed down. For a blackberry fizz, pulse some blackberries and a bit of sugar in a food processor. Strain the juice through a fine-mesh strainer into a pitcher to remove the seeds. Stir in some fresh lime juice and seltzer. Serve the fizz over ice.

Fruit Waters: It sounds fancy to say "infused water" when all you're doing is adding a fresh ingredient or two to your water. Add some sliced strawberries, lemon, or cucumbers to a pitcher of cold water, and then let it sit for a few minutes before serving. The result: calming aroma and subtle flavor.

Fruity Ice Cubes: Add a few blueberries or black-berries, or a strawberry wedge or lemon wedge, to each compartment of an ice cube tray, then top with water. Freeze until firm and add the cubes to a tall glass of water—beautiful!

Homemade Ice Pops: There are all sorts of simple ways to make ice pops—and it's so easy to find molds now. Use fruit juices or, my favorite, brewed tea. I like to add lemon juice, honey, and mint. Pour the mixture into molds and freeze. (For the recipe see page 49.)

Flaxseed Lemonade

V V GF

SERVES 8

This refreshing and vitamin-rich lemonade can be served hot or cold. The soaked flaxseeds thicken the lemonade slightly, and then are strained out for easier digestibility. It has an appealing jelly-like texture.

2 tablespoons flaxseeds
1 cup sugar
Grated zest and juice of 3 large lemons
1 lemon, thinly sliced, for serving

Place the flaxseeds in a saucepan and add 4 cups water. Cover the pan and bring to a boil over high heat. Reduce the heat and simmer for 45 minutes, adjusting the heat as needed to maintain the simmer.

Add the sugar and lemon zest and simmer for 15 to 20 minutes longer or until the sugar dissolves. Remove from the heat and stir in the lemon juice. Strain the mixture through a fine-mesh strainer into a pitcher. Discard the seeds and zest.

Serve hot, at room temperature, or over ice. Garnish each serving with a lemon slice.

Flaxseed Lemonade

Italian Lemonade

V V GF

SERVES 4 TO 6

The Italian twist is basil simple syrup, a suave alternative to the more expected mint sprigs. Pack the lemonade along on your next picnic.

BASIL SIMPLE SYRUP

1 bunch of fresh basil, washed and stemmed
2 cups sugar

LEMONADE

2 cups fresh lemon juice (from 12 to 15 lemons)
2 cups sparkling water or cold tap water
Lemon zest twists, for garnish

For the basil simple syrup: In a saucepan, combine the basil, sugar, and 1 cup water. Bring to a simmer and cook for about 5 minutes or until the sugar dissolves. Strain the syrup through a fine-mesh strainer into a heat-proof bowl or glass measuring cup and cool. Refrigerate until needed. You will have about 2 cups.

For the lemonade: In a large pitcher, mix the lemon juice with the basil simple syrup. Add the sparkling water (or cold tap water) and stir. Serve right away in ice-filled glasses or refrigerate until ready to serve. Garnish each serving with a lemon twist.

Watermelon Agua Fresca

Pretty and Pink

Few foods make me happier than watermelon, whether in a cooling soup, in refreshing *agua fresca,* or just eaten out of hand. Packed with hydrating water (about 92 percent by weight), and sweet but light on calories (about 40 per cup), watermelon is a natural guilt-free heat-beater. No wonder it's a picnic and barbecue staple.

With its high water and fiber content, watermelon also aids in digestion, helping to keep you satisfied; its choline content is believed to help memory and reduce inflammation. And whether you eat the usual red or more exotic orange or yellow varieties, watermelon is packed with antioxidants.

Watermelon Agua Fresca

V V GF

SERVES 4 TO 6

Aguas frescas, Spanish for "cool waters," are sold throughout shops in Mexico and the Caribbean to customers who stop for a thirst-quenching beverage. They're made with fruits, nuts, and flowers, in flavors like mango, almond, and hibiscus. This is one to keep in your water bottle throughout the day.

¼ cup agave syrup
¼ cup packed fresh mint leaves
4 cups chopped seedless red watermelon (about ½ small melon)
¼ cup fresh lime juice (from 2 to 3 limes)

In a small saucepan, bring the agave and ¼ cup water to a simmer over medium heat. Turn off the heat, add the mint, and steep for 15 minutes. Strain the syrup through a fine-mesh strainer and set aside to cool to room temperature.

Put the watermelon and lime juice in a blender. Add ½ cup water and puree until smooth. Strain through the fine-mesh strainer into a large bowl or pitcher and stir in the reserved syrup. Refrigerate until ready to serve.

Green Mint Tea Ice Pops

V GF

MAKES 12 ICE POPS

Who says you have to drink your tea? Start with a pitcher of brewed green tea, add lemon juice, honey, and mint, and you're ready to freeze!

4 cups brewed green tea, chilled
Juice of 1 small lemon
2 teaspoons honey
¼ cup small fresh mint leaves

SPECIAL EQUIPMENT

12 ice pop molds
12 ice pop sticks

Place the green tea in a pitcher and add the lemon juice, honey, and mint leaves. Stir until the honey dissolves. Pour into the molds, filling each mold to the top. Insert an ice pop stick into each and freeze for 4 to 6 hours or until firm.

When ready to serve, run the molds under warm water for a few seconds to release the ice pops.

Green Mint Tea Ice Pops

Mediterranean Chile Chicken Wings

GF

SERVES 2 TO 4

Hot and spicy harissa is a fiery North African chile paste used in cooking and as a condiment. Some prepared brands contain gluten, so if that is a concern for you, make sure to read the label carefully. If you can't find it, use sriracha instead.

⅓ cup sugar
⅓ cup sherry vinegar
⅓ cup harissa
1 pound chicken wings, tips removed and wings split
Vegetable oil cooking spray

In a small saucepan, stir the sugar and vinegar over medium-high heat until the sugar dissolves. Reduce the heat to medium and simmer for 5 minutes longer or until the glaze is slightly thickened. Stir in the harissa and set the pan aside to cool completely.

Put the chicken wings in a resealable plastic bag. Add three-quarters of the glaze and seal the bag (set aside the remaining glaze). Turn the bag upside down several times to coat the chicken wings. Refrigerate the wings and the reserved glaze separately for 2 to 4 hours.

Preheat the oven to 400°F. Spray a small rimmed baking sheet with vegetable oil spray. Pour the contents of the bag, including the liquid, onto the baking sheet, spreading the wings out so they do not touch each other. Bake for 25 to 30 minutes, turning the wings after 12 to 15 minutes of cooking. The wings are done when they are browned and cooked through. Remove from the oven and brush with the reserved glaze.

Preheat the broiler to high. Slide the baking sheet under the broiler or transfer the wings to a broiler pan and broil for about 3 minutes or until the skin is crispy and the glaze is sticky. Serve warm.

Wing It!

A party just isn't a party until the wings arrive. For something so petite, though, deep-fried chicken wings can pack a massive punch of fat and calories—as many as 200 per wing! Eat five or six of those babies and you can see how that adds up, no matter how many celery sticks you load your plate with. Rather than rule them out entirely, though, I was determined to make oven-baked, blue-cheese-free wings that were just as delicious as the ones that made Buffalo famous, and I'm pretty pleased with the results.

All three of these wing recipes are finger-licking good and full of flavor, and not one of them has ever seen the inside of a fryer. Baking them cuts down on the fat and calories and makes cleanup a snap, and the recipes are much easier to scale up for a crowd. Best of all, the wings and their sauces can be prepped and marinated the night before, so all you need to do is spread them onto a baking sheet and bake until cooked through and crisp. Then, pile them on a platter, pass around a big stack of napkins, and dive in without guilt.

Mediterranean Chile
Chicken Wings

Margarita Chicken Wings

Margarita Chicken Wings

GF

SERVES 2 TO 4

All the bright, fresh flavors of a margarita cocktail are found in these wings.

1 pound chicken wings, tips removed and wings split
½ cup silver tequila
1 teaspoon grated orange zest
¼ cup fresh orange juice (from 1 orange)
½ teaspoon grated lime zest
3 tablespoons fresh lime juice (from 2 limes)
2 teaspoons agave syrup
¼ teaspoon kosher salt
4 to 6 pequin chiles, crushed, or ⅛ teaspoon smoked hot paprika
Vegetable oil cooking spray

Put the chicken wings in a resealable plastic bag.

In a small bowl, whisk the tequila with the orange zest and juice, lime zest and juice, agave, salt, and chiles. Pour the marinade over the wings. Seal the bag and turn it upside down several times to coat the wings with marinade. Refrigerate the wings in the bag for 2 to 4 hours.

Preheat the oven to 450°F.

Spray a small rimmed baking sheet with vegetable oil spray. Pat the wings dry and position them on the baking sheet so they do not touch each other. Reserve the marinade in the plastic bag.

Bake the wings for 25 to 30 minutes, turning them after 12 to 15 minutes of cooking. The wings are ready to remove from the oven when nicely browned.

Heat a grill pan over medium-high heat. Transfer the wings to the grill pan and cook over medium-high heat for about 5 minutes or until the wings are golden and crispy. Transfer the cooked wings to a shallow heat-proof dish.

Meanwhile, pour the marinade into a small saucepan and bring to a simmer over medium-high heat. Simmer for 8 to 10 minutes or until the marinade reduces to a thick and sticky glaze. Pour the glaze over the wings and toss to coat. Serve immediately.

Asian Sesame
Chicken Wings

Asian Sesame Chicken Wings

GF

SERVES 2 TO 4

These wings are gingery and citrusy—the perfect Asian combination.

1 pound chicken wings, tips removed and wings split
⅓ cup low-sodium gluten-free tamari
1 tablespoon toasted sesame oil
3 tablespoons grated candied ginger
½ teaspoon grated lime zest
1½ teaspoons fresh lime juice (from 1 lime)
Vegetable oil cooking spray
1 tablespoon chopped fresh cilantro leaves
1 teaspoon toasted white sesame seeds

Put the chicken wings in a resealable plastic bag.

In a small bowl, whisk the tamari with the sesame oil, candied ginger, and lime zest and lime juice. Add 2 tablespoons water, stir well, and pour the marinade over the wings. Seal the bag and turn it upside down several times to coat the wings with the marinade.

Refrigerate the wings in the bag for at least 8 hours or overnight. Turn the bag a few times during marinating, if possible.

Preheat the oven to 400°F.

Spray a small rimmed baking sheet with vegetable oil spray. Pour the contents of the bag onto the baking sheet, spreading the wings out so they do not touch each other. Bake for 25 to 30 minutes, turning the wings after 12 to 15 minutes of cooking. The wings are done when they are golden brown and glazed with the marinade.

Allow the wings to rest at room temperature for 5 minutes. Before serving, sprinkle them with the cilantro and sesame seeds.

Chicken Marsala Meatballs

Chicken Marsala Meatballs

MAKES 24 MEATBALLS

These light, juicy meatballs are one of the most popular antipasti at Giada, my restaurant in Las Vegas. The meatballs, served with cremini mushrooms, make a great appetizer, and can be served over pasta or polenta, or piled on a hero sandwich.

¼ cup panko bread crumbs
2 tablespoons milk, at room temperature
⅓ cup plus 1 tablespoon Marsala wine
1 pound ground chicken breast
¼ cup grated Pecorino Romano, plus more for serving
1 large egg, beaten
2 tablespoons chopped fresh flat-leaf parsley leaves
1 teaspoon kosher salt, divided
⅛ teaspoon freshly ground black pepper
2 tablespoons extra-virgin olive oil, plus more for frying
8 ounces cremini mushrooms, sliced
1 large shallot, minced
1½ teaspoons all-purpose flour
1¼ cups low-sodium chicken broth

In a large bowl, mix together the bread crumbs, milk, and 1 tablespoon of the wine. Let the bread crumbs soak for about 5 minutes. Add the chicken, pecorino, egg, parsley, ½ teaspoon of the salt, and the pepper. Using your hands, gently mix the ingredients together. Do not overmix. Refrigerate for at least 2 hours or overnight.

In a medium skillet, add enough olive oil to come 1 inch up the sides of the pan. Heat the oil over medium-high heat until it registers 350°F on a deep-fry thermometer.

Working quickly, scoop about 2 tablespoons of the chicken mixture into your palms and roll into a ball. Do not handle the meat more than necessary. Repeat with the remaining meat mixture. Gently drop the meatballs, a few at a time, into the hot oil (do not crowd the pan, and let the oil regain its heat between each batch). The meatballs will better retain their shape the colder they are. Fry the balls, rotating them often with a long-handled wooden spoon, until they are golden brown all the way around. (They will continue to cook when added to the sauce later.) Transfer to a paper towel–lined plate and set aside.

In another skillet, heat 1 tablespoon of the olive oil over medium-high heat. Add the mushrooms and cook, stirring often with a wooden spoon, for about 5 minutes, until nicely browned. Add the shallot and the remaining ½ teaspoon salt and cook for another 2 minutes or until the shallot begins to soften.

Reduce the heat to medium and stir in the flour and the remaining tablespoon olive oil to form a paste. Add the remaining ⅓ cup wine and stir until the mixture is smooth. Whisk in the chicken broth and simmer for about 5 minutes or until heated through and smooth.

Add the meatballs to the sauce and simmer for an additional 5 minutes to let the flavors blend and to ensure the meatballs are cooked through. Serve warm, garnished with grated pecorino cheese.

It's All About the Apps

When hosting a get-together at home, I like to offer my guests an assortment of appetizers rather than a more conventional meal. The key is to remember that you're not running a restaurant; one or two hot items that require your supervision is plenty. Round out the spread with some room-temperature options so you're not stuck in the kitchen while everyone else is having fun.

Ricotta and Cinnamon Meatballs

Ricotta and Cinnamon Meatballs

SERVES 8 TO 10

There are meatballs . . . and then there are my meatballs! In this version orzo takes the place of bread crumbs, and as they cook, the orzo absorbs the sauce, adding even more flavor to this already tasty dish.

1 large or 2 small shallots, minced
2 garlic cloves, minced
1 large egg
¼ teaspoon ground cinnamon
⅛ teaspoon ground nutmeg
1 pound ground chuck, 20% fat
¼ cup raw orzo
½ cup whole-milk ricotta cheese
¼ cup fresh basil leaves, chopped, plus whole leaves for garnish
½ teaspoon kosher salt
¼ teaspoon freshly ground black pepper
2 cups marinara sauce, homemade (see page 121) or store-bought
Shaved Parmesan cheese, for serving

In a medium bowl, whisk together the shallots, garlic, egg, cinnamon, and nutmeg. Using a wooden spoon, stir in the meat, orzo, ricotta, and chopped basil. Add ¼ cup water, salt, and pepper and mix well.

Bring the marinara to a simmer in a shallow 12-inch skillet. Form heaping tablespoonfuls of the meat mixture into balls. Drop the meatballs into the simmering sauce. Cover the pot and allow them to simmer for 15 minutes. Serve 3 to 4 meatballs per person, topped with shaved Parm and garnished with fresh basil leaves.

Artichoke Arancini

V V

MAKES ABOUT 25 ARANCINI

Classic arancini are made vegan here by omitting the cheese; they are tasty and unusual.

ARANCINI

3 tablespoons extra-virgin olive oil
3 shallots, minced
3 garlic cloves, minced
½ teaspoon kosher salt
1 cup Arborio rice
1 cup dry white wine
1 tablespoon soy sauce
1 cup unsalted vegetable broth
¾ cup marinated artichoke hearts, cut into ¼-inch pieces
¼ cup fresh basil leaves, chopped

FOR FRYING

1 cup extra-virgin olive oil
1 cup vegetable oil
½ cup all-purpose flour
½ cup unsweetened almond milk
1 cup panko bread crumbs

2 cups warmed marinara sauce, homemade (see page 121) or store-bought, for dipping (optional)

Prepare the arancini: Heat a 3½-quart Dutch oven over medium-high heat. Add the olive oil, shallots, garlic, and salt. Cook, stirring often, for about 2 minutes, until soft and fragrant. Add the rice and toast, stirring constantly to coat in the oil, for about 2 additional minutes. Add the white wine and soy sauce and cook, stirring often, until the wine is almost entirely absorbed.

Combine the vegetable broth and 1 cup water in a measuring cup. Add ¾ cup of the broth mixture to the rice and stir until almost completely absorbed, about 4 minutes. Continue adding the broth, ½ cup at a time, stirring constantly and allowing each addition of broth to be absorbed before adding the next. Cook until the rice is tender but not mushy, about 20 minutes. Stir in the artichokes. Remove the pot from the heat and allow the mixture to cool for 15 minutes. Stir in the basil and spread on a rimmed baking sheet to cool completely, about 20 minutes.

Fry the arancini: Heat the oils in a large heavy-bottomed saucepan or Dutch oven over medium heat until a deep-fry thermometer reaches 350°F.

Set up a station with the flour, almond milk, and panko in separate shallow bowls. Using a small ice cream scoop, scoop about 2 tablespoons of the rice mixture into your hands and gently roll into a ball. Dredge the ball in the flour, then in the almond milk, and then into the panko, packing it on tightly. Continue with the remaining rice mixture. Fry the coated balls in batches of 4 or 5 for about 3 minutes or until golden brown on the outside and warmed through. Drain on paper towels. Serve with warm marinara for dipping if desired.

Hot Italian Sausage-Stuffed Dates

Hot Italian Sausage–Stuffed Dates with Lemon-Basil Crema

GF

MAKES 12 DATES

These sausage-stuffed dates broiled in bacon always get an especially warm welcome. They can easily be assembled well ahead of time, then baked off as needed.

2 tablespoons sour cream, at room temperature
1 tablespoon mascarpone cheese, at room temperature
1 teaspoon grated lemon zest
2 tablespoons fresh lemon juice (from 1 lemon)
¼ teaspoon kosher salt
3 tablespoons chopped fresh basil leaves
12 Medjool dates
2 links hot Italian sausage, casings removed
6 slices bacon (about 4 ounces), halved to make 12 short slices

In a small bowl, whisk together the sour cream, mascarpone, lemon zest and juice, and salt to make the crema. Fold in the basil. Cover and refrigerate for at least 1 hour to let the flavors marry.

Preheat the oven to 400°F.

Make a small lengthwise slit down the center of each date. Remove the pits and open the dates slightly, leaving the bottom intact.

Place about 2 teaspoons of the sausage meat in the cavity of each date. With your fingers, push the sides of the dates up and around the sausage to enclose it a little. Wrap each date with a piece of bacon. Transfer the wrapped dates to a rimmed baking sheet.

Bake the dates for 8 minutes. Remove from the oven and turn over each date. Bake for 8 to 10 minutes (or a little longer), until the bacon is crisp. Serve warm with the lemon-basil crema.

Party On!

When it comes to hosting a large number of guests in a relatively stress-free way, a cocktail party is often the path of least resistence, and for good reason. It's less structured than a dinner party (fewer timing issues to be worried about!), people can come and go as they please, and of course having a killer playlist and a house cocktail or two can do some of the heavy lifting to make sure the mood is appropriately festive. That doesn't mean, though, that you shouldn't put a little thought and effort into the food. If your cocktail parties have been stuck in cheese-and-cracker mode, it's time to move on to some bites that are a bit more memorable.

The best cocktail party foods fall into one of two categories: First, there's the kind that are a play on classics—but elevated. I'm a big fan of one- to two-biters. Think mini mac-and-cheese cupcakes or anything with bacon. The second type is anything in the form of a dip. Guests love to congregate around a big bowl of dip, from a creamy artichoke dip to tomato sauce whipped with mascarpone to a great pesto. Set out a few vehicles for the dips: Seasonal veggies, endive, fennel, crostini, homemade tortilla or pita chips, and grissini are all crowd-pleasers.

Crostini Bar

Heirloom LA makes some of the most striking platters and cocktail spreads I've ever seen, with a riot of different shapes, colors, and textures that make them a magnet for partygoers. Owner Tara Maxey shared her tips for creating an edible centerpiece your guests will want to congregate around:

- Just like assembling a floral bouquet, you need to start your platter with a focal point or three (uneven numbers are best) and build from that.
- Create different heights to make your platter more interesting and dimensional.
- Seasonal produce will be the prettiest and most fragrant, not to mention most flavorful. Get your produce from a local farmers' market, if possible.
- Ask what kind of edible flowers are available. Don't overlook flowering herbs; they are lovely to work with.
- Choose cheeses with different colors and textures, and break them up into slices and crumbles.
- If you are incorporating meats, they will be prettier if you fold the slices rather than arrange them in stacks. Globs of anything are not pretty.
- Place dips and spreads in little bowls or form them into quenelles (small ovals) using two spoons.
- When you mound dip in a bowl, make a little well in the center and add just a bit of olive oil to give it brightness. Top with chopped fresh parsley or edible flowers.

Goat Cheese Toasts

V

SERVES 12

Lots of tangy ingredients make these simple crostini anything but ordinary. Both the crostini and cheese mixture can be prepared ahead of time; use any leftover cheese mixture to fill an omelet or toss with hot pasta and peas.

36 (½-inch-thick) slices baguette bread
3 tablespoons extra-virgin olive oil
8 ounces soft fresh goat cheese
4 ounces cream cheese
2 teaspoons finely chopped fresh flat-leaf parsley leaves
2 teaspoons finely grated lemon zest
Salt and coarsely ground multicolored or black peppercorns
½ cup pitted Sicilian green olives or kalamata olives, finely chopped
2 tablespoons thinly sliced fresh chives

Preheat the oven to 375°F. Arrange the bread slices on 2 large heavy-rimmed baking sheets. Brush the oil over the bread slices. Bake until the crostini are pale golden and crisp, about 15 minutes. (The crostini can be stored in an airtight container for up to 2 days.)

Blend the goat cheese and cream cheese in a food processor until smooth and creamy. Add the parsley and lemon zest. Using the on/off button, pulse just to blend. Season to taste with salt and pepper. If not serving immediately, cover and refrigerate.

To serve, let the cheese mixture stand at room temperature for 1 hour to soften slightly if it has been refrigerated. Spread the cheese mixture over the crostini. Sprinkle with the olives, chives, and pepper. Arrange the toasts on a platter and serve.

Goat Cheese Toasts

Buffalo Grilled Shrimp with Goat Cheese Dipping Sauce

Buffalo Grilled Shrimp with Goat Cheese Dipping Sauce

GF

SERVES 6 TO 8

Shrimp and goat cheese instead of the traditional chicken and blue cheese make this a lighter spin on a game day favorite.

1 pound jumbo shrimp, peeled and deveined
¼ cup plus 2 tablespoons hot sauce
4 garlic cloves, smashed and peeled and coarsely chopped
3 tablespoons extra-virgin olive oil
1 teaspoon grated lemon zest
1 tablespoon finely chopped shallot
¼ teaspoon ground cumin
¼ teaspoon smoked paprika
1 cup heavy cream, at room temperature
⅓ teaspoon plus ½ teaspoon kosher salt
4 ounces fresh goat cheese, at room temperature
1 tablespoon chopped fresh chives
1 tablespoon chopped fresh flat-leaf parsley leaves

In a medium bowl, toss the shrimp with ¼ cup of the hot sauce, the garlic, 2 tablespoons of the oil, and the lemon zest. Cover with plastic wrap and allow to sit at room temperature for 15 minutes. Heat a small saucepan over medium heat and when hot, pour in the remaining tablespoon of oil. Add the shallot and sauté for about 2 minutes to soften. Add the cumin and paprika and continue to cook, stirring with a wooden spoon, for 1 minute longer. Add the heavy cream and ⅓ teaspoon of the salt. Reduce the heat to low and simmer for about 5 minutes, until slightly thickened.

Whisk the goat cheese into the cream sauce a little at a time, until fully incorporated and smooth. Remove from the heat and allow the sauce to cool for 5 minutes. Stir the chives and parsley into the dipping sauce.

Preheat a grill or grill pan to medium-high heat.

Season the shrimp with the remaining ½ teaspoon salt and grill for 2 to 3 minutes on each side or until opaque all the way through. Remove to a clean bowl and toss with the remaining 2 tablespoons hot sauce. Serve with the goat cheese dipping sauce.

Sautéed Shrimp Cocktail

GF

SERVES 4 TO 6

In the classic steakhouse version of this perennial favorite, the shrimp are boiled and often watery-tasting. When they are sautéed and served with a yogurt-mustard dipping sauce, the flavor is much more concentrated and lively.

1¼ cups plain yogurt
2 tablespoons mayonnaise
2 tablespoons whole-grain mustard
1½ tablespoons pure maple syrup
1 teaspoon ground turmeric
¼ cup chopped fresh basil leaves
Salt and freshly ground black pepper
2 tablespoons extra-virgin olive oil
1 pound jumbo shrimp, peeled, tail on, deveined
1 tablespoon herbes de Provence

In a medium bowl, mix together the yogurt, mayonnaise, mustard, maple syrup, and turmeric. When blended, fold in the basil and season to taste with salt and pepper.

In a large skillet, heat the oil over medium-high heat. Add the shrimp and herbes de Provence and season lightly with salt and pepper. Cook for about 3 minutes on each side or until the shrimp are pink and cooked through. Serve the shrimp with the dipping sauce.

Sautéed Shrimp Cocktail

Pizza

Hot, cheesy, savory, and chewy, these crusty slices of heaven are top sellers at my restaurant and others around the world for a reason. I have a special connection to 'za, though. The dough-sauce-and-cheese layered variety we all know can trace its origins to Naples, where my grandfather was from. Some of my earliest kitchen memories are of making pizza with him. When Jade and I spend time tossing and topping dough, it takes me right back to those happy times.

If you don't have the time or the inclination to make your own dough, pick some up at your local pizzeria or the grocery store's freezer. Top with a quick sauce made of canned crushed tomatoes, a sprinkling of shredded mozzarella, and a few leaves of basil. That's it for the basics. Beyond that, just about anything you can think of makes a great pizza topping for a bit of handheld happiness.

The Only Pizza Dough You'll Ever Need

V

MAKES ABOUT 1 POUND

1 cup warm water
1 teaspoon active dry yeast
1 teaspoon honey
2¼ cups flour
1 teaspoon kosher salt
Extra virgin olive oil

To the warm water, add the yeast and honey. Stir to dissolve. Allow the mixture to sit for 3 minutes to make sure the yeast is alive. It should foam and start to bubble.

Place the flour and salt in the bowl of an electric mixer fitted with a dough hook. Add the yeast mixture and mix on low speed until the mixture starts to comes together. Turn the speed up to medium and mix for 8 minutes. The dough should start to pull away from the sides but still remain soft and slighty sticky at the bottom of the bowl. Add an extra tablespoon of flour if needed. Coat your hands in a bit of olive oil and form the dough into a ball. Place the dough in a bowl that is coated in olive oil. Cover with a towel and allow to sit in a warm place for 1 hour or until doubled in size. Knock down the dough and cut into 4 equal pieces if making small pizzas or simply reform into a ball and allow the dough to proof for an additional hour. The dough is now ready to use.

Roasted Acorn Squash and Gorgonzola Pizza

V

SERVES 4

This sweet, spicy, and salty combo is unique and completely addictive.

1 (1-pound) acorn squash
2 tablespoons pure maple syrup
1 tablespoon extra-virgin olive oil
1 teaspoon crushed red pepper flakes
½ teaspoon kosher salt
½ teaspoon freshly ground black pepper
All-purpose flour, for rolling the dough
1 pound pizza dough, homemade (opposite) or store-bought
1 cup shredded whole-milk mozzarella cheese
½ cup crumbled Gorgonzola cheese
1 cup arugula

Preheat the oven to 375°F. Line a rimmed baking sheet with parchment paper.

Slice the squash in half through the stem and scoop out the seeds. Slice the squash into ½- to ¾-inch-thick half-moons and place in a medium bowl. Toss the squash with the maple syrup, olive oil, red pepper flakes, ¼ teaspoon of the salt, and ¼ teaspoon of the pepper. Arrange the squash on the prepared baking sheet and bake until tender and golden, 20 to 25 minutes. Leave the oven on.

On a flour-dusted piece of parchment paper, roll the pizza dough into a circle 13 inches in diameter. Transfer the pizza and parchment paper to a baking sheet. Sprinkle the dough with the mozzarella and Gorgonzola. Bake until the crust is golden and cooked through, 25 to 30 minutes. Peel the skin off the squash pieces and arrange the squash atop the hot pizza. Scatter the arugula over it all and season with the remaining ¼ teaspoon salt and ¼ teaspoon pepper. Slice and serve.

Roasted Acorn Squash and Gorgonzola Pizza

Focaccia with Tangerine and Fennel

Focaccia with Tangerine and Fennel

V V

SERVES 4 TO 6

A great appetizer, this focaccia is sweet and savory. I happen to love tangerines, but you can substitute any kind of orange or cherries for an equally delicious dish.

3 tablespoons extra-virgin olive oil
1 pound pizza dough, homemade (see page 64) or store-bought
½ tangerine, peeled and sliced thin, seeds removed
½ fennel bulb, cored, shaved thin on a mandoline
½ teaspoon fennel seeds
1 teaspoon coarse sea salt, for sprinkling

Preheat the oven to 400°F. Brush the bottom and sides of a 9 x 13-inch rimmed baking sheet with 2 tablespoons of the olive oil.

Stretch the pizza dough to fit the pan, pushing out the dough with your hands as needed. Using a pastry brush, cover the top of the dough with the remaining tablespoon of oil. Evenly distribute the tangerine slices, the shaved fennel, and the fennel seeds, pushing the items gently into the dough using your fingertips. Sprinkle with the salt.

Bake the focaccia until golden brown, 25 to 30 minutes. Cut into slices and serve.

Pizza Bianca

SERVES 6

This may be the simplest pizza recipe I know and also one of the best. Flattened pizza dough is sprinkled with salt and thyme, baked for 15 minutes, then topped with slices of mortadella. Addictive.

1 pound pizza dough, homemade (see page 64) or store-bought
All-purpose flour, for rolling the dough
2 teaspoons extra-virgin olive oil
1 tablespoon chopped fresh thyme leaves
¾ teaspoon kosher salt
½ pound thinly sliced mortadella sausage

Position an oven rack in the center of the oven and preheat the oven to 450°F. Roll out the dough on a lightly floured work surface to ½ inch thick. Transfer the dough to a heavy large baking sheet. Using a fork, pierce the dough all over.

Drizzle the oil over the dough. Sprinkle with the thyme and salt. Bake until golden, about 15 minutes. Remove from the oven and drape the mortadella over the pizza. Cut into wedges or squares, and serve.

Pizza Bianca

Roasted Mushroom and Kale Pizzette

V

SERVES 6

Canapé-size pizzette are the perfect choice for game-day gatherings. Earthy mushrooms and kale combined with pungent Gorgonzola make a party bite that's hard to pass up (and sneakily healthy).

8 ounces button mushrooms, stemmed and sliced
1 teaspoon extra-virgin olive oil, plus more for brushing and drizzling
½ teaspoon kosher salt
All-purpose flour, for rolling the dough
1 pound pizza dough, homemade (see page 64) or store-bought
¼ cup shredded mozzarella cheese
1 small bunch of Tuscan kale (about 4 leaves), ribs removed, leaves sliced into ribbons
2 ounces Gorgonzola cheese, crumbled

Position a rack in the center of the oven and preheat the oven to 400°F. Line 2 baking sheets, one rimmed, with parchment paper.

On the rimmed baking sheet, toss the mushrooms with the olive oil and salt, then spread the mushrooms in an even layer. Roast for 8 to 10 minutes, until they are golden brown. Set the mushrooms aside and increase the oven temperature to 475°F.

On a lightly floured surface, roll out the pizza dough to ¼ inch thick. Using a 3-inch round cookie cutter, cut out circles in the dough and transfer them to the second lined baking sheet. Brush the dough circles lightly with olive oil.

Place a teaspoon of mozzarella on each circle, then top with the mushrooms and kale, then the Gorgonzola. Drizzle a little more olive oil over each pizzette and bake until golden and bubbly, about 10 minutes. Arrange the pizzette on a platter and serve immediately.

Roasted Mushroom and Kale Pizzette

Mini
Eggplant
Parmesan

Mini Eggplant Parmesan

V

SERVES 6 TO 8

These small eggplant bites are crisp and light. Japanese eggplants are the perfect size and shape for these bite-size portions, plus they have thin skins, which makes them easy to slice.

SAUCE

2 tablespoons extra-virgin olive oil
1 shallot, chopped
1 large garlic clove, minced
1 cup marinara sauce, homemade (see page 121) or store-bought
¼ cup finely chopped fresh basil leaves
1 teaspoon dried oregano
⅛ teaspoon crushed red pepper flakes
¼ teaspoon balsamic vinegar, plus more to taste
¼ teaspoon kosher salt
⅛ teaspoon freshly ground black pepper

EGGPLANT

1 cup panko bread crumbs
½ cup all-purpose flour
2 large egg whites
2 Japanese eggplants, sliced ¼ inch thick on the diagonal
⅔ cup extra-virgin olive oil
½ cup (packed) coarsely grated whole-milk mozzarella cheese
½ cup finely grated Parmesan cheese
Small fresh basil leaves, for garnish

For the sauce: Place the oil in a heavy medium saucepan. Add the shallot and garlic to the saucepan. Stir over medium heat until very fragrant, about 2 minutes. Add the marinara sauce, basil, oregano, and red pepper flakes. Simmer the sauce, stirring often, until the flavors blend and the sauce thickens slightly, about 5 minutes. Mix in the vinegar, salt, and pepper, then more vinegar if desired. Puree the sauce in a blender. Cool, cover, and chill. The sauce can be made up to 2 days ahead of time.

For the eggplant: Put the panko and flour in separate medium bowls. Whisk the egg whites in a third bowl until broken up and very frothy. Dip each eggplant slice first in flour, then in egg whites, and finally in panko to coat completely. Arrange the eggplant slices on paper towels and let them sit at room temperature. The eggplant can be prepared to this point up to 2 hours ahead of time.

Heat the oil in a heavy medium skillet over medium-high heat for 2 to 3 minutes until shimmering and hot. Cook half of the eggplant slices for 1 to 2 minutes on each side or until deep golden brown on both sides. Taking care not to break the crispy crust, transfer the eggplant to a paper towel–lined plate. Fry the remaining eggplant slices and let them rest at room temperature. The eggplant can be cooked to this point up to 1 hour ahead of time.

Preheat the oven to 350°F.

Toss the mozzarella and Parmesan cheeses in a small bowl until blended.

Spread 1 generous teaspoon of sauce on each eggplant slice. Top with a rounded teaspoon of cheese and spread out to cover the slice. Press lightly to adhere. Transfer the eggplant slices to a rimmed baking sheet and bake for about 12 minutes or until the cheese melts and the eggplant is heated through and crisp.

Transfer the eggplant slices to a platter and garnish each with 2 small basil leaves. Let them stand for 2 to 3 minutes to cool a bit before serving.

Salads & Seasons

If I go more than a day without a big bowl of greens, I feel it, and not in a good way. Fresh, clean, minimally manipulated salads are the prettiest and most improvisational way to ensure you get your veggies 365 days of the year. Actually, I would happily eat a salad for breakfast, lunch, and dinner, especially as the term encompasses such a wide variety of dishes, from a simply dressed bowl of fresh leafy greens to heartier mixtures with few or no greens at all. Truth be told, when it comes to salads, there really are no rules except that the ingredients be fresh, unprocessed, and lightly tossed with a complementary dressing that's been made from scratch. (If I haven't yet persuaded you to walk right past the bottled-dressing aisle of your supermarket, turn directly to page 74, where you'll discover The Only Vinaigrette You'll Ever Need.) Don't limit your salad-making moments to the summer months, either; made with a base of cooked grains or winter's sturdy greens, a cold-weather salad is anything but an oxymoron and everything I want in a casual and healthy meal.

Herbed Cucumber Salad

V GF

SERVES 2 TO 4

Herbs give this dressing its punch of flavor without excess oil and salt. Sweet, crunchy, tangy, and herby—it's satisfying without weighing you down.

- 1 medium cucumber, quartered lengthwise and cut into ½-inch wedges
- 1 pint yellow cherry tomatoes, halved
- 2 jarred roasted red peppers, sliced into strips
- 2 tablespoons white balsamic vinegar
- 2 tablespoons extra-virgin olive oil
- ¼ teaspoon kosher salt
- ⅛ teaspoon freshly ground black pepper
- ¼ cup loosely packed fresh flat-leaf parsley leaves
- ¼ cup loosely packed fresh mint leaves
- ¼ cup loosely packed fresh dill fronds
- ½ cup crumbled feta cheese

In a large bowl, combine the cucumber wedges, tomatoes, roasted red peppers, vinegar, olive oil, salt, and pepper. Add the parsley, mint, dill, and feta and toss gently to combine. Allow the salad to sit for at least 10 minutes before serving to allow the flavors to marry.

Herbed Cucumber Salad

Herb Salad with Yogurt Dressing

V GF

SERVES 4

This salad makes a delicious side to many dishes. The herbs are fresh, light, and super-flavorful. The citrus and za'atar in the dressing bring the herbs to a whole other level!

DRESSING

- ⅓ cup nonfat plain Greek yogurt
- 1 teaspoon za'atar
- ¼ teaspoon grated lemon zest
- 2 teaspoons white balsamic vinegar
- 1 tablespoon extra-virgin olive oil
- ¼ teaspoon kosher salt

SALAD

- ½ cup fresh basil leaves
- ¾ cup fresh flat-leaf parsley leaves
- ¼ cup fresh mint leaves
- ¼ cup fresh tarragon leaves
- ¼ cup dill fronds

For the dressing: In a small bowl, whisk together the yogurt, za'atar, lemon zest, and vinegar. Continue whisking while drizzling in the olive oil. Season with the salt and whisk in ½ teaspoon water. Refrigerate until ready to use.

For the salad: In a medium bowl, gently toss all of the herbs together using your hands so as not to bruise them. On a platter or large plate, spread ½ cup of the dressing. Pile the tossed herbs in the middle of the dressing so that as people serve themselves they can spoon some dressing onto the herbs.

Herb Salad with Yogurt Dressing

The Only Vinaigrette You'll Ever Need

The Only Vinaigrette You'll Ever Need

V V GF

MAKES 1 CUP

A jar of this classic dressing in your refrigerator is like that little black dress in your closet—it goes with anything and everything from a warm lentil or potato salad to a plate of delicate Bibb lettuce, radishes, and avocado. Leftover dressing will keep for up to two weeks in the refrigerator, so make a double batch while you're at it. Just shake or whisk to combine before using. It can be brushed on chicken breasts or fish before grilling; used as a marinade for flank steak; served with boiled shrimp or lobster; drizzled on steamed or roasted vegetables; tossed with farro, quinoa, and other cooked grains; or added by the tablespoon to bowls of hearty soups.

1 small shallot, minced
¼ cup apple cider vinegar
1 teaspoon Dijon mustard
1 teaspoon chopped fresh thyme leaves
¾ teaspoon agave syrup
½ teaspoon kosher salt
¾ cup extra-virgin olive oil

Place the shallot in a fine-mesh strainer and rinse under warm water; drain well. Transfer the shallot to a bowl, add the vinegar, and allow to sit at room temperature for 5 minutes. Add the mustard, thyme, agave, and salt and whisk to combine. Continue whisking and slowly drizzle in the olive oil until fully incorporated and emulsified.

Whipped Ricotta with Greens

V GF

SERVES 4 TO 6

Sure, it's a salad, but it's also a pretty and filling first course, which is how we serve it in my Vegas restaurant. Pureeing store-bought ricotta with olive oil and salt gives it an incredibly smooth and sexy texture that goes perfectly with the crunch of raw vegetables.

RICOTTA

1 cup whole-milk ricotta cheese, chilled
2 teaspoons extra-virgin olive oil
⅛ teaspoon kosher salt

DRESSING

1 cup packed fresh basil leaves
2 tablespoons toasted pine nuts (see Cook's Note)
2 tablespoons white balsamic vinegar
¼ teaspoon crushed red pepper flakes
½ teaspoon kosher salt
3 tablespoons extra-virgin olive oil

SALAD

1 cup heirloom cherry tomatoes, halved or quartered depending on the size
18 sugar snap peas (about ¼ pound), trimmed and cut in half
3 cups baby kale or frisée

For the ricotta: Place the ricotta, olive oil, and salt in a food processor. Blend for 30 seconds or until light and smooth. Remove to a bowl and set aside.

For the dressing: Place the basil, pine nuts, vinegar, red pepper flakes, and salt in a food processor. With the motor running, drizzle in the olive oil until a smooth dressing is formed. Set aside.

For the salad: In a large bowl, toss the tomatoes, snap peas, and baby kale with the dressing.

To assemble: Divide the whipped ricotta among 4 to 6 small salad plates. Spread the ricotta across the bottom of each plate. Place some of the dressed vegetable salad on top of the cheese, leaving a bit of the cheese exposed on the side.

Cook's Note: To toast the pine nuts, place them in a small sauté pan over medium-high heat for 2 to 3 minutes, stirring regularly, until just starting to turn golden. This method works well with other types of nuts.

Grilled Caprese Salad

Grilled Caprese Salad

V GF

SERVES 4 TO 6

In this take on mozzarella caprese, grilling the tomatoes really brings out their flavor, while olives balance the sweetness.

1 cup pitted marinated olives, roughly chopped
¼ cup packed basil, chopped
¼ cup plus 2 tablespoons extra-virgin olive oil
3 large tomatoes, sliced ⅓ inch thick
½ teaspoon kosher salt
1 pound fresh mozzarella cheese, sliced ⅓ inch thick

In a small bowl, mix together the olives, basil, and ¼ cup of the olive oil. Set aside.

Preheat a grill pan over medium-high heat. Lay out the tomato slices and season on all sides with the salt and the remaining 2 tablespoons of olive oil. Place the tomato slices on the preheated grill and grill for about 2 minutes per side or until the edges are beginning to brown.

Transfer the tomatoes from the grill to a platter, and while still hot, shingle with the mozzarella cheese slices to warm and soften the cheese. Spoon the olive mixture over the top and serve.

Roman Caprese Salad

V GF

SERVES 6

I tend to think of a classic recipe as a stepping-stone to fun, new recipes. Using the dish as a point of departure, you can transform it with the simple addition of an ingredient. Here an assortment of olives upgrades this traditional mozzarella, tomato, and basil salad.

1 cup balsamic vinegar
1 cup pitted green and black olives, halved
1 cup fresh ciliegine (mozzarella balls)
¼ cup chopped fresh flat-leaf parsley leaves
2 tablespoons capers, rinsed and drained
1 garlic clove, thinly sliced
8 fresh basil leaves, shredded
½ teaspoon freshly ground black pepper
6 tablespoons extra-virgin olive oil
1 pound vine-ripened heirloom tomatoes (about 3 tomatoes)

In a small saucepan, cook the balsamic vinegar over low heat until thick, syrupy, and reduced to ¼ cup, about 20 minutes. Set aside to cool.

In a small bowl, combine the olives, mozzarella, parsley, capers, garlic, basil, pepper, and olive oil and toss to coat well.

To serve, slice the tomatoes into ¼-inch-thick rounds and place, slightly overlapping, on a serving plate. Spoon the olive-mozzarella mixture over the tomatoes. Drizzle the reduced balsamic over the salad and serve.

Roman Caprese Salad

Eggplant and Zucchini Scapece

Eggplant and Zucchini Scapece

V V GF

MAKES 20 SCAPECE

The veggies are grilled just enough to cook off the raw flavor, but not enough to make them mushy. Once marinated in the zesty vinaigrette, their texture becomes dense and meaty.

SCAPECE VINAIGRETTE

2 tablespoons white balsamic vinegar
1 tablespoon apple cider vinegar
4 tablespoons extra-virgin olive oil
1 teaspoon lemon zest
1 garlic clove, smashed and peeled
1 tablespoon chopped fresh mint
1 teaspoon kosher salt

SCAPECE

2 Japanese eggplant, sliced 1/16 of an inch thick lengthwise on a mandoline
2 medium zucchini, sliced 1/16 of an inch thick lengthwise on a mandoline

For the vinaigrette: In a small bowl whisk together the balsamic, cider vinegar, olive oil, lemon zest, garlic, mint, and salt. Set aside to let the flavors mingle.

For the scapece: Meanwhile, preheat a grill pan over medium high heat. Gently toss the eggplant and zucchini slices with the salt and olive oil. Grill the slices for about 2 minutes per side or until they are nicely marked and pliable but not overcooked. Remove from the grill and brush each slice with the scapece vinaigrette.

Place a zucchini strip on a board lengthwise. Lay a slice of eggplant parallel to it, lining up the sides farthest from you. If there is a little overlap, that is okay. Begin rolling at the end closest to you and roll until it is rolled up like a scroll. Drizzle a bit more dressing over the top. Place on a plate and chill until ready to serve. Just before serving spoon a little more dressing over the top.

Better Wedge Salad

Better Wedge Salad

SERVES 4

Radicchio and romaine stand in for iceberg and smoked almonds for bacon in this play on the classic wedge salad.

DRESSING

¼ cup low-fat buttermilk
1 tablespoon extra-virgin olive oil
½ cup low-fat plain Greek yogurt
¼ teaspoon onion powder
½ teaspoon garlic powder
⅛ teaspoon cayenne pepper
½ teaspoon kosher salt
1 tablespoon chopped dill

1 head radicchio
2 tablespoons olive oil
¼ teaspoon kosher salt
2 small heads romaine lettuce
½ cup smoked almonds, chopped
⅓ cup crumbled Gorgonzola dolce

For the dressing: In a medium bowl, whisk together the buttermilk, oil, yogurt, onion powder, garlic powder, cayenne, salt, and dill. Allow to sit for 1 hour in the refrigerator to let the flavors mingle. Preheat a grill pan over medium-high heat.

Cut the radicchio into 6 wedges and drizzle with the olive oil and salt. Place the wedges on the grill and cook for 2 minutes per side or until slightly browned and wilted. Place the wedges on a platter.

Meanwhile, quarter the romaine and nestle it in between the wedges of radicchio. Dollop the dressing around the platter and scatter the smoked almonds and Gorgonzola over the top.

Shaved Vegetable Salad with Goat Cheese Vinaigrette and Walnuts

Shaved Vegetable Salad with Goat Cheese Vinaigrette and Walnuts

V GF

SERVES 4

Who said salad has to be mostly lettuce? This version is a tangle of zucchini and carrots, which are shaved into long strips and tossed with a tart and creamy vinaigrette.

2 medium zucchini, trimmed
3 medium carrots, trimmed and peeled
¾ teaspoon kosher salt
1½ tablespoons extra-virgin olive oil
1 tablespoon white balsamic vinegar
2 ounces fresh goat cheese
2 teaspoons thyme leaves
¼ teaspoon freshly ground black pepper
½ cup toasted walnuts (see Cook's Note, page 75), chopped
¼ cup fresh flat-leaf parsley leaves, chopped

Using a vegetable peeler, shave the zucchini and carrots into long thin strips. Place the strips in a serving bowl and toss with ½ teaspoon of the salt.

In a the bowl of a food processor, combine the olive oil, balsamic vinegar, goat cheese, thyme, 1 teaspoon water, the remaining ¼ teaspoon salt, and the pepper. Puree until smooth. Drizzle the dressing over the vegetables and toss to coat.

Garnish the salad with the walnuts and parsley. Serve.

Grilled Stone Fruit Salad with Orange-Herb Vinaigrette

Grilled Stone Fruit Salad with Orange-Herb Vinaigrette

V GF

SERVES 6

With fresh orange juice, mustard, honey, and fragrant basil and thyme, this vinaigrette has a sweet-tart thing going on, echoing and enhancing the flavors of the summery salad. The nectarines, apricots, and plums take on a smoky edge from the grill, and the walnuts offer some welcome crunch.

ORANGE-HERB VINAIGRETTE

Juice of 1 medium orange
2 teaspoons apple cider vinegar
2 teaspoons Dijon mustard
1 teaspoon raw honey
1 tablespoon finely chopped fresh basil leaves
1 teaspoon finely chopped fresh thyme leaves
¾ teaspoon kosher salt
⅛ teaspoon freshly ground black pepper
¼ cup extra-virgin olive oil

SALAD

2 medium nectarines, pitted and halved
2 medium apricots, pitted and halved
2 medium plums, pitted and halved
1 tablespoon extra-virgin olive oil
½ teaspoon kosher salt
¼ teaspoon freshly ground black pepper
4 cups baby arugula
1 pint cherry or grape tomatoes
¼ cup toasted walnuts (see Cook's Note, page 75), chopped

For the vinaigrette: In a medium bowl, combine the orange juice, vinegar, mustard, honey, basil, thyme, salt, and pepper. Whisk in the olive oil to incorporate.

For the salad: Put a grill pan over medium-high heat or preheat a gas or charcoal grill.

Put the nectarines, apricots, and plums in a medium bowl. Drizzle with the olive oil, sprinkle with the salt and pepper, and toss to coat. Grill the fruit until charred and slightly softened, about 2 minutes per side.

Place the arugula on a platter. Arrange the grilled fruit and the tomatoes and walnuts over the greens. Drizzle with the vinaigrette and toss gently to coat.

Grilled Panzanella Salad

SERVES 4 TO 6

Tuscan panzanella salad is traditionally made with cubes of stale bread and summer tomatoes and perhaps some onion and basil, all tossed with a vinaigrette. I like to grill the bread along with some other seasonal vegetables for a rib-sticking salad. Enjoy this on its own or as an accompaniment to grilled seafood or chicken.

6 (1½-inch-thick) slices rustic wheat bread
2 medium zucchini, halved lengthwise
2 Italian eggplants, halved lengthwise
2 small fennel bulbs, halved lengthwise and cored
4 medium heirloom tomatoes, halved
2 large scallions, trimmed
½ cup plus 2 tablespoons extra-virgin olive oil
¾ teaspoon kosher salt
½ teaspoon freshly ground black pepper
¾ cup chopped fresh basil leaves (about 1 bunch)
¼ cup white balsamic vinegar

Place a grill pan over medium-high heat or preheat a gas or charcoal grill.

Arrange the bread slices and all of the vegetables in a single layer on a heavy rimmed baking sheet. Drizzle with ½ cup of the oil and season with ½ teaspoon of the salt and the pepper. Grill in batches until grill-marked and tender, 3 to 4 minutes per side. (The fennel may need a few more minutes.) Transfer to a cutting board. When cool enough to handle, cut the bread into 1-inch cubes and transfer to a large bowl. Chop the vegetables into ¾-inch pieces and add to the bowl. Add the basil and toss together with the bread and vegetables to gently combine.

In a small bowl, whisk together the remaining 2 tablespoons oil, the balsamic vinegar, and the remaining ¼ teaspoon salt.

Drizzle the dressing over the salad and toss until coated. Serve immediately.

Grilled Panzanella Salad

Asian Radish Slaw

V V GF

SERVES 4

This recipe is a delicious reason to practice your knife skills! The combination of sweet grapes, green herbs, and Asian flavorings is especially refreshing.

½ teaspoon finely grated peeled fresh ginger
2 teaspoons brown rice vinegar
1 teaspoon toasted sesame oil
1 teaspoon vegetable oil
¼ teaspoon kosher salt
1 cup finely sliced napa cabbage
1 black radish, julienned
4 red radishes, julienned
1 cup quartered red seedless grapes
¼ red bell pepper, cored, seeded, and finely diced
2 tablespoons chopped fresh cilantro leaves
1 tablespoon basil chiffonade (fresh basil leaves cut into fine strips)
1 tablespoon chopped fresh chives

In a medium bowl, whisk together the ginger, vinegar, sesame oil, vegetable oil, and salt until combined. Add the cabbage, radishes, grapes, bell pepper, cilantro, basil, and chives. Using your hands, gently toss the slaw together, bringing up the dressing from the bottom of the bowl. Serve immediately or refrigerate for up to 2 hours before serving.

Asian Radish Slaw

Knife Skills

Like most cooks, I have a food processor in my kitchen, but I find lately that I'm relying on it a lot less often than I used to. When it comes to preparing basic family meals, there's something very satisfying and relaxing about cutting ingredients by hand. The repetitive motion, the quiet sound of knife meeting board, the smell of garlic or herbs as their fragrant oils are released remind me of the pleasures of cooking in a way that firing up an appliance just can't.

There are other good reasons food, and particularly vegetables, is generally better cut by hand—some scientific, some aesthetic. Taking a knife to your carrots, potatoes, or onions will give you more uniform pieces so they will all cook in precisely the same amount of time, from hearty cubes for a stew to the tiny dice known as brunoise. The kind of coarse chopping you will get from a food processor yields irregularly shaped pieces, and also releases a vegetable's liquid, so it becomes soggy when cooked. Clean knife cuts give your veggies a nice, consistent surface that browns evenly, and develop that great depth of flavors you want in a soup, a braise, or a roast.

Precise knife cuts are also less likely than the repeated exposure to the blades of a hand chopper or processor to cause the edges of delicate vegetables and fruits to turn brown.

When you are chopping or dicing, let the knife do the work, using a smooth, forward-rocking motion, not downward pressure. You're just there to guide it. It's when you apply pressure that the knife can slip and cause an accident, as well as squash the thing you are cutting. Think of pushing the knife away from you, rocking from the front of the blade to the back, rather than pivoting up and down on the point like a paper cutter.

Put the knife right up against your curled-under fingers and get used to the feeling of rocking the knife against your knuckles. This way it is virtually impossible to cut yourself. Practice finding your rhythm and motion on a vegetable that's somewhat soft, like a potato or an onion. Cut it in half to give yourself a stable base, then slowly work your way from right to left (assuming you're a righty), moving the knife a bit to the left after each cut and scooting your fingers back just enough to keep the blade snugly up against those curled-under fingers. Aim for nice, even slices before you progress to dicing or finer cuts like chiffonade and brunoise. You'll be amazed at the difference having well-prepped vegetables makes in the flavor and appearance of the finished dish, and how Zen-like the process can be!

No More Soggy Salads

This may be painfully obvious, but it bears repeating: The single best way to ensure you're getting something wholesome and healthy at lunchtime rather than mindlessly refueling at the nearest fast-food joint (or grazing from an open fridge) is to eat something you've made yourself. For a lot of us, that means lunch has to be not just tasty but transportable. And while you'd be hard-pressed to improve on a big tossed salad for your midday meal—especially if you're trying to nix sandwiches and pastas to minimize wheat in your diet, up your veggie intake, and/or go meatless for a meal or two each day—it's hard to work up much enthusiasm for a slick mess of faded greens that have drowned in their own dressing when you break out that plastic container come noon.

There are a few ways around this conundrum. First, consider a salad that is sturdy enough to stand up to dressing. Grain salads, pasta salads, or salads made with chunky raw or cooked veggies (think Greek salads, for instance) tend to survive better than those made with more tender ingredients. Another tactic is to transport your salad and dressing separately, to be combined and tossed just before eating. You might even stash a jar of vinaigrette (my "one-and-only" version on page 74 or any customized variation thereof) in the office fridge.

A fun option to consider is the Shaker Salad, a cleverly compiled selection of greens, grains, and other goodies that miraculously retains its crispy crunch for hours and tastes freshly made when you serve it up. The trick is in the layering: Start with the dressing, then load in the heaviest, wettest ingredients, such as cooked beans, chopped tomatoes or cucumber, or cubes of tofu or avocado. Shredded cabbage, lettuce, arugula, kale, or other delicate ingredients come next, with any finishing crunchy bits, like sunflower seeds, going in last, never coming into contact with the soggifying elements until you are ready to shake and serve.

Shaker Salad

V GF

SERVES 1

If you're tired of limp greens and soggy veggies when you pack a salad for lunch, this one is for you. By layering the ingredients over the dressing, with the most delicate ones on top, everything stays fresh and perky until you are ready to shake and serve. Plus it's so pretty in the jar.

1 tablespoon ready-made hummus
1 tablespoon fresh lemon juice (from 1 lemon)
1½ tablespoons extra-virgin olive oil
⅛ teaspoon kosher salt
¼ cup canned black-eyed peas, rinsed and drained
⅓ cup red seedless grapes, cut in half
1 celery stalk, chopped
3 tablespoons crumbled feta cheese
1 cup chopped radicchio (about ¼ head)
1 cup loosely packed chopped romaine (about 2 leaves)
1 tablespoon slivered almonds

In a small bowl, whisk together the hummus, lemon juice, olive oil, and salt. Pour the dressing into the bottom of a wide-mouth quart-size canning jar or any resealable container. On top of the dressing layer the peas, grapes, celery, feta, radicchio, romaine, and almonds. Seal the container and refrigerate for up to 6 hours. When ready to eat, shake the jar to coat and mix the entire salad in the dressing.

Shaker Salad

Winter Salads

In the spring, when the produce aisles are bursting with tender lettuces, salads are the first things we think of making. But the colder months also offer plenty of hardy, nutrient-packed pleasures that make wonderful salads, and they are the perfect complement to the flavors of hearty braises and winter fare. Pair dark, leafy greens like kale, collards, escarole, chard, and mustards with grains and legumes like quinoa, farro, barley, lentils, and black beans and you have the makings of a substantial, satisfying meal. Nuts and cheeses are another great way to add some heft, while lemon zest, dried fruits, and fresh herbs lend brightness and another layer of flavor.

When eaten raw, some winter greens can be a bit chewy, but don't let that deter you. If there are ribs, remove them. Then roll up a stack of leaves cigar-fashion and slice across the bundle. You can also soften greens by letting them sit with a bit of olive oil and salt or by massaging the dressing into the greens (yes, get in there with your bare hands and *squeeze!*). A warm vinaigrette will also help soften the greens.

It's also worth noting that winter greens tend to hold up longer than delicate lettuces in the fridge, so make a big batch for dinner tonight and you've got tomorrow's lunch in the bag.

Hummus Salad

V V GF

SERVES 4

I always have these healthy ingredients around, so it's easy to toss this salad together at the last minute. If you happen to have some za'atar—a Middle Eastern spice blend of thyme, oregano, and sesame seeds—in the spice cabinet, sprinkle it over the top.

⅓ cup extra-virgin olive oil
1 garlic clove, sliced
3 tablespoons tahini
3 tablespoons fresh lemon juice (from 2 lemons)
5 cups shredded kale
½ teaspoon kosher salt
1 (15-ounce) can chickpeas, rinsed and drained
¼ cup slivered sun-dried tomatoes (optional)
Za'atar (optional)

Warm a small sauté pan over medium heat. Add the olive oil and the sliced garlic and cook just until the garlic is fragrant. Allow to cool slightly.

In a large bowl, whisk together the tahini and lemon juice. Slowly add the warmed garlic oil, whisking constantly. Add the kale, salt, chickpeas, and sun-dried tomatoes, if using, and gently toss together, bringing the dressing up from the bottom to coat everything evenly. Serve, sprinkled with za'atar, if desired.

Pomegranate Brussels Sprouts Salad

V GF

SERVES 4

This salad has everything I love in a salad: contrasting colors, textures, and fresh, bright flavors. Seeding fresh pomegranates can be messy work, but fresh pomegranate seeds, or arils, are now available in many markets.

2 tablespoons pomegranate molasses
1 teaspoon Dijon mustard
2 teaspoons agave syrup
½ teaspoon kosher salt
¼ cup extra-virgin olive oil
1 pound Brussels sprouts, shaved thin
1 small bunch of Tuscan kale, ribs removed, leaves sliced into thin ribbons
⅓ cup pomegranate seeds
⅓ cup Marcona almonds, coarsely chopped
4 ounces Gorgonzola dolce cheese, shaved or crumbled (see Cook's Note)

In a large bowl, whisk together the pomegranate molasses, mustard, agave, and salt. Drizzle in the olive oil while whisking constantly, until the mixture is emulsified.

Add the Brussels sprouts and kale to the bowl. Toss to coat in the dressing, working the greens a bit roughly with your hands to help soften them. Fold in the pomegranate seeds and almonds. Top with shaved or crumbled Gorgonzola and serve.

Cook's Note: To shave the Gorgonzola dolce, place the cheese in the freezer for at least 2 hours. Using a vegetable peeler, shave strips of cheese over the salad. By the time the cheese hits the greens, it will be thawed and ready to eat.

Pomegranate Brussels Sprouts Salad

Squeeze the juice of half a lemon in a large bowl and add the endives and apple. Toss to coat so they don't turn brown. Add the corn and cheese and toss. Place the avocado cubes in another bowl and squeeze the second half lemon over them. Toss very gently to coat and add to the salad. Cut the pomegranate in half, if using. Hold over a cutting board, cut side down, and use a wooden spoon to lightly beat the skin, causing the seeds to fall onto the board. Repeat with the other half. Sprinkle the seeds over the salad.

To make the dressing, juice the remaining 2 lemons into a medium bowl. Gradually add the olive oil, whisking constantly, and season with the salt and pepper. Just before serving, pour the dressing over the salad and toss gently.

Raffy's Holiday Salad

V GF

SERVES 4

A perfect winter salad, this is full of colors, flavors, and textures that will set your taste buds tingling: crunchy apple, crisp endive, and creamy avocado.

3 lemons
4 Belgian endives, ends trimmed and cut into 1-inch slices
1 medium green apple, cored and cut into small cubes
⅔ cup corn kernels, cut from ½ ear of corn and simmered for 3 minutes or defrosted frozen corn
4 ounces Gruyère cheese, cut into 1-inch cubes
½ avocado, pitted and cut into 1-inch cubes
1 small pomegranate (optional)
¼ cup plus 2 tablespoons extra-virgin olive oil
1 teaspoon sea salt
½ teaspoon freshly ground black pepper

Beet, Olive, and Kale Salad

V GF

SERVES 4 TO 6

Beets are available in colors ranging from red, yellow, and orange to purple. There are even candy-striped beets. Mix varieties for this winter salad.

BEETS

6 medium beets, trimmed and scrubbed (different colors if available)
8 garlic cloves, peeled and smashed
6 fresh thyme sprigs
6 fresh rosemary sprigs
¼ cup extra-virgin olive oil
1 teaspoon kosher salt

SALAD

1 orange
2 teaspoons apple cider vinegar
2 tablespoons extra-virgin olive oil
1 small bunch of Tuscan kale, ribs removed, leaves sliced thin
¼ teaspoon kosher salt
½ cup crumbled feta cheese
½ cup Castelvetrano olives, pitted and quartered
½ cup hazelnuts, toasted and peeled (see page 75)

Preheat the oven to 350°F.

For the beets: On a large piece of aluminum foil, place the beets, garlic, thyme, and rosemary.

Beet, Olive, and Kale Salad

Drizzle with the oil and sprinkle with the salt. Bring the foil up and around the beets and seal to create a small package. Place on a baking sheet and bake for about 1½ hours or until the beets are tender when pierced with the tip of a knife. Allow the beets to cool slightly. When cool enough to handle, peel the beets by simply rubbing off the skin with a paper towel or by using a small paring knife. Cut the beets into bite-size pieces. Set aside.

For the salad: Grate the zest from the orange and reserve. Working over a bowl, use a sharp knife to cut off the remaining peel and pith, then cut between the membranes to free the segments. Squeeze the membranes over the bowl to capture the juice.

In a large bowl, whisk together 2 tablespoons of the orange juice, the orange zest, apple cider vinegar, and olive oil. Add the beets and toss. Massage the kale lightly with the salt and add the kale to the beets along with the feta, olives, and orange segments. Toss gently. Top with the nuts and serve.

Farro and Arugula Salad

Farro and Arugula Salad

V

SERVES 4

Farro is an umbrella term for unhulled grains from the wheat family. It has a nutty flavor, much like brown rice, that goes well with all kinds of dark greens. If you cook up a batch on the weekend, this is a quick weeknight side or meatless entrée.

⅓ cup plus 2 tablespoons extra-virgin olive oil
1 small shallot, diced
1 cup farro, rinsed
2 fresh oregano sprigs
1 teaspoon kosher salt
Juice of 1 large lemon
Juice of 1 orange
½ cup dried cherries or 1 cup fresh cherries, pitted and halved
½ cup toasted walnuts (see Cook's Note, page 75), chopped
½ English cucumber, peeled and chopped into ¼-inch pieces
1 (5-ounce) container baby arugula
4 ounces fresh goat cheese

Heat a medium saucepan over medium-high heat. Add 2 tablespoons of the olive oil and the shallot and cook, stirring often with a wooden spoon, until the shallot has softened and is fragrant, about 3 minutes. Add the farro and toast in the olive oil, stirring often, for about 4 minutes. Reduce the heat to medium and add the oregano, ½ teaspoon of the salt, and 2 cups water to the pan. Bring to a simmer and cook, stirring occasionally, for about 25 minutes until the farro is cooked through and tender. Remove the oregano sprigs, drain, and set aside.

In a large bowl, whisk together the lemon juice, orange juice, the remaining ⅓ cup olive oil, and the remaining ½ teaspoon salt. Add the warm, cooked farro and toss to coat. Add the cherries, walnuts, cucumber, and arugula. Mix well to combine. Crumble in the goat cheese and toss gently just to mix through.

Lentil and Carrot Salad

V GF

SERVES 4 TO 6

Crunchy carrots, leafy spinach, and a bit of sharp ricotta salata are tossed with lentils for a salad I never tire of.

LENTILS

1 cup French lentils (*lentilles du Puy*), picked over and rinsed
1 teaspoon ground cumin
½ teaspoon ground coriander
2 teaspoons kosher salt

SALAD

2 tablespoons fresh lemon juice (from 1 lemon)
¼ cup extra-virgin olive oil
1 teaspoon za'atar
¼ teaspoon ground cumin
¼ teaspoon kosher salt
3 carrots, peeled and julienned
4 cups baby spinach, coarsely chopped
½ cup fresh mint leaves, coarsely chopped
½ cup shaved ricotta salata cheese

For the lentils: In a medium saucepan, combine the lentils, cumin, coriander, salt, and 3 cups water. Place over medium heat and bring to a simmer. Reduce the heat to maintain the simmer, partially cover, and cook for about 25 minutes or until tender and cooked through. Drain any remaining liquid.

For the salad: In a large bowl, whisk together the lemon juice, olive oil, za'atar, cumin, and salt. Add the hot lentils and the carrots to the dressing and toss gently. Allow the mixture to cool to room temperature. Add the spinach, mint, and ricotta salata and toss to combine.

Lentil and Carrot Salad

Brown-Bagging It

Lunchtime meals have done in even the most well-intentioned eaters because time and budget often lead us to make choices based on convenience rather than health. Even if you have access to a company cafeteria or a convenient take-out option, it's hard to know what's in that creamy soup or overstuffed sandwich.

That's why packing lunch from home is a tradition deserving of a revival. Forget the PB&J and greasy brown paper bag—there are loads of snazzy cooler bags and storage containers that will keep hot stuff hot and cold stuff cold for hours. No time to scramble around making lunch in the morning? Repurpose last night's leftovers and include a piece of fruit or two to add some fresh flavors, plus a small bag of almonds or cut-up veggies for a midafternoon snack. Better still, plan ahead and use an hour or two on the weekend to cook up a big pot of soup and some sturdy salads that you can dole out over the course of the week.

Bringing your own lunch allows you to control portion size much more easily, enabling you to stick to any dietary goals you may have set. And because it's ready when you are, there is less danger that you will succumb to the birthday cake left in the coffee room when the twelve o'clock munchies set in.

Orzo Salad with Fresh Citrus and Red Onion

SERVES 4 TO 6

Orzo is my pasta of choice for salads that will be served chilled or at room temp because the rice-like shapes are less likely to become soggy. Citrus makes this a lot more lively and interesting than your run-of-the-mill pasta salad. Cook the orzo in vegetable broth if you want to make a vegetarian/vegan version.

ORANGE OIL

½ cup extra-virgin olive oil
1 orange, zested

SALAD

8 cups low-sodium chicken broth
1 pound orzo
1 orange
1 pink grapefruit
1 small red onion, thinly sliced
¼ cup fresh mint leaves
¼ cup fresh basil leaves
½ cup shaved fennel
1 teaspoon coarse salt
½ teaspoon freshly ground black pepper

For the orange oil: In a small bowl, combine the olive oil and the orange zest. Set aside.

For the salad: In a large saucepan, bring the chicken broth to a boil over high heat. Add the pasta and cook, stirring occasionally, until tender but still firm to the bite, 10 to 12 minutes. Drain the pasta and dump it onto a large rimmed baking sheet. Spread it out into a single layer and let cool for 10 minutes.

Meanwhile, using a small knife, cut all the peel and pith off the orange and grapefruit. Holding the fruit over a large bowl, cut between the membranes to release the segments into the bowl and catch the juices. Add the onion, mint, basil, fennel, salt, pepper, and cooled orzo.

Add the reserved orange oil to the pasta. Toss all the ingredients together and serve.

Fusilli Salad with Sun-Dried Tomato Vinaigrette

V V GF

SERVES 4 TO 6

Gluten-free spirals are perfect for a room-temp pasta salad; to make the dish vegan or dairy-free, omit the cheese or substitute a half cup of chickpeas for extra protein.

DRESSING

½ cup sun-dried tomatoes
1 tablespoon apple cider vinegar
3 tablespoons extra-virgin olive oil
Juice of 1 orange
½ teaspoon kosher salt
¼ teaspoon freshly ground black pepper

SALAD

1 (8-ounce) package ancient-grain gluten-free fusilli, such as TruRoots brand
3 cups baby arugula, chopped
¾ cup pitted kalamata olives, chopped
½ cup packed fresh basil leaves, chopped
¼ teaspoon kosher salt
¼ teaspoon freshly ground black pepper

For the dressing: Place the sun-dried tomatoes, vinegar, olive oil, orange juice, salt, and pepper in the bowl of a food processor. Pulse to combine. The mixture should be slightly chunky but pourable. Set aside.

For the salad: In a large pot of boiling, salted water, cook the pasta according to the package directions. Drain and rinse in cold water.

In a large bowl, toss together the cooked pasta, arugula, olives, basil, and the dressing. Season with the salt and pepper and serve.

Fusilli Salad with Sun-Dried Tomato Vinaigrette

Soups & Stews

I can't think of any other foods that marry comfort and convenience better than the recipes in this chapter. Virtually every soup can be made ahead of time and reheated (or served chilled, as the case may be), and most lend themselves very well to freezing, too, so you can make a big batch and stockpile some to defrost and serve at a moment's notice. I love to send Jade to school with a container of soup to reheat at lunchtime (her classroom has a microwave, but you could also use an insulated vacuum bottle), and after a long day sometimes a bowl of warm soup and a quick, simple salad is all the dinner that I really need or want. Coming home and seeing that pot in the fridge ready to be rewarmed just takes a huge weight off of my shoulders at the end of the day.

Soups and stews are also a great reason to bring out the slow cooker, an appliance that I've only recently come to appreciate, or the pressure cooker, both of which reduce the hands-on time and pot-watching required to make a deeply flavorful meal. I love the idea that I can put some ingredients on to cook in the morning, then run errands, take Jade to her riding lessons or for a bike ride, and come home to a warming, virtually instant meal. In this chapter you'll find slow-simmered soups and others that are quick to make and refreshingly flavorful—in other words, a recipe to fit any occasion.

Aunt Raffy's Quinoa and Ceci Soup

GF

MAKES 5 CUPS

Ceci is the Italian word for chickpeas or garbanzo beans. Quinoa is most frequently used in salads, but I love it in soups, too.

1 teaspoon extra-virgin olive oil
1 small onion, coarsely chopped
2 celery stalks, coarsely chopped
4 medium carrots, peeled and coarsely chopped
½ teaspoon kosher salt
4 Roma tomatoes, coarsely chopped
¼ teaspoon freshly ground black pepper
3 fresh rosemary sprigs
3 fresh oregano sprigs
3 fresh thyme sprigs
1 (15.5-ounce) can ceci (chickpeas), rinsed and drained
2 cups low-sodium chicken broth
⅓ cup quinoa, rinsed and drained

Heat the oil in a large saucepan over medium heat. Add the onion, celery, carrots, and salt and cook, stirring occasionally, until the vegetables begin to soften. Add the tomatoes, pepper, rosemary, oregano, and thyme and cook until the tomatoes begin to break down, about 5 minutes. Add the ceci, broth, and 1 cup of water, and bring to a boil. Reduce the heat to low and simmer for 15 minutes.

Carefully pour the soup through a strainer into a bowl, separating the solids. Remove the large herb sprigs and puree the vegetables and ceci in a blender or food processor until smooth; set aside. Pour the broth back into the saucepan and add the quinoa. Cook the quinoa until tender, about 10 minutes. Lower the heat, add the vegetable puree, and simmer for 5 more minutes.

Aunt Raffy's Quinoa and Ceci Soup

Chilled Watermelon-Basil Gazpacho

V V GF

SERVES 6

There's nothing more refreshing than this chilled soup, which comes together quickly in the blender. While tomato may be traditional, using watermelon in a starring role makes for an appealing twist. The seasonings—fresh herbs, lime, salt, and pepper—ensure this soup, despite the watermelon, is savory, not sweet.

1 (5-pound) seedless watermelon, rind removed and flesh chopped (6 cups)
1 medium heirloom tomato, chopped
2 tablespoons extra-virgin olive oil
2 limes
¾ cup fresh basil leaves, finely chopped
¼ cup fresh mint leaves, finely chopped
½ teaspoon kosher salt
¼ teaspoon freshly ground black pepper

In a blender or food processor, combine the watermelon, tomato, and olive oil. Zest one of the limes and squeeze out the juice; add the zest and juice to the blender and puree until the mixture is smooth. Pour the soup into a large bowl and stir in the basil, mint, salt, and pepper. Chill the soup for at least 3 hours before serving.

To serve, pour the soup into chilled bowls. Cut the remaining lime into wedges and use to garnish the bowls.

Chilled Watermelon-Basil Gazpacho

Italian White Bean, Pancetta, and Tortellini Soup

SERVES 4 TO 6

With beans, pancetta, and cheese, this broth-based soup is packed with protein and filling enough to make a meal.

3 tablespoons olive oil
4 ounces pancetta, chopped
3 large shallots, chopped
1 carrot, peeled and chopped
2 garlic cloves, chopped
1 (15-ounce) can cannellini beans, rinsed and drained
4 cups chopped Swiss chard (1 bunch, trimmed)
6 cups low-sodium chicken broth
1 (9-ounce) package fresh cheese tortellini
½ teaspoon kosher salt
¼ teaspoon freshly ground black pepper

In a large heavy soup pot, heat the olive oil over medium-high heat. Add the pancetta, shallots, carrot, and garlic and cook, stirring occasionally, until the pancetta is crisp, about 5 minutes.

Add the beans, Swiss chard, and broth. Bring the soup to a boil over medium-high heat, then reduce the heat to a simmer. Add the tortellini and cook for 8 minutes. Season with salt and pepper and serve.

Pastina Soup

SERVES 4

When Italians talk about comfort food, this is what they mean. I often make it for Jade when she's feeling under the weather; the mild flavors and soft texture are easy on her tummy but warming and filling. The trick to perfect pastina soup is to cook the little pasta shapes in the broth so that they soak up a lot of the liquid. The final "soup" is a cross between a risotto and a very thick stew.

1 tablespoon extra-virgin olive oil
1 celery stalk, finely chopped
1 carrot, peeled and finely chopped
2 shallots, minced
3 fresh thyme sprigs
¾ teaspoon kosher salt
1 (2-inch) piece of Parmesan rind
4 cups low-sodium chicken broth
1¼ cups little star pasta (stelline)
1 cup frozen peas, thawed
½ cup freshly grated Parmesan cheese
1 teaspoon grated lemon zest (optional)

Heat a medium saucepan over medium heat. Add the olive oil, celery, carrot, and shallots and cook, stirring frequently, until the vegetables are softened, about 5 minutes.

Add the thyme, salt, Parmesan rind, chicken broth, and 1 cup of water. Bring to a simmer and cook for 10 minutes.

Add the pasta and stir with a wooden spoon to prevent sticking to the pan. Return to a simmer and continue to cook for 8 to 10 minutes more, or until the pasta is cooked and the liquid is slightly thickened.

Remove the thyme sprigs and Parmesan rind. Stir in the peas. Ladle the soup into bowls and top with the grated cheese and lemon zest if desired.

Pastina Soup

Pass the Soup

Healthy, restorative, and as easy to make as it is to eat, this brothy bean and veggie soup is too good to keep to yourself.

There is something so satisfying about stirring up a big batch of soup, watching a handful of humble ingredients transform into a complexly flavorful and sustaining bowlful of goodness. Most soups can be scaled up to serve a crowd with very little additional effort, so next time you haul out the soup pot, double or triple the recipe so you have some to share. You won't have to think too hard to come up with a list of worthy recipients: someone with a new baby or a new home, the student struggling to get through finals and pack up for winter break, the neighbor whose kitchen renovation is almost but not quite done, the friend succumbing to the first cold of the season—any and all of them would be thrilled to receive a jar of soup ready to heat and serve. Soup is so much more personal than a bottle of wine and more likely to be used than a gift certificate. Add a loaf of bread or a simple green salad with a jar of dressing and you will have made someone very happy indeed.

"House" Soup

SERVES 8 TO 10

Like many soups, this one was created to use up odds and ends, so feel free to substitute other grains for the farro and to swap out (or leave out entirely) the beans. Just don't omit the cheese rind or lemon; they give the broth a lovely savory flavor.

2 tablespoons extra-virgin olive oil, plus more for drizzling
1 leek, white and tender green parts, washed well and finely chopped
2 carrots, 1 peeled and finely chopped, 1 peeled and sliced
½ fennel bulb, cored and finely chopped
Kosher salt
½ teaspoon crushed red pepper flakes
¾ cup dried small white beans, such as navy
½ to ¾ cup farro
1 (15-ounce) can diced tomatoes
2 quarts low-sodium chicken broth
2 to 3 fresh thyme sprigs
1 (2 x 3-inch) piece of Parmesan rind
½ lemon
13 ounces turkey kielbasa or Polish kielbasa, cut into half-moons
4 to 5 large leaves of Tuscan kale, ribs removed, chopped
Freshly grated Parmesan cheese, for serving (optional)

Heat the oil in a large soup pot over medium heat. Add the leek, carrots, and fennel, season with about ½ teaspoon salt and the red pepper flakes, and sauté slowly until very soft but not browned.

Add the beans and farro and toast for a minute or two, then add the tomatoes with their juices and the chicken broth, thyme, Parmesan rind, and half lemon. Bring to a boil, then reduce the heat to a steady simmer and cook for about 40 minutes or until the beans are tender but not mushy; they should be firm and separate. Season to taste with salt.

Add the kielbasa, kale, and sliced carrot. Cook until the kale and carrot are tender, about 15 minutes. Remove and discard the thyme sprigs, Parm rind, and lemon (squeeze it into the soup before discarding). Serve with a drizzle of olive oil and a sprinkle of grated Parm if you like.

Smart Cooking with a Slow Cooker

The slow cooker is a time-pressed cook's secret weapon. Plan ahead, do a little bit of work upfront, and a few hours later, there you have it: the home-cooked dish of your dreams. No wonder slow-cooker recipes are so popular. Most of us probably associate this appliance with the hearty soups and stews of fall and winter, but this handy tool lends itself to lighter dishes during the spring and summer as well.

Skeptical? Well, unlike the hot burners on the stovetop or the hot air in your oven, the heating element of a slow cooker is completely self-contained. Translation: It won't make a hot kitchen even hotter. If you have the outdoor space and a power source, you can even take the cooker outside and avoid cooking in the kitchen altogether. What's even better: The slow cooker does most of the work, meaning you're free to get outside and head off to the pool, beach, or wherever you go to escape the heat.

The meals you can make with a slow cooker are ideal for year-round entertaining. Seafood stews and light soups for summer parties; hearty stews or pot roasts for winter events—whatever you're serving, have your guests help themselves, and put dishes of accompaniments on the side so they can add them to suit their own tastes.

Slow-Cooker Lentil, Kale, and Mushroom Soup

V V GF

SERVES 6

Here's a hearty, filling, and totally vegan soup that has plenty of protein thanks to the lentils.

2 teaspoons extra-virgin olive oil
2 carrots, peeled and diced
2 celery stalks, diced
1 medium leek, washed well and finely chopped
1 small celery root, peeled and diced
1 teaspoon ground cumin
1 teaspoon ground turmeric
1 teaspoon ground coriander
½ teaspoon kosher salt
¼ teaspoon ground cinnamon
¼ teaspoon freshly ground black pepper
1 cup sliced cremini mushrooms
1 (15-ounce) can diced fire-roasted tomatoes
1 cup lentils, picked over and rinsed
4 cups low-sodium vegetable broth
5 large Tuscan kale leaves, ribs removed, chopped

In a 5- to 6-quart slow cooker, place the oil, carrots, celery, leek, celery root, cumin, turmeric, coriander, salt, cinnamon, and pepper and toss to coat. Add the mushrooms, tomatoes, lentils, and vegetable broth and stir to combine. Cover and cook on high for 4 to 5 hours, until the lentils are tender.

Stir in the chopped kale and allow to wilt for 5 minutes in the warm soup before serving.

Slow-Cooker Beef and Kabocha Squash Stew

SERVES 6

If you can't find kabocha squash, then substitute any winter squash, such as acorn, butternut, or Hubbard.

2 tablespoons extra-virgin olive oil
1 large onion, diced
2 garlic cloves, finely chopped
1 tablespoon chopped fresh rosemary leaves
1 tablespoon chopped fresh thyme leaves
2 tablespoons all-purpose flour
1 teaspoon kosher salt
¼ teaspoon freshly ground black pepper
2 pounds stew beef, trimmed and cut into 2-inch cubes
½ cup Marsala wine
1 pound kabocha squash, peeled, seeded, and cut into 1-inch pieces
¼ cup chopped sun-dried tomatoes
3 cups beef broth
Crusty bread, for serving
2 tablespoons chopped fresh flat-leaf parsley leaves

In a large sauté pan, heat the olive oil over medium-high heat. Add the onion, garlic, rosemary, and thyme and cook for about 4 minutes or until the onion is tender.

Meanwhile, place the flour, salt, and pepper in a large bowl. Add the beef cubes and toss gently to coat. Add the beef to the pan in batches and cook, turning occasionally, until the beef is browned on all sides and golden around the edges, about 5 minutes. Add the Marsala and use a wooden spoon or spatula to scrape up the browned bits from the bottom of the pan.

Transfer the beef and pan juices to the slow cooker. Add the squash, sun-dried tomatoes, and broth and stir to combine. Cover and cook on high for 4 to 5 hours, or on low for 8 hours, until the beef and squash are tender. Serve with crusty bread and a sprinkle of parsley.

Slow-Cooker Black Bean and Pork Stew

GF

SERVES 6

Black beans and the mild heat of smoked andouille sausage will warm chilly trick-or-treaters, skiers, and other cold-weather sports lovers.

- 4 ounces pancetta, diced
- 1 large onion, diced
- 2 garlic cloves, minced
- 2 pounds boneless pork shoulder, trimmed and cut into 1-inch cubes
- ½ teaspoon kosher salt
- ¼ teaspoon freshly ground black pepper
- 2 pork or chicken andouille sausage links, halved lengthwise and cut into 1-inch pieces
- 2 cans black beans, rinsed and drained
- 2 cups low-sodium chicken broth
- 1 cup cooked white rice (optional)
- ¼ cup queso blanco, crumbled
- 2 plum tomatoes, diced
- 2 tablespoons chopped fresh cilantro leaves

Place the pancetta in a medium skillet over medium-high heat and cook for about 4 minutes, until it begins to brown. Add the onion and garlic and cook for another minute, until the onion begins to soften. Transfer the pancetta mixture to a 5- to 6-quart slow cooker.

Sprinkle the pork with the salt and pepper, add to the skillet (working in batches, if necessary, to avoid crowding the pan), and cook for 1 to 2 minutes per side, until the cubes are golden brown all over. Transfer the pork to the slow cooker, then add the sausage, black beans, and chicken broth, stirring to combine.

Cover and cook on high for 4 to 5 hours or on low for 8 hours, until the pork and beans are tender. Gently break up the pork pieces with a wooden spoon or shred with 2 forks. Serve alone or over rice, garnished with queso blanco, tomato, and cilantro.

Slow-Cooker Black Bean and Pork Stew

Make-Ahead Cioppino

GF

SERVES 6

Although Cioppino is fairly quick to make, you can make things even easier on yourself if you cook up the tomato base in advance. To serve, just reheat the flavorful broth, add the raw seafood, and you're good to go in about 10 minutes. It's a fantastic solution for weeknight entertaining.

2 tablespoons extra-virgin olive oil
1 large fennel bulb, cored and thinly sliced (stalks and fronds removed)
1 onion, chopped
3 large shallots, chopped
3 large garlic cloves, minced
2 teaspoons kosher salt, plus more to taste
¾ teaspoon crushed red pepper flakes
¼ cup tomato paste
1 cup dry white wine
1 (28-ounce) can diced tomatoes
4 cups fish stock
1 bay leaf
1 thyme sprig
½ pound Manila clams, scrubbed
½ pound mussels, scrubbed and debearded
½ pound raw shrimp, peeled and deveined
½ pound skinless salmon fillet, cut in chunks

Heat a 5-quart Dutch oven over medium-high heat. Add the oil, fennel, onion, shallots, and garlic. Cook, stirring often, for 5 minutes or until the vegetables are beginning to soften. Stir in the salt and red pepper flakes and cook 2 minutes.

Add the tomato paste and cook, stirring constantly, until the paste darkens slightly in color, about 2 minutes. Deglaze with the white wine and simmer for 3 minutes to reduce slightly. Add the diced tomatoes with their juices, fish stock, bay leaf, and thyme sprig. Simmer uncovered for about 30 minutes.

Stir in the clams and mussels and cover with the lid. Steam the shellfish for 5 minutes. Remove the lid and stir in the shrimp and salmon; cover and continue cooking until the salmon and shrimp are cooked through and the clams and mussels are open, about 5 minutes more. Discard the bay leaf, thyme, and any clams and mussels that do not open. Serve immediately

Make-Ahead Cioppino

Chilled Red Pepper Soup

GF

SERVES 6 TO 8

My aunt Carolyna often greets guests with shot glasses or espresso cups of this bright soup. Make it at least an hour before serving, to give it time to chill, or up to two days ahead.

3 tablespoons extra-virgin olive oil
2 medium onions, chopped
3 large garlic cloves, crushed
2 carrots, peeled and chopped
2½ cups low-sodium chicken broth
10 large red bell peppers, cored, seeded, and cut into 1-inch pieces
2 bay leaves
¼ teaspoon crushed red pepper flakes
Salt and freshly ground black pepper
Greek yogurt or crumbled feta cheese

Heat the oil in a large pot over medium heat. Add the onions and cook until slightly translucent, 2 to 3 minutes. Add the garlic and carrots and cook for 1 minute. Add the chicken broth, bell peppers, bay leaves, and red pepper flakes. Cover and simmer for 30 minutes. Remove from the heat. Remove the bay leaves and discard.

Using a regular blender or an immersion blender, puree the mixture. Season to taste with salt and black pepper. Allow the mixture to cool in the refrigerator for at least 1 hour or up to 2 days. Garnish each serving with a dollop of yogurt or feta.

Chilled Red Pepper Soup

Spicy Tomato and Lentil Gazpacho

Spicy Tomato and Lentil Gazpacho

V GF

SERVES 4 TO 6

Yes, lentils in a chilled soup. They give this traditional summer favorite a bit more heft and some protein as well.

1 pound (about 4 cups) ripe cherry tomatoes
2 medium cucumbers, peeled and chopped, or 4 Persian cucumbers, chopped
1 jalapeño chile, seeded and coarsely chopped
2 scallions, coarsely chopped, plus 1 scallion, sliced thin on the diagonal, for garnish
1 cup lentils, rinsed, cooked, and drained
2 tablespoons extra-virgin olive oil
2 tablespoons fresh lemon juice (from 1 lemon)
2 to 3 teaspoons hot sauce, such as Tabasco
1½ teaspoons kosher salt, plus more to taste
Crème fraîche, for garnish

In a blender, puree the tomatoes, cucumbers, chile, chopped scallions, lentils, oil, lemon juice, hot sauce, and salt until smooth. Taste and add more salt, if needed. Refrigerate for 2 hours or until ready to serve.

To serve, pour the gazpacho into soup bowls, top with a dollop of crème fraîche, and sprinkle with a few scallion slivers.

Pressure Cooker Curried Cauliflower Soup

V V GF

SERVES 6

This velvety soup was developed by Bruce Weinstein and Mark Scarbrough, who have done a lot to help me love my pressure cooker! The soup has lots of mellow sweet notes that get a spike from the pickled ginger.

2 tablespoons canola or vegetable oil
1 large yellow onion, chopped
½ tablespoon yellow curry powder
1 (2-pound) head of cauliflower, cored, trimmed, and coarsely chopped
½ cup dry vermouth or dry, oaky chardonnay
1¾ cups canned coconut milk (not cream of coconut)
1½ cups vegetable broth
3 tablespoons chopped pickled ginger (sushi ginger)

Heat the oil in a 6-quart stovetop pressure cooker set over medium heat. Add the onion; cook, stirring often, until softened, about 4 minutes.

Stir in the curry powder; cook for less than a minute, just until aromatic. Add the cauliflower and vermouth; cook for 1 minute, stirring all the while. Pour in the coconut milk and broth; stir well.

Lock the lid onto the pot. Raise the heat to high and bring the pot to high pressure (15 psi). Once this pressure has been reached, reduce the heat as low as possible while maintaining this pressure. Cook for 10 minutes. Use the quick-release method to bring the pot's pressure back to normal.

Unlock and open the pot, and stir in the ginger. Use an immersion blender to puree the soup in the cooker or ladle the soup in batches into a standard blender and puree, taking the knob out of the center of the lid and covering its hole with a clean kitchen towel.

Serve the soup garnished with a bit of pickled ginger.

Pressure Cooker Curried Cauliflower Soup

Pastas & Risottos

Like many people of Italian heritage, I consider pasta, especially the cheesy, baked variety, the ultimate comfort food. When I was growing up, my mother served my brother, sister, and me pasta several times a week and we never got tired of it—in fact, it never seemed like the same dish at all.

What I know now that I didn't know then is that pasta is also the ultimate *convenience* food. For those nights when I walk in the door without a fixed notion of what I'm going to make for dinner, nine times out of ten the answer is pasta and a salad, often made with pantry ingredients and whatever fresh veggies I have in the crisper. And ten times out of ten, that meal makes me completely happy. If you've put pasta on the back burner because of concerns about carbs and gluten in your diet, you'll find options here that will help you get this weekday staple back in the rotation, and I know you'll be glad it's there.

Go-Green Carbonara with Peas

V

SERVES 4 TO 6

Carbonara is luscious but über-rich, definitely a dish I would call an occasional indulgence. Swapping out the bacon for a minty pesto and fresh (or frozen) peas ups the veggie quotient in the dish and instantly makes it a bit less of a guilty pleasure.

BASIL-MINT AIOLI

1 garlic clove, minced
2 large egg yolks (see Cook's Note)
2 teaspoons mustard
1 teaspoon fresh lemon juice (from 1 lemon)
¼ cup finely chopped fresh basil leaves
1 tablespoon finely chopped fresh mint leaves
½ teaspoon kosher salt
¼ teaspoon freshly ground black pepper
½ cup grapeseed oil
½ cup extra-virgin olive oil

PASTA CARBONARA

1 pound linguine
2 cups fresh peas, or frozen peas, thawed
1 cup shaved Pecorino Romano cheese
½ teaspoon kosher salt
½ teaspoon freshly ground black pepper
4 tablespoons (½ stick) unsalted butter
4 to 6 large eggs

For the aioli: In a food processor, combine the garlic, egg yolks, mustard, lemon juice, basil, mint, salt, and pepper and process to a smooth consistency, about 20 seconds. With the machine running, slowly drizzle in the grapeseed and olive oils. Set the aioli aside while you make the pasta. Basil-mint aioli can be kept, covered, in the refrigerator for up to 3 days.

For the pasta: Bring a large pot of salted water to a boil over high heat. Add the linguine and cook, stirring occasionally, until tender but still firm to the bite, 8 to 10 minutes. Reserve 1 cup of pasta water, drain the pasta, and transfer to a large bowl. Add 1 cup of the aioli, the peas, cheese, salt, and pepper and toss gently to combine, using the reserved pasta water to loosen the aioli as needed. Place the pasta on a long rectangular serving dish. Cover to keep warm while you fry the eggs.

Place the butter in a medium skillet over medium-high heat. Add the eggs and sprinkle with salt and pepper. Fry the eggs to your liking. Place the eggs on top of the pasta and serve immediately.

Cook's Note: There are some dangers associated with eating raw eggs, especially for those with compromised immune systems. To reduce the risk of salmonella or other food-borne illnesses, use only fresh, properly refrigerated, clean grade A or AA eggs with intact shells or packaged eggs that have been treated to destroy salmonella by pasteurization or another approved method.

Go-Green Carbonara with Peas

Pasta Rules

I feel strongly that pasta—any kind of pasta—can be part of a healthful diet. But with so many health-conscious cooks trying to cut down on carbs in general, and those containing gluten and refined wheat in particular, unfortunately pasta has fallen into the verboten category. It makes me sad that so many people consider pasta the enemy, something to be indulged in only occasionally and atoned for afterward.

I couldn't imagine life without pasta, and neither should you. After a long day of work there are few things that are quicker to prepare or are a better vehicle for a variety of nutritious, seasonal ingredients, with meat or without. Those facts alone should earn pasta at least an occasional place on your weekly meal plan. If you've been sidelining pasta, here are some easy ways to get it back into the game:

Revisit portion size. I've said it a million times: a little bit of everything but not too much of anything. Nowhere is that more relevant than when it comes to the servings of pasta we routinely dole out. A two-ounce portion of pasta—yes, that's an eighth of a box—is actually plenty to satisfy that pasta craving without filling you up. Try it. I bet you will be surprised.

Reverse the proportions. Instead of pasta topped with a bit of sauce, bulk up your sauce with extra veggies, low-fat sausage, seafood, or beans, so there is more sauce than pasta in each serving.

Use pasta as an accent. In brothy dishes with a base of stock, wine, or even dairy, all you need is a little bit of pasta to add body and substance. I especially love a frutti di mare with lots of seafood and a bit of tomato in the broth and a small handful of fregola or other shaped pasta to soak up the delicious sauce instead of bread.

Try alternative pastas. If you or a family member have been diagnosed with celiac disease, regular pasta may indeed be off the menu permanently at your house. But in recent years there has been an explosion of pastas made from gluten-free ingredients like rice, legumes like lentils, quinoa, and spelt (which is tolerated by some who can't eat wheat), and they look and taste every bit as good as the original. Experiment to see which kinds you like best—and cook them carefully, as some can become mushy just past al dente.

Go grainless. Who says noodles have to be made of flour—or any other grain, for that matter? Spaghetti squash is an old standby, but lots of other vegetables can be shredded, lightly cooked, and sauced as you would your favorite noodles. If you have a spiralizing tool, see Vegetable Noodles (page 151) for a delicious zucchini "pasta" you can make in minutes. Shirataki noodles, made of tofu or tubers, are completely carb-free and totally slurpable in Asian or Italian dishes.

Brown Butter Tortellini

Brown Butter Tortellini

V

SERVES 2 TO 4

Browned butter lends a rich, nutty depth to prepared tortellini, which is simple enough to become a weeknight staple. Use a fancy high-fat European butter if you want to push this over the top.

1 (9-ounce) package fresh cheese tortellini
4 tablespoons (½ stick) unsalted butter
¾ cup frozen peas, thawed
⅓ teaspoon kosher salt
1½ tablespoons chopped fresh dill
1 teaspoon grated lemon zest
2 teaspoons fresh lemon juice (from 1 lemon)
¼ cup freshly grated Parmesan cheese, plus more for serving

Bring a large pot of salted water to a boil over high heat. Add the tortellini and cook for 1 minute less than the package directions, about 7 minutes. Drain the pasta, reserving ½ cup of the cooking water.

Heat a medium skillet over medium heat. Melt the butter, then cook until the solids begin to brown, 2 to 3 minutes. You may have to scrape the bottom of the pan with a wooden spoon to release the brown bits from the bottom; keep an eye on it. It should smell nutty and appear golden brown, not black.

When the butter is browned, add the cooked pasta, the peas, and salt to the skillet and toss gently to coat in the butter. Add about ¼ cup of the reserved pasta water, the dill, lemon zest and juice, and cheese. Cook for another minute, stirring gently to coat the pasta evenly and adding the remaining ¼ cup pasta water if needed. Serve topped with more cheese if desired.

Pasta Primavera with Summer Vegetables

V

SERVES 6

Flipping the usual pasta-to-veggie ratio on its head, this dish is the perfect way to use the bounty of your CSA box or trip to the farmers' market. It's clean and light and won't weigh you down.

2 medium zucchini or 1 large zucchini, cut into thin strips
4 pattypan squash (or yellow and green squash), cut into thin strips
1 onion, thinly sliced
6 mini sweet peppers, sliced into quarters
1 head of broccoli, chopped into small pieces
½ cup olive oil
Kosher salt and freshly ground black pepper
½ pound farfalle (bow-tie pasta)
5 Tuscan kale leaves, sliced into thin ribbons
15 cherry tomatoes, halved
1 cup freshly chopped fresh basil leaves
1 tablespoon fresh lemon juice (from 1 lemon)
½ cup freshly grated Parmesan cheese

Preheat the oven to 450°F.

On a large heavy rimmed baking sheet, toss the zucchini, pattypan squash, onion, sweet peppers, and broccoli with ¼ cup of the oil, salt, and pepper to coat. Transfer half of the vegetable mixture to another large heavy rimmed baking sheet and arrange evenly on both sheets. Bake until the vegetables are tender and begin to brown, stirring after the first 10 minutes, about 20 minutes total.

Meanwhile, cook the pasta in a large pot of boiling salted water until al dente, tender but still firm to the bite, about 8 minutes. Drain, reserving 1 cup of the cooking liquid.

Toss the pasta with the roasted vegetables, kale, cherry tomatoes, basil, and enough reserved cooking liquid to loosen. Add the remaining ¼ cup olive oil and the lemon juice and season with salt and pepper to taste. Sprinkle with the Parmesan and serve immediately.

Bottom of the Box Bonus

Unlike Americans, who tend to cook their pasta by the package, Italians cook pasta in smaller amounts and consume smaller portions. My mother was always adding a handful of broken long pasta or shaped pasta to soups or fish stews, and often she would boil up just a few ounces to serve with the braising sauce from the meat we'd eat after the pasta course. As a result, her pantry ended up with lots of pasta odds and ends: an ounce of shells or farfalle, a dozen strands of linguine or capellini, a half package of fusilli or penne. When the leftover situation reached critical mass, she would boil up all these odd lots together for a dish known affectionately in some households as "rubbish" pasta. Sometimes it was the basis of a soup that also incorporated the bits and pieces of vegetables or meat left in the fridge; other times she would toss the cooked pasta with a simple sauce or pesto and call it a day. As kids, my brother and sister and I always loved the novelty of so many different shapes in our bowl or plate; as an adult I appreciate it as a practical and economical practice that helps clear out the cupboard. It also creates a dish with a variety of textures, as some pieces will be cooked to a silky softness while the chunkier pieces will retain a toothy al dente bite, a surprisingly sophisticated result given its humble beginnings.

Pasta e Fagioli with Mussels

SERVES 3 OR 4

Using a mixture of pasta shapes and sizes gives this dish an unusual texture, as some pieces will remain chewy while others are quite tender. It's also a smart way to use up those odds and ends you have kicking around in the pantry.

Kosher salt
3 cups mixed dry pasta
2 tablespoons extra-virgin olive oil
1 onion, finely chopped
1 carrot, peeled and finely chopped
1 celery stalk, finely chopped
1 garlic clove, halved
½ teaspoon crushed red pepper flakes
4 plum tomatoes, chopped
2¼ pounds mussels, scrubbed and debearded
1 (15-ounce) can cannellini beans, rinsed and drained

Bring a large pot of water to a boil and add a tablespoon of salt. Add the pasta and cook until the biggest, thickest pieces are just al dente. This could be as short as 7 minutes or up to 12 minutes, depending on what is in your mixture.

While the pasta cooks, heat the oil in a large skillet with a lid over medium-high heat. Add the onion, carrot, celery, garlic, and red pepper flakes and cook until softened, 3 to 4 minutes. Add the tomatoes, reduce the heat to medium, and cook for about 10 minutes. Add the mussels in a single layer, cover the pan, and cook until the mussels have opened, 7 to 10 minutes, shaking occasionally.

Remove the mussels from their shells, returning the meat and any juices to the skillet. (Discard any mussels that do not open.) Stir in the beans and add a pinch of salt. Mix gently.

When the pasta is done cooking, drain it (reserving 1 cup of the cooking liquid), then add to the skillet with the beans and sauce; add some of the reserved cooking water if needed to loosen. Cook over medium heat for a minute to blend the flavors, and serve.

Pasta e Fagioli with Mussels

Is Gluten-Free Here to Stay?

Only five years ago the special diet section of the grocery story was limited to a few boxes of "dietetic" sugar-free cookies and pudding mixes. Today there is a huge selection of products meant to make cooking and eating easier for those with intolerances and allergies to various ingredients, from nuts to lactose to gluten. Buyer beware, though: In many cases products substitute one questionable ingredient for another. Gluten-free products, for example, very often rely on highly processed carbohydrates such as cornstarch or potato flour, making them allergen-free but not particularly nutritious. It's easy to eat a lot of extra calories' worth of refined carbs if you overindulge.

That said, with food allergies on the rise, every cook needs a few good gluten-, dairy-, and nut-free recipes up her sleeve for accommodating guests and just making things a little lighter. I have never been specifically diagnosed with a food allergy, but I've observed that I feel better, my digestion is improved, and I experience less bloating when I ease off on the gluten and dairy (a tough admission for an Italian girl to make!). I don't avoid them entirely—there's still nothing I love better than a simple plate of capellini dressed with lemon and Parmesan—but it's an occasional treat rather than an everyday event. The upside is that I've discovered a whole world of alternative foods, such as pastas made from brown rice or quinoa, that have introduced new flavors and textures to my repertoire.

So buy a box or two of rice crackers to allow your friends with gluten sensitivities to enjoy the cheese plate along with everyone else, then serve one of these delicious, healthful, naturally allergen-free pastas or risottos for the main event. They are perfect for anyone who is avoiding wheat—or not!

Gluten-Free Penne with Lemon-Cumin Chicken and Pesto

GF

SERVES 4 TO 6

With so many people avoiding gluten either by choice or necessity, it's a good idea to have a few gluten-free dishes like this one up your sleeve when guests stop by. Use whichever g-free pasta you like best; the zesty pesto is flavorful to stand up to even hearty varieties.

LEMON-CUMIN CHICKEN

¼ cup extra-virgin olive oil
Zest of 1 large lemon
¼ cup fresh lemon juice (from 1 large lemon)
2 garlic cloves, minced
1 tablespoon ground cumin
1 teaspoon kosher salt
¼ teaspoon crushed red pepper flakes
4 (4-ounce) boneless, skinless chicken breasts

PESTO

1½ packed cups fresh mint leaves (about 1 large bunch)
1 packed cup baby spinach leaves
½ cup freshly grated Parmesan cheese
⅓ cup chopped toasted walnuts (see Cook's Note, page 75)
1 garlic clove, smashed and peeled
2 teaspoons fresh lemon juice (from 1 lemon)
½ teaspoon kosher salt
½ teaspoon freshly ground black pepper
½ cup extra-virgin olive oil

Vegetable oil cooking spray
1 pound gluten-free brown rice penne

For the chicken: In a medium bowl, whisk together the oil, lemon zest and juice, garlic, cumin, salt, and red pepper flakes until smooth. Add the chicken and toss until coated with the marinade. Cover and refrigerate for at least 4 hours or overnight. (The chicken can also be marinated in a resealable plastic bag.)

For the pesto: In a food processor, blend the mint, spinach, Parmesan, walnuts, garlic, lemon juice, salt, and pepper until chunky. With the machine running, slowly add the olive oil until smooth. Transfer the pesto to a large bowl.

Place a grill pan over medium-high heat or preheat a gas or charcoal grill. Spray the grill lightly with vegetable oil spray. Remove the chicken from the marinade and discard the marinade. Pat the chicken dry with paper towels. Grill the chicken until cooked through, 4 to 5 minutes on each side. Transfer the chicken to a cutting board and allow to rest before slicing into 2-inch pieces.

Bring a large pot of salted water to boil over medium-high heat and cook the pasta according to package directions. Drain the pasta, reserving 1 cup of pasta water. Transfer the pasta to the bowl with the pesto and toss gently to coat, adding reserved pasta water to loosen if necessary. Add the chicken and toss gently to combine. Serve immediately.

Gluten-Free Penne with Lemon-Cumin Chicken and Pesto

Gluten-Free Pasta with Butternut Squash and Marjoram

V V GF

SERVES 4 TO 6

I've always loved the simplicity of this dish, which traditionally featured wheat pasta and nuts. To "free" it up, I've swapped roasted squash cubes for the nuts and used brown rice pasta, making it gluten-, nut-, and dairy-free.

1 (1-pound) butternut squash, peeled, seeded, and cut into ½-inch pieces
2 tablespoons extra-virgin olive oil
1½ teaspoons kosher salt
⅛ teaspoon cayenne pepper
1 pound brown rice spaghetti
4 tablespoons Meyer lemon olive oil or citrus olive oil
2 large red onions, cut into ¼-inch-thick rings
½ teaspoon freshly ground black pepper
2 teaspoons chopped fresh marjoram leaves

Preheat the oven to 375°F.

In a medium bowl, toss the squash with the olive oil, ½ teaspoon of the salt, and the cayenne. Spread the squash on a rimmed baking sheet and roast for 25 minutes or until tender and golden around the edges.

Bring a large pot of salted water to a boil. Add the spaghetti and cook according to the package directions, until tender but still firm to the bite, stirring often. Drain, reserving 1 cup of cooking liquid.

Meanwhile, heat 2 tablespoons of the lemon olive oil in a large heavy skillet over medium heat. Add the onions and sauté until tender and beginning to brown, about 15 minutes.

Add the remaining 1 teaspoon salt and the black pepper. Stir in the marjoram and sauté until fragrant, about 1 minute. Add the cooked pasta, roasted squash, and the remaining 2 tablespoons lemon olive oil. Toss with enough reserved cooking liquid, ¼ cup at a time, to moisten. Transfer to bowls and serve.

Calabrian Chile Pasta

V

SERVES 4

The cool thing about this dish is that you don't need to boil the pasta separately; it all cooks together in one pan, with the heat of the hot pasta softening the tomatoes and warming the peppers just the right amount. It's quick and easy and just one pan to wash! Roasted piquillo peppers are mild and sweet, not spicy. They are available at many specialty food stores, but if you can't locate them, regular roasted red peppers can be substituted. There is no substitute for the hot pepper paste, but crushed red pepper flakes would be delicious, too.

1 pound penne
2 teaspoons kosher salt
1 cup grated Pecorino Romano cheese
1 pint cherry tomatoes, quartered
½ cup diced roasted piquillo peppers
3 tablespoons Calabrian hot pepper paste
⅓ cup chopped fresh chives
1 teaspoon grated lemon zest
1 teaspoon fresh lemon juice (from 1 lemon)
⅓ cup extra-virgin olive oil

In a 10-inch high-sided skillet, bring 1 inch of water (about 4 cups) to a boil over high heat. Add the penne and salt. Cook, stirring often, until the pasta is al dente, about 9 minutes. There should be a little water left in the pan.

Sprinkle the pecorino cheese on top of the pasta and toss to coat. Add the cherry tomatoes, piquillo peppers, hot pepper paste, chives, lemon zest and juice, and olive oil. Mix to combine and serve.

Parmesan Marinara

V GF

MAKES ABOUT 3 CUPS

There are few things more satisfying than peeking in your freezer and seeing a few homemade staples ready and waiting for use. This all-purpose tomato sauce is the perfect example; make a double or even triple batch when you have a little extra time and you'll never have to buy jarred sauce again. Trust me, you'll use it for literally everthing. Because it has only a handful of ingredients, using the best quality you can find is essential. I like San Marzano tomatoes, which come from just outside Naples—they're the best—and Parmesan rinds for an extra punch of flavor.

4 tablespoons olive oil
2 garlic cloves, smashed and peeled
1 (28-ounce) can whole San Marzano tomatoes, crushed by hand
1 small red onion, peeled and halved
1 carrot, peeled and halved
2 fresh basil sprigs
2 (2-inch) pieces of Parmesan rind
1 bay leaf
½ teaspoon kosher salt

In a medium-size deep skillet or wide saucepan, heat 2 tablespoons of the olive oil over medium heat. Add the garlic and sweat until fragrant. Add the tomatoes and their juices, red onion, carrot, basil, Parmesan rind, bay leaf, and salt. Reduce the heat to low and simmer, stirring often with a wooden spoon, for about 25 minutes. Stir in the remaining 2 tablespoons olive oil and simmer for an additional 5 minutes.

Allow the sauce to cool to room temperature. Discard the onion, carrot, basil, rind, and bay leaf. Pass the sauce through a food mill or puree it with an immersion blender and chill completely. The sauce will keep for 4 or 5 days in the refrigerator, or transfer to freezer containers and freeze for up to 3 months.

Parmesan Marinara

Name Your Shape

If you're stuck in a pasta routine of bowl after bowl of plain old spaghetti, you're missing out. Whether it's a short cut or long, the way the shapes interact with the sauce has a big impact on the finished dish. There are literally hundreds of different cuts out there, many of the most unusual made by artisanal producers who use heirloom grains and favor old-fashioned methods and brass dies for extruding the pasta. Expect to cook these a little bit longer and enjoy the way the roughened, toothy edges capture your sauce.

Bucatini (boo-kah-TEEN-ee; "little holes") Hailing from Rome and the surrounding Lazio, these strands are hollow, like thick tubular spaghetti. A versatile pasta, it's often served simply with a red sauce, or with butter or olive oil and a bit of grated Parmesan.

Capellini (ka-pull-EE-nee; "little hairs") Also known as angel hair pasta, these long, thin noodles cook quickly and go best with light sauces that won't weigh them down. Think olive oil, garlic, and lemon, or a simple tomato-basil sauce.

Casarecce (ka-sa-RAY-cheh; "homemade") Narrow, rolled, and twisted tubes, this pasta is as rustic as its homey name suggests. Try it with chunky sauces or in casseroles.

Conchiglie (kohn-KEEL-yeh; "shells") These come in various sizes, from very large ones meant for stuffing, to very small ones, which are called conchigliette. Shells are good with meat sauces, and the small ones work in any dish in which you'd use elbow macaroni.

Croxetti (kro-KET-tee; "little crosses") Like coins of pasta, these disks are stamped with different patterns. They date back to the Middle Ages, when wealthy families had them adorned with their coats of arms—the ultimate edible status symbol. Serve with a simple, light sauce, or just a bit of olive oil.

Farfalle (far-FALL-eh; "butterflies") Often called bow-tie pasta, these pretty butterfly shapes taste best with simple olive oil– or tomato-based sauces that may incorporate ingredients such as peppers, chicken, or arugula. They are also great for a pasta salad.

Fettuccine (fet-too-CHEEN-eh; "little ribbons") Similar to linguine but thicker and wider, these noodles are suitable for many sauces, including those that are cream-based or made with meat.

Fregola Sarda (FREG-o-lah SAR-dah; "little Sardinian fragments") These bead-like bits of pasta hail from Sardinia. Similar to Israeli couscous, they are thought to have come to the island with immigrants from the Genovese colony in Tunisia. A traditional fregola preparation includes tomato sauce and clams.

Fusilli bucati (foo-ZEE-lee boo-CAH-tee; from the Italian for "spun" and "hole") Similar to fusilli, which look like corkscrews, these noodles look more like bedsprings. They are a good choice for thick-and-hearty sauces because all the "goodness" gets trapped inside the spiral rather than just coating the exterior.

Gigli (GEE-lee; "lilies") Resembling a flower, with a bell-like shape and ruffled edges, gigli stands up best to thick sauces and the chunky ingredients of a casserole.

Girelle (gee-REL-eh; "swivels") This shape takes its name for its corkscrew-like turns. Try it with ingredients that can cling to its substantial curves, such as a pesto and vegetables.

Gramigna (gra-MEEN-ya; "weed") Small, grass-like curls of pasta, these noodles cling to most ingredients. They lend themselves to light sauces with a few small chunks of meat or sausage.

Linguine (lin-GWEE-neh; "little tongues") These long, flat strands are slightly curved in their cross section, like the tongues they are named after. They stand up to sturdier sauces, such as a pesto, tomato, or mushroom sauce, or those with flavorful ingredients, such as shellfish.

Macaroni (mak-a-ROW-neh) Most commonly used in the United States in macaroni and cheese or pasta salads, these curved tubes make an ideal ingredient for soups and stews, such as pasta e fagioli.

Mafalda (ma-FAL-da; named after Princess Mafalda of Savoy) These flat, wide, ribbon-like noodles have wavy ridges that make them look a little like narrow strips of lasagna. They go best with light, delicate sauces that cling to their smooth sides.

Orecchiette (or-ay-KYET-tay; "little ears") Resembling their namesake ears, these round, curved pieces hail from southern Italy, and they are often served with broccoli rabe and sausage.

Paccheri (pa-KER-ee; "open-handed slap") These short, wide tubes were said to have been invented during the Renaissance for use in smuggling garlic across the Alps into what is now Austria. This variety is suited to thick sauces, which cause them to make a slapping sound when eaten.

Penne (PEN-eh; "quills") These small tubes may be smooth or ridged (*rigate*). Penne is best used in soups, in pasta salads, and with thicker sauces and casseroles because the ingredients and sauces can penetrate the inside of the pasta. Penne rigate are ideal for meat, vegetable, or butter-and-oil-based sauces because the ridges hold the sauce.

Riccioli (REE-key-oh-lee; "little curls") Short, wide, and with a twist, these pieces stand up to chunkier ingredients like meat and cheese.

Rigatoni (ree-gah-TOE-nee; "ridged") This wide, ridged, tube-shaped pasta has holes on either end that are large enough to capture pieces of vegetables in a sauce. In addition, this kind of pasta is perfect for baked dishes made with sauce and cheese.

Strozzapreti (strote-za-PRAY-tee; "priest chokers") There are a few legends about how this short, rolled pasta got its colorful name. One says that Roman housewives who made it would "choke" the dough with such force, it looked as if they could choke a priest. Serve it as you would penne, with meat, vegetables, or just butter and oil.

Tagliatelle (tall-yuh-TELL-eh; from the Italian *tagliere*, "to cut") A ribbon that's generally narrower than fettuccine, this versatile pasta lends itself to various sauces, but is traditionally served with Bolognese or other meaty sauces.

Trofie (TROH-fee) This short, tapered, twisted pasta from Genoa pairs well with pesto and other simple sauces.

Parsley-Lemon Pesto with Farfalle

MAKES 1 CUP

With parsley available year-round, you can enjoy this pesto any time you need a dose of springtime.

- 2½ cups (tightly packed) fresh flat-leaf parsley leaves (about 2 ounces)
- ⅓ cup toasted pine nuts (see Cook's Note, page 75)
- 1 to 2 teaspoons grated lemon zest
- 2 tablespoons fresh lemon juice (from 1 lemon)
- ½ cup extra-virgin olive oil
- ⅓ cup freshly grated Parmesan cheese
- ½ teaspoon kosher salt
- ½ teaspoon freshly ground black pepper
- 1 pound farfalle or other pasta

In the bowl of a food processor, combine the parsley, pine nuts, and lemon zest and juice. Process for a few seconds to chop. With the machine running, gradually add the oil, blending until the mixture is thick.

Transfer the pesto to a large bowl. Stir in the Parmesan, salt, and pepper. (If not using right away, transfer the pesto to a jar and refrigerate for up to 3 days.)

Bring a large pot of salted water to a boil over high heat. Add the pasta and cook for 8 to 10 minutes or until the pasta is al dente. Drain the pasta, reserving 1 cup of pasta water.

Add the pasta to the pesto. Using a large spoon or rubber spatula, toss the pesto with the pasta, adding pasta water as needed to thin the sauce. Serve warm or at room temperature.

Pesto

In America, "pesto" generally refers to the familiar green mixture of basil, garlic, Parm, and pine nuts. In Italy, though, the word refers to the preparation—pounding ingredients together using a mortar and pestle to make a paste that is then thinned with olive oil to a sauce-like consistency.

Virtually anything can be the basis of a pesto, from chiles or kale to pistachios or walnuts. Swirl a dollop of cilantro pesto into a tomato or black bean soup, smear some rosemary pesto under the skin of your chicken before you roast it, or use chervil pesto as the basis for a delicate dressing to toss with spring greens. Mix it with mayonnaise to perk up a sandwich or chicken salad, spoon some onto your baked potato, and, oh yeah, toss it with any kind of pasta for an instant burst of green goodness.

Brown Rice Pasta with Creminis and Creamy Cauliflower

V V GF

SERVES 4

This is not only gluten-free, but thanks to the creamy pureed cauliflower sauce, it's also dairy-free.

1 small or ½ large head of cauliflower, cut into florets (about 1 pound)
2 garlic cloves, smashed and peeled
Kosher salt
5 ounces frozen spinach, thawed, squeezed dry, and drained well
2 tablespoons chopped fresh basil leaves
1 teaspoon grated lemon zest
1 teaspoon fresh lemon juice (from 1 lemon)
¼ cup plus 2 tablespoons extra-virgin olive oil
8 ounces cremini mushrooms, sliced ⅛ inch thick
1 shallot, minced
1 (12-ounce) package brown rice pasta
1 cup cherry tomatoes, halved (optional)

Place the cauliflower and garlic in a medium saucepan, cover with cold water, and bring to a boil over high heat. Reduce the heat to medium to maintain a simmer, salt the water well, and cook for about 15 minutes or until the cauliflower is completely tender. Drain well.

To the bowl of a food processor, add the cooked cauliflower and garlic, drained spinach, basil, lemon zest and juice, and ¼ cup of the olive oil. Puree until smooth and creamy, scraping down the sides as needed. Season with ¾ teaspoon salt and pour the mixture into a large bowl.

Place a medium skillet over medium-high heat. Add the remaining 2 tablespoons olive oil to the skillet. When the oil is hot, add the mushrooms. Spread them evenly over the pan and allow to cook undisturbed on the first side for 4 minutes, until golden brown. Stir with a wooden spoon, add the shallot, and continue cooking until both sides of the mushrooms are browned. Season with ¼ teaspoon salt and transfer the cooked mushrooms and shallot to the bowl with the creamy cauliflower.

Meanwhile, bring a large pot of salted water to a boil. Cook the rice pasta according to package directions. Drain well, reserving 1 cup of pasta water. Add the cooked pasta to the cauliflower-mushroom mixture and toss well, adding pasta water as needed to loosen. Stir in the tomatoes, if using, and serve.

Brown Rice Pasta with Creminis and Creamy Cauliflower

Go Vegan Part Time

I've always admired Mark Bittman's writing, both on food policy and politics as well as his useful *How to Cook Everything* books. We met one morning to talk about his book *VB6: Eat Vegan Before 6:00* and why being a part-time vegan works for weight loss and well-being.

Giada: Before you started eating vegan part time you were diagnosed with some pretty serious health issues. I'm surprised your doctor didn't just put you on drugs.

Mark Bittman: The first doctor I saw wanted to, but when I went for a second opinion, that one said, "Just be vegan." He was right!

GDL: How did you come up with the VB6—vegan until six p.m., then eat what you want after—approach?

MB: I like rules. This was a simple rule that I found easy to follow. No counting calories, no weighing things, no points.

GDL: Take me through a day: What do you eat when you get up?

MB: Just what we're eating now: oatmeal topped with olive oil and some fruit. Tapenade and oatmeal are amazing. Or try pesto. Oatmeal is like rice—almost anything can go on it. Some mornings I make a pot of farro or wheat berries to eat throughout the week. Yesterday, for instance, I had leftover spinach and mushrooms.

GDL: How do you eat on the road? Because I find it hard. I always have almonds in my bag—they keep me going and help me avoid bad stuff.

MB: I try to have fruit for breakfast. I always have a banana or an apple in my bag. They're portable and delicious. And I eat a lot of nuts, too. Airport food is the worst—everything has cheese in it, and it's terrible cheese! It's very difficult to eat well when you're on the move. If I come back from a trip and haven't gained weight, I consider that a good trip.

GDL: And if you did gain weight?

MB: Then I do strict VB6 for a week or two.

GDL: Are you also very conscious of portion control? I find that's critical for me.

MB: I don't pig out anymore. Maybe it's an age thing. I find I get full pretty fast, and I've learned to stop eating when I'm full. So I no longer attempt to finish anything; as soon as I'm satisfied I just stop.

GDL: Is there anything you've cut back on that you miss?

MB: I eat way less dairy—I don't like it and I don't tolerate it as well as I used to. Yogurt and cheese are fermented so they are in a sense predigested. Once you start thinking like a part-time vegan, you just can't stop, especially when you get into the flexitarian meals, which combine just a little meat—like one pound for four people instead of two pounds—with lots of vegetables and grains.

Orecchiette with Cauliflower and Bread Crumbs

Orecchiette with Cauliflower and Bread Crumbs

SERVES 4

Italians often add bread crumbs to pasta dishes for texture and color; here they are the secret ingredient that makes a simple pantry meal sing.

1 head of cauliflower, chopped into ½-inch pieces
5 tablespoons extra-virgin olive oil
Kosher salt
1 pound orecchiette pasta
⅓ cup fresh bread crumbs
½ cup plus 2 tablespoons freshly grated Parmesan cheese
4 garlic cloves, chopped
5 anchovy fillets packed in oil, chopped
½ teaspoon crushed red pepper flakes
3 tablespoons chopped fresh flat-leaf parsley leaves

Preheat the oven to 400°F. On a rimmed baking sheet, toss together the cauliflower, 2 tablespoons of the olive oil, and ½ teaspoon salt. Roast for 20 to 25 minutes, turning the cauliflower midway through, until golden brown and cooked through. Set aside.

Bring a large pot of salted water to a boil. Add the pasta and cook for 10 to 12 minutes or until al dente. Drain well, reserving 1½ cups of pasta water.

Heat a large sauté pan over medium heat. Add the bread crumbs and toast until fragrant and golden brown, about 3 minutes. Remove to a small bowl and mix with 2 tablespoons of the Parmesan cheese.

In that same large sauté pan, heat the remaining 3 tablespoons olive oil over medium-high heat. Add the garlic and anchovies and stir with a wooden spoon, breaking up the anchovies to help them dissolve in the oil. This will take about 2 minutes. Add the red pepper flakes and the cauliflower and toss gently to coat.

Add to the pan the cooked pasta, half of the reserved pasta water, the remaining ½ cup cheese, and the parsley. Toss to coat, and simmer for another 2 minutes, adding additional pasta water as needed to moisten. Sprinkle with the bread crumb mixture and drizzle with more olive oil if desired.

Olive Oil

If you've ever shopped for olive oil in a specialty food shop, you've probably noticed that the prices can vary wildly and wondered what makes some so costly—and whether they're worth the extra expense. The answer is . . . maybe . . . if you know exactly what you're getting.

Like wine aficionados, olive oil experts have their own vocabulary to describe the important characteristics of oil. In the best oils, a balance of fruity, bitter, and pungent qualities should be evident. A vivid green color, though attractive, is not always indicative of flavor, nor is the variety of olive or country of origin a sure guarantee of good (or poor) quality. A fine bottle of oil should indicate the date of press, and once the oil is more than six months old it is probably not worth a premium price. After another three months or so, the oil will have lost its unique characteristics.

To assess the bouquet of a young oil, pour a small amount of oil into a small glass bowl and an equal amount of supermarket oil into a second bowl. One at a time, cup your hand over the bowl, then swirl the oil to warm it from the heat of your hand. When you uncover the dish you should be able to get a good whiff of the grassy, peaty, herbaceous, or fruity aromas. If, on the other hand, you detect aromas of gasoline, plastic, or other chemicals, it's likely your bottle was produced using some shortcuts to extract the oil from the fruit, or has been adulterated with other ingredients.

Precious extra-virgin oils should be reserved to drizzle over soups, pastas, seafood dishes, and in dressings; for everyday use in cooked sauces or marinades, a good-quality mass-produced oil will do just fine.

Short-Rib Lasagna

SERVES 6 TO 8

A great make-ahead meal that can be frozen and reheated. Use the short rib braising liquid as a base for soup or toss with pasta another night.

RIBS

2 tablespoons extra-virgin olive oil
2½ pounds beef short ribs
Kosher salt and freshly ground black pepper
1 onion, coarsely chopped
4 garlic cloves, smashed and peeled
2 (4-inch) fresh rosemary sprigs
2 cups red wine, such as pinot noir
2 cups beef broth

FILLING

1½ cups milk
1 cup heavy cream
1½ cups (6 ounces) freshly grated Pecorino Romano cheese
1 cup (4 ounces) shredded mozzarella cheese
1 small bunch of Tuscan kale, ribs removed, leaves chopped
¼ cup chopped fresh basil leaves
2 garlic cloves, minced

12 lasagna noodles (about 10 ounces)
Butter, for greasing the baking dish
3½ cups marinara sauce, homemade (see page 121) or 1 (25-ounce) jar
½ cup freshly grated Parmesan cheese
Extra-virgin olive oil, for drizzling

For the ribs: In a large Dutch oven or heavy stockpot, heat the oil over medium-high heat. Season the ribs with 2 teaspoons salt and 1 teaspoon pepper. Add the ribs to the pot and cook for about 4 minutes on each side, until brown. Remove the ribs and set aside. Add the onion, garlic, and rosemary to the pot. Season with salt and pepper. Cook for 5 minutes, until the onion is translucent and soft. Increase the heat to high. Add the wine and use a wooden spoon to scrape up the brown bits that cling to the bottom of the pot. Add the beef broth and ribs to the pan.

Bring the mixture to a boil. Reduce the heat to a simmer, cover the pot, and cook for 2½ to 3 hours, until the meat is very tender. Remove the ribs and set aside until cool enough to handle, about 20 minutes. Reserve the cooking liquid for another use or discard along with the bones. Using 2 forks, shred the meat into 2-inch-long pieces (to yield approximately 2¼ cups shredded meat).

For the filling: In a medium heavy saucepan, bring the milk and cream to a simmer over medium heat. Reduce the heat to low. Add the cheeses and whisk until melted and the sauce is smooth. Remove the pan from the heat and stir in the kale, basil, and garlic.

Bring a large pot of salted water to a boil over high heat. Add the pasta and cook until just tender but still firm to the bite, stirring occasionally, 8 to 10 minutes. Drain and set aside.

Place an oven rack in the center of the oven. Preheat the oven to 400°F. Butter a 9 x 13-inch glass baking dish. Spread 1 cup of the marinara sauce in the bottom of the prepared baking dish. Lay 3 noodles over the marinara. Spread one-third of the filling mixture evenly along each noodle. Sprinkle with one-third of the shredded short ribs. Repeat with the remaining noodles and filling, making 3 layers of filling and ending with pasta. Spoon the remaining marinara sauce on top and sprinkle with the Parmesan cheese. Drizzle with olive oil and bake until the lasagna is heated through and the cheese is beginning to brown, about 25 minutes. Cool for 10 minutes. Cut into squares and serve.

Short-Rib Lasagna

Creamy Spinach and Mushroom Lasagna

V

SERVES 6 TO 8

Fresh pasta sheets make for a more tender lasagna, so if you have a good source for fresh pasta, by all means use it here. You'll appreciate the difference. But even with dried lasagna noodles this is a great option to keep in mind for meatless meals.

1 tablespoon unsalted butter, at room temperature, for greasing the baking dish

VEGETABLES

3 tablespoons extra-virgin olive oil, plus extra for drizzling
1 medium onion, chopped
12 ounces cremini mushrooms, cleaned and quartered
1 teaspoon kosher salt
½ teaspoon freshly ground black pepper

SAUCE

2 cups heavy cream, at room temperature
1¾ cups whole milk, at room temperature
⅓ cup all-purpose flour
2 cups (8 ounces) freshly grated Pecorino Romano cheese
3½ cups (14 ounces) shredded mozzarella cheese
2 (5-ounce) bags baby spinach, coarsely chopped
¼ cup packed chopped fresh basil leaves
2 garlic cloves, minced
1 teaspoon kosher salt
½ teaspoon freshly ground black pepper

8 (8 x 5-inch) fresh lasagna noodles or 12 dried lasagna noodles

Preheat the oven to 350°F. Butter a 9 x 13-inch glass or ceramic baking dish. Set aside.

For the vegetables: In a large nonstick skillet, heat the oil over high heat. Add the onion, mushrooms, salt, and pepper. Cook, stirring frequently, until the onion is soft and any liquid from the mushrooms has evaporated, about 20 minutes.

For the sauce: In a heavy 5-quart saucepan, bring the cream, milk, and flour to a simmer over medium heat, whisking constantly for 3 minutes. Reduce the heat to low. Add the pecorino and 2 cups of the mozzarella cheese. Whisk until the cheeses have melted and the sauce is smooth. Remove the pan from the heat and stir in the spinach, basil, garlic, salt, and pepper. Add the mushroom mixture to the sauce and stir to combine. Set aside to cool slightly.

Creamy Spinach and Mushroom Lasagna

If using dried pasta, bring a large pot of salted water to a boil, then add the dried lasagna noodles and cook for 6 to 8 minutes until just tender. Drain and cool slightly before using.

Spread 1 cup of the sauce over the bottom of the prepared baking dish. Arrange 2 sheets of fresh pasta or 3 boiled lasagna noodles on top in a single layer. Spread with 2 cups of sauce. Repeat the layers with the remaining pasta sheets and sauce, ending with sauce. Sprinkle with the remaining 1½ cups mozzarella cheese. Drizzle with olive oil and bake for 30 to 35 minutes, until the filling is bubbling and the top is golden. Cool for 20 minutes. Cut into squares and serve.

Pasta Pizza

SERVES 4

Another family favorite from my childhood, this was a quick and easy dish my mother made from leftover cooked pasta. Feel free to incorporate any kind of pasta, vegetables, and cheese that you have on hand.

2 eggs
¾ cup grated Parmesan cheese, plus more for serving
½ teaspoon kosher salt
¼ teaspoon freshly ground black pepper
3 cups cooked spaghetti (about ½ pound dried)
⅓ cup diced salami, prosciutto, or ham
⅓ cup frozen edamame or peas, thawed, or chopped cooked broccoli
1 to 2 tablespoons olive oil
Crushed hot red pepper flakes (optional)

In a small bowl, beat the eggs until well combined. Stir in the Parmesan, salt, and pepper and mix well.

In a large bowl, toss together the pasta, diced meat, and vegetables; using your hands generally gets the job done most efficiently. Add the egg mixture and mix again, being sure to distribute the eggs thoroughly.

Heat 1 tablespoon of the oil in a medium skillet over medium-high heat. When hot but not smoking, add the pasta mixture, pressing evenly into the pan with the back of a spatula. Reduce the heat to medium and cook without stirring for 5 to 6 minutes or until the bottom of the cake is browned and crisp and releases from the pan (you may need to run a spatula or knife around the edge of the pan to nudge it free). Press down on the pasta as it cooks now and then to ensure it is making good contact with the bottom of the pan.

Cover the pan with a large plate and carefully flip it over, inverting the pasta cake onto the plate. Add a bit more oil to the pan if it looks dry, then slide the pasta cake back into the pan. Cook for another 5 to 6 minutes or until golden.

Slide the pasta cake onto a cutting board and cut it into wedges. Serve hot, sprinkled with Parmesan and red pepper flakes if desired.

Kitchen Remedies

When I was growing up, my nonna would take the sting out of a sunburn with a milk-soaked cloth, or cure a cough with a glass of hot water, lemon, and honey. Her generation relied on home remedies for health and beauty treatments, and today, this all-natural approach has newfound appeal as we learn more about the unwanted ingredients in so many packaged goods. Here are some tried-and-tested cures.

Witch Hazel: Get rid of morning puffiness by soaking two cotton pads in chilled witch hazel and placing them on your closed eyes for a minute or two.

Olive Oil: Drizzle a few tablespoons into your bathwater for softer skin. Rub some onto your cuticles if they are dry or cracked.

Baking Soda: Use as a skin-softening body scrub, work it through wet tresses as a shampoo alternative, or mix it with equal parts water to make a 15-minute acne spot treatment.

Aloe Vera: The leaves of this succulent plant contain a gel that soothes minor burns or sunburn. It can reduce the appearance of wrinkles and stretch marks and take the bite out of razor nicks, too. Grow an aloe vera plant in a pot, or purchase a tube of pure aloe vera gel.

Ginger: To settle an upset stomach, peel and chop a half-inch piece of gingerroot and steep it in boiled water for a few minutes. Sip.

Chamomile: Hot chamomile tea will make you sleepy and help you get your beauty rest; a cooled version can be poured over your scalp to prevent and treat dandruff.

Pasta Pizza

10-inch timbale

Spring Pasta Timbale

SERVES 4 TO 6

This is an impressive-looking dish for a spring dinner gathering. The pasta is wrapped in grilled zucchini before baking, which not only keeps it moist, but also adds flavor throughout the whole dish. You can make individual servings in four 10-ounce ramekins if you prefer.

4 medium zucchini, sliced lengthwise into ¼-inch-thick strips
¼ cup plus 2 tablespoons extra-virgin olive oil
½ teaspoon kosher salt
¼ teaspoon freshly ground black pepper
½ pound penne
2 medium shallots, diced
½ pound Italian pork sausage, casings removed
1½ cups cherry tomatoes, quartered
¼ cup Marsala wine
½ cup frozen peas, thawed
½ bunch of asparagus, chopped fine
1 cup diced provolone piccante cheese (about 4 ounces)
1 cup freshly grated Pecorino-Romano cheese
½ cup chopped fresh basil leaves

Place a grill pan over medium-high heat or preheat a gas or charcoal grill. Using a pastry brush, lightly brush the zucchini slices with ¼ cup of the olive oil and sprinkle with the salt and pepper. Grill the zucchini until tender and colored with grill marks, about 4 minutes per side. Set aside.

Bring a large pot of salted water to a boil over high heat. Add the pasta and cook, stirring occasionally, until tender but still firm to the bite, 8 to 10 minutes. Drain the pasta.

Meanwhile, warm the remaining 2 tablespoons olive oil in a large skillet. Add the shallots and sauté until tender, about 3 minutes. Add the sausage and brown the meat, breaking it into bite-size pieces with a wooden spoon, about 5 minutes. Add the tomatoes and the Marsala and cook until the liquid has evaporated, about 3 minutes. Turn off the heat. Add the peas and asparagus and stir to combine. Add the provolone, ¾ cup of the Pecorino-Romano, the basil, and the cooked pasta. Set aside.

Preheat the oven to 350°F. Line a 9-inch springform pan with the grilled zucchini. Be sure that the slices overlap and hang over the edge. Fill with the pasta mixture, pressing down to make sure the pan is filled evenly. Fold the zucchini slices over the top of the pasta and add more slices on top to completely enclose the timbale.

Bake the timbale until warmed through and the cheese has melted, about 30 minutes. Transfer the timbale to a wire rack and let it rest for 10 minutes to set.

To serve, invert the timbale onto a platter and release the sides and bottom of the pan. Sprinkle with the remaining ¼ cup Pecorino-Romano and cut into wedges to serve.

Individual timbale

Lighter Macaroni and Cheese

Lighter Macaroni and Cheese

GF

SERVES 6

This lightened-up version is also gluten-free. Greek yogurt gives it the rich, creamy texture of cream and butter without the fat, and the rice cereal adds a boost of fiber and the perfect crunch.

1 (12-ounce) bag rice flour penne, such as Bionaturae
1 teaspoon extra-virgin olive oil
1 shallot, minced
½ cup low-sodium chicken broth
1 (15-ounce) container part-skim ricotta cheese
¼ cup fat-free plain Greek yogurt
1 cup (about ¼ pound) shredded Gruyère or Emmentaler cheese
½ teaspoon chopped fresh thyme leaves
1 teaspoon kosher salt
¼ teaspoon cayenne pepper
½ cup oven-toasted rice cereal, such as Chex, crushed
2 tablespoons freshly grated Parmesan cheese

Bring a large pot of salted water to a boil. Add the penne and cook according to package directions, just until al dente. Drain well, reserving ⅓ cup of pasta water for the sauce.

Heat a 3-quart ovenproof pot over medium heat. Add the olive oil and shallot and cook, stirring often, until the shallot has softened and become translucent. Add the chicken broth and bring to a simmer.

Preheat the broiler to high.

Turn off the heat and add the ricotta, yogurt, Gruyère, thyme, salt, cayenne, and reserved pasta water. Whisk until combined. Add the cooked pasta and fold it into the sauce until it is well coated.

In a small bowl, mix the crushed rice cereal with the Parmesan. Sprinkle the mixture over the pasta and broil for 3 to 5 minutes or until golden brown on top and bubbly.

Stock Up

One of the keys to putting together a quick-and-easy meal—or any meal, for that matter—that's stress-free and delicious is to have a well-stocked pantry. Here are some of the staples I can't cook without.

Extra-virgin olive oil: A less expensive oil for sautéing garlic and onions, and a pricey one for drizzling over salads, oatmeal, vegetables, and seafood. Store in a cool, dark place.

Fresh garlic: Choose garlic heads that are firm, not hard and dried out. Store in a cool, dark place, but not in the refrigerator.

Red pepper flakes: These go in everything! If they've been in your pantry for more than six months or their color isn't a vibrant red, they've lost their heat.

Canned or jarred Italian tuna: Choose tuna packed in olive oil—it has more flavor.

Marinara sauce: I prefer to make my own (see page 121) and store it in the freezer, but if you don't have time, choose one that has as few added flavorings and sugars as possible.

Dried herbs: Oregano, rosemary, thyme, and herbes de Provence are my basics.

Vinegars: A good balsamic vinegar for salads and both red and white wine vinegars.

Onions: These keep well, so I keep on hand red, Spanish, and a sweet variety, such as Vidalia, as well as shallots.

Capers: A fast way to add zing to salads, sauces, and meat or fish dishes. Those packed in salt are best; rinse well before using.

Anchovies: Mashed into dressings, sauces, or vegetable purees, they add a subtle depth of flavor.

Nuts: I like to keep almonds, walnuts, and hazelnuts on hand to add crunch to salads, cookies, and pasta. Store in the freezer.

Dried pasta: I keep long strands such as spaghetti and linguine, short tubes like penne and rigatoni, and other shapes like shells, orecchiette ("little ears"), and farfalle (bow ties) as well as a box of brown rice pasta for guests who can't eat gluten.

Canned cannellini beans: Italian beans, also known as Tuscan white beans.

Fusilli with Tuna, Capers, and Almonds

SERVES 4

If the phrase "pantry meal" suggests lackluster dishes that lack vibrancy and kick, this recipe will be a revelation. Made with ingredients straight off the shelf, it's full of flavor and loaded with nutrients—and it has great texture, too.

1 pound fusilli
⅓ cup extra-virgin olive oil
3 garlic cloves, peeled and crushed
1 (28-ounce) can diced tomatoes, drained
½ teaspoon crushed red pepper flakes
¼ teaspoon kosher salt
3 tablespoons capers, rinsed and drained
1 (7.76-ounce) jar tuna in olive oil, drained and flaked
½ cup freshly grated Parmesan cheese, plus more for serving
¼ cup chopped fresh flat-leaf parsley leaves
½ cup toasted almonds (see Cook's Note, page 75), chopped

Bring a large pot of salted water to a boil over high heat. Cook the pasta until al dente, about 8 minutes. Drain well, reserving 1 cup of pasta water.

Meanwhile, heat a large skillet over medium-high heat for about 2 minutes. Add the oil and garlic and cook for 3 minutes or until the garlic is lightly browned and fragrant. Add the drained tomatoes, red pepper flakes, and salt to the pan, reduce the heat to medium, and cook, stirring often, for about 5 minutes.

Add the capers and tuna and cook for an additional minute. Add the drained pasta, the Parmesan, and about ½ cup of the pasta water. Stir to combine. Add the parsley and almonds and toss, adding more pasta water if needed. Serve with more cheese, if desired.

Fusilli with Tuna, Capers, and Almonds

Spiced Kabocha Squash Risotto

Spiced Kabocha Squash Risotto

V GF

SERVES 4 AS AN ENTRÉE OR 6 AS A SIDE DISH

Kabocha squash has a mild, nutty flavor and smooth texture similar to that of butternut squash, which can be substituted for the kabocha. You will recognize it by its deep green skin and flattened cylindrical shape. A touch of vanilla makes this both sweet and savory.

4 cups low-sodium vegetable broth
1 large vanilla bean
¼ teaspoon ground cinnamon
⅛ teaspoon cayenne pepper
½ medium kabocha squash, peeled and cut into 1-inch cubes
3 tablespoons unsalted butter
¾ cup finely chopped onion
1½ cups Arborio rice or medium-grain white rice
¾ cup dry white wine
½ cup freshly grated Parmesan cheese
¾ teaspoon kosher salt
2 tablespoons chopped fresh flat-leaf parsley leaves

In a medium saucepan, warm the broth and 1 cup water over medium-high heat. Cut the vanilla bean in half lengthwise. Scrape out the seeds and add them, the bean, cinnamon, and cayenne to the broth. Bring to a simmer, then reduce the heat to low.

Add the squash to the simmering broth and cook until tender, about 5 minutes. Using a slotted spoon, remove the squash to a side dish. Turn the heat on the broth to very low and cover to keep warm.

Meanwhile, in a large heavy saucepan, melt 2 tablespoons of the butter over medium heat. Add the onion and sauté until tender but not brown, about 3 minutes. Add the rice and stir to coat with the butter. Add the wine and simmer until the wine has almost completely evaporated, about 3 minutes. Add ½ cup of the simmering broth and stir until almost completely absorbed, about 2 minutes.

Continue cooking the rice, adding the broth 1 cup at a time, stirring constantly and allowing each addition of the broth to be absorbed by the rice before adding the next, until the rice is tender but still firm to the bite and the mixture is creamy, about 20 minutes total.

Discard the vanilla bean and turn off the heat. Gently stir in the cooked squash, the Parmesan cheese, the remaining tablespoon of butter, and the salt. Transfer the risotto to a serving bowl. Garnish with the parsley and serve immediately.

Artichoke Risotto

GF

SERVES 4 TO 6

Using frozen artichokes hearts makes this quick and easy enough for a weeknight; fresh mint, chives, and peas make it memorable.

¼ cup extra-virgin olive oil
1 tablespoon unsalted butter
1 (9-ounce) package frozen artichoke hearts, thawed and cut into bite-size wedges
1 large or 2 small shallots, minced
1 cup Arborio rice
1 teaspoon kosher salt
1 cup dry white wine, at room temperature
3½ cups low-sodium chicken broth
½ cup frozen peas, thawed
½ cup (3 ounces) crumbled feta cheese
¼ cup chopped fresh mint leaves
¼ cup finely chopped fresh chives
¼ teaspoon freshly ground black pepper
1 tablespoon fresh lemon juice (from 1 lemon)

Heat 2 tablespoons of the olive oil and butter in a medium saucepan over high heat. Add the artichoke hearts and reduce the heat to medium high. Cook, stirring occasionally, until the hearts are beginning to brown, about 10 minutes. Remove to a plate and set aside.

To the same pan, add the remaining 2 tablespoons olive oil and the shallots and cook for 1 minute, stirring regularly. Add the rice and salt and stir, using a wooden spoon, to coat all of the kernels in the oil. Continue to cook for 3 minutes or until the rice is sizzling. Add the wine and continue to stir until the wine is almost entirely absorbed.

Continue cooking the rice, adding the broth 1 cup at a time, stirring constantly and allowing each addition of the broth to be absorbed by the rice before adding the next, until the rice is tender but still firm to the bite and the mixture is creamy, about 20 minutes total.

Stir in the peas, cheese, herbs, and pepper. Gently stir in the browned artichoke hearts and the lemon juice and serve.

Chorizo Risotto

SERVES 4

This risotto has a definite south-of-the-border vibe. Serve it with an avocado-and-orange salad.

2 jalapeño chiles
½ small jicama, julienned
1 teaspoon fresh lime juice (from 1 lime)
½ teaspoon kosher salt
3½ cups low-sodium chicken broth
½ pound raw Mexican chorizo
1 white onion, diced small
1 red bell pepper, cored, seeded, and diced small
1 cup Arborio rice
1 cup light beer
¾ cup crumbled Cotija cheese

Over an open flame, char the jalapeños until completely blackened, about 6 minutes. Place in a small bowl, cover with plastic wrap, and steam for 5 minutes. Peel off the charred skin and remove the stems and seeds, then slice thin. In a small bowl combine with the jicama, lime juice, and ¼ teaspoon of the salt. Toss well.

In a medium saucepan, bring the chicken broth to a simmer. Keep warm. In a medium Dutch oven cook the sausage over medium heat, breaking it into bite-size pieces with a wooden spoon, until almost completely cooked through, about 4 minutes. Add the onion and bell pepper and cook, stirring often, until the vegetables have softened slightly, about 3 minutes. Season with the remaining ¼ teaspoon salt.

Add the rice to the pan and stir to coat the rice with the oil in the pan for 2 to 3 minutes. Deglaze the pan with the beer and cook, stirring constantly, until all of the liquid is completely absorbed, about 3 minutes. Add 1 cup of simmering broth and stir until almost completely absorbed, about 4 minutes.

Continue cooking the rice, adding the broth ¾ cup at a time, stirring constantly and allowing each addition of broth to absorb before adding the next, until the rice is tender but still firm to the bite and the mixture is creamy, about 20 minutes total. Remove from the heat and stir in the cheese. Serve, topping each portion with a spoonful of the jalapeño-jicama slaw.

Chorizo Risotto

Eating Clean

It's taken me a long time to realize that when I don't eat the way I know is best for me, I can't function the way I want and need to, and I just don't feel like myself. While I try to make an effort to eat good-for-me foods most of the time, I'm only human. I go through periods when I'm just not able to prioritize a healthy meal over the other items on my To Do list, and other times when, well, let's just say my choices are not what they should be. So when I want to help my body get back on track, I turn to foods like these that are a little simpler, a little cleaner, but still nutritious and satisfying.

For me, clean eating means dairy, sugar, and alcohol are strictly off-limits. I may even go all in with a liquid cleanse for a couple of days to kick-start things. That's what works for me, but listen to your own body and do what feels right for you. The results more than make up for any deprivation you may feel in passing up the foods that do a number on your digestion (or waistline) for a few days.

My Mini Cleanse

For the past few years, the word *cleanse* has become synonymous with *juice fast*. But these programs aren't for everyone. Especially in the winter I find my body tolerates something cooked and warm better than it does cold, raw juices. For me, my special Detox Soup is the answer. It's warm and comforting, exactly what my body wants. And, like many people, I find it's a satisfying and more sustainable meal replacement than raw juices.

I do a cleanse a few times a year—after I've been on the road, after finishing filming my shows for Food Network, and after the holidays, when I've had one too many cups of eggnog. I also like to cleanse when I'm doing an important photo shoot, such as a magazine cover, because it helps me de-puff.

Detox Soup

GF

SERVES 4

This broth is a fantastic tune-up for your body. It's packed with anti-inflammatory veggies and spices such as garlic and ginger, to help with liver function and aid digestion.

2 bone-in chicken breasts (about 1½ pounds)
3 lemongrass stalks, trimmed and pounded
1 (4-inch) piece of fresh ginger, peeled and sliced
1 carrot, peeled and cut into large pieces
1 celery stalk, cut into large pieces
1 shallot, peeled and halved
1 bay leaf
½ teaspoon black peppercorns
1 dried Thai chile
1 teaspoon kosher salt
6 cups cold water
1 (5-ounce) package baby spinach, washed and coarsely chopped

To a large Dutch oven or soup pot add the chicken, lemongrass, ginger, carrot, celery, shallot, bay leaf, black peppercorns, Thai chile, and salt. Add the water and place over medium heat. Bring the soup to a simmer, skimming off any residue that may come to the top. Cook for 45 minutes or until the chicken is cooked through. Turn off the heat and allow the soup to cool for about 30 minutes.

Remove the chicken from the soup and shred the meat, discarding the bones and skin. Strain the stock and return the liquid to the pot. Add the shredded chicken back in the stock, along with the spinach, and bring the soup to a simmer over medium-high heat. Serve immediately.

Jade's Spa Water

V V GF

SERVES 4

A special treat my daughter, Jade, makes for my breakfast-in-bed trays, this can be made with most any fruit that is in season. Try it with grapes and oranges, or peaches and kiwi. Just keep it fun and fresh.

1 cup red grapes
1 pint fresh strawberries, hulled and sliced
2 kiwis, peeled and sliced
2 cups cubed watermelon
Ice (optional)

Thread a grape, a piece of strawberry, and a piece of kiwi on each of 4 small wooden skewers or toothpicks. Set aside until ready to serve. Add the rest of the fruit to a pitcher. Add 2 quarts cold water and refrigerate for 30 minutes.

Pour the spa water into four 16-ounce water glasses. Add ice if desired and serve, garnished with a fruit skewer.

Detox Soup

Bring on the Broth

Everything old is new again. Including bone broths. Wise cooks never tossed out poultry carcasses or meat bones. They put them in a large pot with some aromatics and vegetables and water and let them simmer for hours, then used the resulting broth as the base of soups and sauces or as a sustaining curative for those feeling under the weather.

What *is* new is the notion of broth as a meal replacement, a nourishing and warm beverage both higher in protein and lower in carbs (and sugars) than the juices that generally form the basis of a liquid detox. While juices can quickly be metabolized and cause spikes (and the accompanying plunges) in blood sugar that leave fasters ravenous between juice fixes, many people find bone broth leaves them feeling satiated longer and without the ups and downs they experience on a pure juice diet. I know I always feel better when I detox with a cup of warm and comforting Bone Broth or Detox Soup. But even for those not on a cleanse, a cup of homey hot broth is appealing and satisfying.

Making Bone Broth is a simple project. Most supermarkets sell packages of beef shins marked "soup bones" and may even offer chicken "frames"—rib cages from which the breast fillets have been removed—for a song. If you don't see them, ask. If you are in the habit of cutting up your own chickens, save any bony parts you don't use, including necks, backs, and wing tips, in the freezer until you've accumulated 2 or 3 pounds. Then defrost, simmer, and sip. I use readily available beef oxtail and chicken carcasses.

Once the bones are briefly roasted to develop some color and caramelization, they are left to simmer slowly on a back burner for hours (even days, if you like), until every drop of flavor and goodness is extracted from the solids. An occasional skim and the addition of some veggies and other flavorings along the way is all the attention the broth requires. Chill the broth overnight to allow the fat to rise to the surface, then skim off the solidified fat, transfer to storage containers, and refrigerate or freeze until needed.

Bone Broth

GF

MAKES ABOUT 9 CUPS

This broth is made without salt, because it can become too salty as the liquid reduces. Season to taste before adding to soups or sauces, or sipping from a mug.

2 pounds beef bones
2 (6-ounce) pieces of oxtail
2 tablespoons extra-virgin olive oil
1 onion, halved through the equator
2 tablespoons tomato paste
2 raw chicken carcasses
4½ quarts cold water
3 carrots, washed and cut in 3 pieces each
1 small celery root, peeled and cut in 6 chunks
1 head of garlic, halved through the equator
Stems from 1 bunch of flat-leaf parsley
1 bay leaf
6 large sprigs of thyme
Kosher salt, to taste

Preheat the oven to 400°F.

Place the beef bones and the oxtail on a rimmed baking sheet. Drizzle and rub the bones and oxtails with 1 tablespoon of the olive oil to coat them evenly. Roast for 20 minutes, until the bones are fragrant and golden brown.

In a large stockpot, heat the remaining tablespoon of olive oil over medium heat. Place the onion in the pot, cut side down, and cook for about 5 minutes or until both cut sides are a deep, even brown. Remove and set aside. Add the tomato paste to the pot and cook, stirring constantly, until the tomato paste is caramelized and a shade darker in color, about 2 minutes. Add the beef bones, oxtail, and the chicken carcasses to the pot and cover with the water. Bring to a simmer over medium-high heat, then reduce the heat as needed to just maintain a gentle simmer. Cook for 2½ hours, skimming any impurities or grease that may float to the surface.

Add the browned onion, the carrots, celery root, garlic, parsley stems, bay leaf, and thyme sprigs to the stockpot and continue to simmer gently for an additional 3 hours. Strain the stock through a fine-mesh strainer. Cool to room temperature, then refrigerate if not using immediately. Before using or sipping, season with salt if desired.

California Lettuce Cups

V V GF

MAKES 4 TO 6 SERVINGS

It doesn't get much cleaner, fresher, or California-inflected than these pretty salad cups.

¼ cup fresh lime juice (from 2 to 3 limes)
2 tablespoons extra-virgin olive oil
¾ teaspoon kosher salt
¼ teaspoon freshly ground black pepper
2 avocados
1 cup ruby red grapefruit segments (from 2 or 3 grapefruit; see Cook's Note)
½ cup toasted almonds (see Cook's Note, page 75), coarsely chopped
1 serrano chile, coarsely chopped
½ cup fresh cilantro leaves, coarsely chopped
1 head of Boston or butter lettuce, leaves separated, washed, dried, and left whole

In a small bowl, whisk together the lime juice, olive oil, ½ teaspoon of the salt, and the pepper. Set the dressing aside.

Halve each avocado and remove the pit. Scoop the flesh from the halves with a large spoon and dice it into bite-size pieces. Combine the avocado with the grapefruit, almonds, chile, and cilantro leaves. Toss gently with the dressing and the remaining ¼ teaspoon salt. Spoon the mixture into the lettuce leaves and serve.

Cook's Note: **To segment (or supreme) a grapefruit, working on a cutting board, cut off the top and the bottom, and stand the grapefruit on one of the flat ends. Holding the grapefruit steady, slice downward, following the contour of the fruit to cut off all the peel and pith. Holding the grapefruit in the palm of your hand over a bowl to catch the juices, gently free each segment by cutting along the membranes on each side, and place the fruit segments in the bowl. Continue cutting until all of the segments are released, then discard the membranes and seeds.**

California Lettuce Cups

Zucchini Spaghetti with Sun Gold Tomato Sauce

Zucchini Spaghetti with Sun Gold Tomato Sauce

V GF

SERVES 4 TO 6

Star anise is the secret ingredient that brings this vivid sauce to life. Add your zucchini "noodles," top with some Parmesan and a bit of fresh thyme, and there you have it: Even an avid pasta lover won't miss the pasta.

4 medium zucchini
2 tablespoons olive oil
2 garlic cloves, minced
¼ teaspoon crushed red pepper flakes
1 star anise
4 fresh thyme sprigs, plus 2 teaspoons chopped fresh thyme leaves for sprinkling
4 cups Sun Gold or cherry tomatoes, halved
1½ teaspoons kosher salt
¼ teaspoon freshly ground black pepper
2 teaspoons sherry vinegar
¼ cup freshly shaved Parmesan cheese

Attach the zucchini to a spiral slicer or use a julienne peeler or Microplane slicer to slice the zucchini into thin strips. Set the noodles aside in a large bowl while you make the sauce.

Heat the oil in a large saucepan over medium heat. Add the garlic, red pepper flakes, star anise, and thyme and cook until fragrant, about 1 minute. Add the tomatoes, ½ teaspoon of the salt, the pepper, and the vinegar and stir gently to combine. Cook the sauce, stirring occasionally, until the tomatoes have released their juices, about 8 minutes.

Discard the star anise and thyme sprigs and add the zucchini noodles and remaining teaspoon of salt. Toss gently to coat the noodles with the sauce and cook for another 2 minutes to warm the noodles. Serve with the shaved Parmesan and a sprinkle of fresh thyme.

Vegetable Noodles

I am unabashedly pro-pasta. Give me a bowl of noodles, a vibrant, fresh sauce, and a fork to swirl it with and I'm a happy woman. But much as I might want to, I can't eat pasta every day.

That's why I'm a big fan of spiral slicers that let you carve up long, thin, noodle-like slices of zucchini, squash, carrots, cucumbers, or pretty much any vegetable you can imagine. You get a meal with a lot fewer carbohydrates and calories, but with all the fiber and vitamins from your whole-food veggie ingredients—and all the twirling pleasure of real pasta. It's a big win-win.

Start with washed, raw vegetables, then, depending on your spiral slicer model, either twist or crank to slice up spaghetti-like strands or wider, pappardelle-like ribbons. Sweet potatoes and carrots make for nice, sweet noodles, and a mix of summer squash and carrots creates a colorful salad. But zucchini is perhaps the most versatile and an easy veggie on which beginners can hone their noodle-cutting skills.

These noodles are super-fast to make because the thinly sliced veggies cook up quickly in a sauté pan with a bit of olive oil, no boiling water needed. Just add the strands to your sauce and you have a healthy, satisfying plateful in minutes.

Pan-Roasted Asparagus with Crispy Fried Egg

V

SERVES 1

There are a lot of appealing textures and colors in this meatless main for one, and it's rich without being heavy. It should go without saying it would make a lovely breakfast, too.

BREAD CRUMB GREMOLATA

1½ teaspoons extra-virgin olive oil
2 tablespoons panko bread crumbs
¼ teaspoon grated lemon zest
Pinch of crushed red pepper flakes
Pinch of salt
2 tablespoons chopped fresh flat-leaf parsley leaves
1 tablespoon freshly grated Parmesan cheese

ASPARAGUS

1 tablespoon extra-virgin olive oil, plus more for drizzling
¼ pound thin asparagus, trimmed
Pinch of salt
1 large egg

For the gremolata: Heat a medium skillet over medium heat. Add the olive oil and bread crumbs and toast, stirring often with a wooden spoon, until golden brown. Place the bread crumbs in a small bowl and add the lemon zest, red pepper flakes, and salt. Stir well, then allow the mixture to cool to room temperature. Stir in the parsley and cheese.

For the asparagus: Wipe out the pan, then add 1 teaspoon of the olive oil and heat over medium-high heat. Add the asparagus and a pinch of salt and cook for 4 to 5 minutes, stirring and flipping the spears often until they are bright green, cooked through, and slightly browned. Remove to a serving plate.

To the same pan add the remaining 2 teaspoons olive oil and place over medium-high heat. Carefully crack the egg into the pan, season it with salt, and reduce the heat slightly. Cook for 2 to 3 minutes or until the edges are light brown and crispy and the whites are just set; the yolk should still be runny. Using a slotted spatula, carefully slide the egg on top of the asparagus. Sprinkle everything with the gremolata and a drizzle of olive oil if desired.

Tuna, White Bean, and Bitter Greens Salad

GF

SERVES 4

Tuna packed in olive oil, canned beans, and endive, radicchio, and fennel are available throughout the winter. Think of this main course as a winter salade niçoise.

1 tablespoon capers, rinsed, drained, and chopped
2 tablespoons fresh lemon juice (from 1 lemon)
1 teaspoon Dijon mustard
¼ cup extra-virgin olive oil
¾ teaspoon kosher salt
1 (15-ounce) can cannellini beans, rinsed and drained
1 (6.35-ounce) jar tuna packed in olive oil, drained
2 Belgian endives, cut into 2-inch pieces
1 small head of radicchio, cut into 2-inch pieces
1 small fennel bulb, cored, shaved on a mandoline or thinly sliced with a knife
½ cup lightly packed fresh flat-leaf parsley leaves

In a large bowl, whisk together the capers, lemon juice, and mustard. Continue whisking and drizzle in the olive oil in a steady stream until emulsified. Whisk in ¼ teaspoon of the salt.

Add the beans and tuna to the dressing, flaking the tuna into bite-size pieces with a fork as you add it to the bowl. Toss lightly to coat. Add the endives, radicchio, shaved fennel, parsley leaves, and the remaining ½ teaspoon salt to the tuna mixture. Using your hands, toss the salad together, bringing the dressing up from the bottom of the bowl until everything is coated evenly.

Tuna, White Bean, and Bitter Greens Salad

Dairy-Free Risotto with Mushrooms and Peas

V V GF

SERVES 6

When I'm eating clean, I avoid dairy, but I still love something rich and creamy for dinner. This risotto does the trick, as Arborio rice releases starch as it cooks, creating a creamy consistency even without the addition of dairy. Peas and mushrooms add earthy and fresh notes to this naturally gluten-free, vegan dish.

5¾ cups vegetable broth
½ ounce dried porcini mushrooms
¼ cup extra-virgin olive oil
2 cups finely chopped onions
10 ounces white mushrooms, finely chopped
2 garlic cloves, minced
1 teaspoon kosher salt
¼ teaspoon freshly ground black pepper
1½ cups Arborio rice or medium-grain white rice
⅔ cup dry white wine
½ cup frozen peas, thawed

In a medium heavy saucepan, bring the broth to a simmer. Add the porcini mushrooms. Cover and set aside until the mushrooms are tender, about 5 minutes. Using a slotted spoon, transfer the mushrooms to a cutting board and chop them. Cover the broth and keep warm over very low heat.

In a large heavy saucepan, heat the olive oil over medium heat. Add the onions and sauté until tender, about 8 minutes. Add the white mushrooms, porcini mushrooms, and garlic; sauté until the mushrooms are tender and the juices evaporate, about 10 minutes.

Stir in the salt, pepper, and rice and cook for an additional minute. Add the wine; cook, stirring often, until the liquid is absorbed, about 2 minutes. Add 1 cup of the hot broth; simmer over medium-low heat until the liquid is absorbed, stirring often, about 3 minutes.

Continue to cook until the rice is just tender and the mixture is creamy, adding more broth by cupfuls and stirring often, about 28 minutes. Just before serving, stir in the peas.

Roasted Cauliflower and Quinoa Salad

Roasted Cauliflower and Quinoa Salad

V V GF

SERVES 4

This is a nice, light entrée for a mostly broth- or juice-based day. Cauliflower and quinoa provide enough heft and protein to qualify this as a main; grapes, tangerine juice, and spinach add bright flavor and lots of healthy nutrients.

1 large head of cauliflower, cut into bite-size florets
¼ cup plus 2 tablespoons extra-virgin olive oil
¾ teaspoon kosher salt
¾ cup quinoa, rinsed and drained
1 teaspoon tangerine zest
3 tablespoons tangerine juice (from 1 tangerine)
1 tablespoon plus 1 teaspoon apple cider vinegar
2 tablespoons chopped fresh tarragon leaves
2 cups red seedless grapes, halved
3 cups baby spinach, coarsely chopped
½ cup chopped walnuts

Preheat the oven to 425°F. On a rimmed baking sheet, toss the cauliflower with 2 tablespoons of the olive oil and ½ teaspoon of the salt. Roast until the cauliflower is golden brown on the edges and tender all the way though, about 25 minutes. Cool to room temperature.

Bring a medium pot of salted water to a boil over high heat. Add the quinoa and cook for 20 minutes or until tender. Drain well and cool to room temperature.

In a large bowl, whisk together the tangerine zest and juice, vinegar, and the remaining ¼ cup olive oil. Season with the tarragon and the remaining ¼ teaspoon salt. Add the quinoa, roasted cauliflower, grapes, spinach, and chopped walnuts. Toss gently with a large spoon to coat everything with the dressing, and serve.

Matcha Chicken Tenders with Soy Citrus

SERVES 4

Matcha is finely powdered green tea that has powerful antioxidant properties. It gives simple breaded tenders a brilliant green color and unusual flavor you just may find addictive.

SAUCE

2 tablespoons soy sauce
½ teaspoon orange zest
¼ cup fresh orange juice (from 1 to 2 oranges)
1 teaspoon toasted sesame oil
1 teaspoon rice wine vinegar
1 teaspoon agave syrup

CHICKEN

1½ cups panko bread crumbs
2 teaspoons matcha powder
½ cup all-purpose flour
1 teaspoon kosher salt
2 large eggs, beaten
1 pound chicken tenders

Preheat the oven to 400°F. Line a baking sheet with parchment paper.

For the sauce: In a small bowl, whisk together the soy sauce, orange zest and juice, sesame oil, rice vinegar, and agave. Set aside to allow the flavors to marry while you prepare the chicken.

For the chicken: In a pie plate or shallow bowl, mix together the panko and matcha powder. In a separate shallow bowl, mix together the flour and ½ teaspoon of the salt. Place the beaten eggs in a third shallow bowl. Working with one tender at a time, dredge in the seasoned flour, then the egg, followed by the matcha panko.

Place the tenders on the prepared baking sheet. Bake for 10 minutes or until lightly golden and cooked through. Sprinkle with the remaining ½ teaspoon salt. Serve with the dipping sauce on the side.

Matcha Chicken Tenders with Soy Citrus

Fennel Snapper in Parchment

GF

SERVES 4

For an entrée that's as gorgeous as it is good for you, I bake snapper fillets in parchment paper with some fennel, kale, and slices of orange for a bit of brightness. (I also love that cleanup is a cinch!)

1 small bunch of Tuscan kale, ribs removed, leaves sliced thin
1 small head of fennel, halved, cored, and thinly sliced from root to tip
1½ teaspoons kosher salt
4 tablespoons extra-virgin olive oil
12 thin orange slices (from about 1½ oranges)
4 (6-ounce) fillets of snapper or other flaky fish
½ teaspoon fennel pollen

Preheat the oven to 450°F. Cut 4 large pieces of parchment paper into 4 x 14-inch hearts by folding the paper in half and cutting half of a heart shape, as if making a valentine. Set aside.

In a medium bowl, toss together the kale, fennel, 1 teaspoon of the salt, and 2 tablespoons of the olive oil.

Open the parchment hearts so that the tips are toward you. Place 2 slices of orange on the right side of each heart, close to the center. Divide the vegetable mixture on top of the orange slices. Place a piece of fish on top of each mound and season with the fennel pollen and the remaining ½ teaspoon salt. Drizzle evenly with the remaining 2 tablespoons olive oil.

Top each fillet with one of the remaining orange slices. Close the heart to make a half heart, and rotate it so the mound is facing you and the tip is pointed away. Begin to make small folds, each one overlapping the last, around the edge of the package to seal the edges. When you get to the tip, fold the remaining point under the packet.

Place the packets on a rimmed baking sheet and bake for 12 to 15 minutes or until the packets are slightly brown and puffed. Remove from the oven and, using scissors or a small paring knife, carefully cut open the top of each packet, as the steam will escape. Serve in the parchment for easy cleanup.

Piquillo Pepper and Macadamia Pesto with Broiled Cod

GF

SERVES 4

Simple broiled cod pairs perfectly with this light dill-based savory pesto that's full of healthy fats and bright colors.

PESTO

1 (9.8-ounce) jar roasted piquillo peppers
½ cup unsalted macadamia nuts
¼ teaspoon kosher salt
2 tablespoons extra-virgin olive oil
3 tablespoons chopped fresh dill

FISH

Vegetable oil cooking spray
4 (6-ounce) cod fillets
½ teaspoon kosher salt
1 teaspoon chopped fresh thyme leaves
½ teaspoon grated lemon zest
2 tablespoons extra-virgin olive oil
½ lemon, cut into 4 wedges, for garnish (optional)

Preheat the broiler. Place a rack in the middle of the oven.

For the pesto: In the bowl of a food processor, place the peppers, nuts, salt, and olive oil. Puree until the mixture is smooth, scraping down the sides with a rubber spatula as needed. Stir in the dill and set aside.

For the fish: Spray a rimmed baking sheet with vegetable oil spray. Place the fillets on the baking sheet and season with the salt. In a small bowl, mix together the thyme, lemon zest, and olive oil. Brush the fillets with the olive oil mixture. Place under the broiler and cook for 6 to 8 minutes or until the fish is opaque, flaky, and cooked through.

Spoon about ¼ cup of the pesto on each plate and place a piece of cod in the middle of the sauce. Serve with a lemon wedge if desired.

Piquillo Pepper with Macadamia Pesto with Broiled Cod

Seared Cod with Tangerine and Arugula

GF

SERVES 4

Fish and citrus go together like tomato and mozzarella; this fresh salsa-like salad of tangerine or orange, arugula, and olives elevates a simple piece of seared fish to guest-worthy fare.

2 tangerines or small oranges
½ teaspoon chopped fresh oregano leaves
½ teaspoon Dijon mustard
2 tablespoons plus 4 teaspoons extra-virgin olive oil
1¼ teaspoons kosher salt
4 cups baby arugula
⅓ cup pitted green olives, halved
4 (6-ounce) skinless cod fillets
½ teaspoon freshly ground black pepper

Zest both tangerines into a medium bowl. Place a strainer over the bowl. Cut off the top and bottom of each tangerine, stand on a flat end, and use a sharp knife to slice off the rind, following the curve of the fruit. Holding the fruit over the strainer, use a paring knife to carefully cut between the membranes and free the segments. When you've released all the segments, squeeze the juice from the remaining membranes. Reserve the juice and segments separately.

To the zest and juice in the bowl, add the oregano, mustard, 4 teaspoons of the olive oil, and ¼ teaspoon of the salt. Whisk well to combine. Set aside ¼ cup of the dressing. To the remaining dressing add the tangerine segments, arugula, and olives. Toss gently to combine.

In a large pan, heat the remaining 2 tablespoons olive oil over medium-high heat. Dry the fish well. Season each fillet with ¼ teaspoon of the remaining salt on both sides. Place the fillets flesh side down in the heated pan. Cook for 3 minutes undisturbed or until the fillets are golden brown and release easily from the pan.

Flip the fillets and season the tops with the pepper. Cook for an additional 3 minutes or until cooked through. Transfer the fish to serving plates and drizzle with the reserved dressing. Spoon some of the salad alongside each portion.

Herbed Striped Bass with Winter Kale Salad

GF

SERVES 4

Fresh and *clean* are two words that describe this simple meal to a T. You can substitute any flaky white fish for the striped bass if it's not available; cod or snapper would also be fine choices.

SALAD

⅓ cup apple cider
¼ cup apple cider vinegar
2 teaspoons whole-grain mustard
3 tablespoons extra-virgin olive oil
1 medium sweet potato, peeled and cut into 1-inch pieces
1 teaspoon kosher salt
½ bunch of Tuscan kale, ribs removed, leaves thinly sliced crosswise (about 4 cups)
1 apple, such as Honeycrisp, cut into ½-inch pieces

FISH

4 (4-ounce) center-cut skinless striped bass fillets
3 tablespoons extra-virgin olive oil
¼ cup chopped fresh dill (about ½ bunch)
1 teaspoon grated lemon zest
¾ teaspoon kosher salt
1 lemon cut in 8 wedges, for serving

Preheat the oven to 450°F.

For the salad: In a small saucepan, combine the cider and vinegar and bring to a simmer over medium-high heat. Cook for 4 minutes or until slightly reduced. Whisk in the mustard and return to a simmer, then remove from the heat and whisk in 1 tablespoon of the olive oil. Set aside.

On a rimmed baking sheet, toss the sweet potato with the remaining 2 tablespoons olive oil and ½ teaspoon of the salt. Roast for 20 minutes, flipping the pieces halfway through to ensure they cook evenly. Remove the sweet potato from the oven but don't turn the oven off.

Toss the kale and apple together in a large bowl. Add the hot sweet potato pieces, the cider dressing, and the remaining ½ teaspoon salt. Set aside to let the flavors mingle until ready to serve.

For the fish: Place the fish fillets on a rimmed nonstick baking sheet (or line the baking sheet with parchment paper). In a small bowl, whisk together the olive oil, dill, and lemon zest. Season the fish with the salt and spoon the herbed oil evenly over the fillets. Bake the fillets for 5 to 8 minutes or until the fish is cooked through and flakes when prodded with a fork.

To serve, spoon some of the salad onto each dinner plate and top with a piece of the fish. Serve with a couple of lemon wedges on the side.

Herbed Striped Bass with Winter Kale Salad

Mindful Cooking

Much has been written about mindful eating, but I think the term can also be applied to the way we approach cooking.

Like most working moms, I have plenty of nights when it seems like a race to get something easy, quick, and nutritious on the table; the cooking part happens almost on autopilot.

Other times, though, when I'm a little less rushed, a little less distracted, and can really focus on the process of cooking itself, I am able to reconnect with the joy I find in the kitchen. Stirring a risotto, watching the rice transform from hard and opaque to translucent to snowy and creamy, or shelling the first fresh peas of the season, hearing the sound the pod makes as it pops open, the velvety feel as I run my finger along the inside to free the peas—at those moments I feel fully present, with all of my senses engaged.

Next time you are just going through the motions of making a meal, try to be more aware of the moment, and give yourself over to the task rather than trying to wrestle it to the ground. You might find that it feels a little less like work and instead becomes something centering and calming that brings you happiness, too.

Superfood Fudge Torte

V

MAKES 8 SERVINGS

If you're like me and can't go too long without a little bit of chocolate in your life, even when you're eating super clean, go ahead, have a small slice of this torte. Made with agave, it's not supersweet.

BLUEBERRY AND SPINACH PUREE

1¼ cups baby spinach
½ cup fresh or frozen blueberries, thawed and drained
½ teaspoon fresh lemon juice

TORTE

Vegetable oil spray
6 tablespoons (¾ stick) unsalted butter
¾ cup semisweet chocolate chips
1 large egg
2 teaspoons pure vanilla extract
½ cup light agave syrup
¼ cup brown rice flour
2 tablespoons flax meal
1 tablespoon unsweetened cocoa powder
¼ cup rolled oats, ground in a food processor
¼ teaspoon kosher salt

SPICED YOGURT TOPPING

¾ cup nonfat plain Greek yogurt
2 teaspoons pure maple syrup
¼ teaspoon ground cinnamon

For the blueberry and spinach puree: Bring the spinach and 2 tablespoons water to a boil in a medium saucepan. Turn the heat down to low and simmer for 10 minutes.

Combine the spinach, blueberries, and lemon juice in a food processor or blender. Process on high until smooth, stopping occasionally, if necessary, to scrape the sides. Add a little more water if necessary, to make a smooth puree. Set aside.

For the torte: Preheat the oven to 350°F. Spray the bottom only (not the sides) of a 9-inch pie plate with vegetable oil spray. Put the butter and chocolate chips in a heat-proof bowl. Set over a saucepan of simmering water. Stir until the butter and chocolate are melted. Set aside to cool.

Meanwhile, in another bowl, whisk together the egg, vanilla, agave, and the blueberry and spinach puree. Stir in the cooled chocolate mixture.

In a mixing bowl, stir together the brown rice flour, flax meal, cocoa powder, oats, and salt. Add to the chocolate mixture and stir to combine; do not overmix. Pour the batter into the prepared pie plate. Bake until a cake tester or wooden skewer inserted into the center comes out clean, 20 to 25 minutes.

For the spiced yogurt topping: While the torte is baking, in a small bowl combine the yogurt, maple syrup, and cinnamon until smooth.

Allow the torte to cool completely in the pan before cutting into 8 wedges. Add a dollop of the spiced yogurt topping to each serving.

Sweet Dreams

Getting plenty of uninterrupted sleep has been shown to be just as important to our health as eating well and exercising regularly. For years I've had a semi-serious coffee addiction, and I was rarely seen without a caffè Americano. Recently, though, I've been trying to give the caffeine a rest so I can rest better! (Caffeine, I've learned, stays in your system for hours and can disrupt sleep patterns even if you don't drink coffee in the evening.)

I still enjoy having something to sip on while I sort through the events of the day and wind down. Herbal tea is one obvious choice, although I've found out not all teas are created equal when it comes to helping me relax and slow things down. Green tea, for instance, can have nearly as much caffeine as black tea, depending on the variety and form you choose. And many innocuous-sounding fruit- or spice-flavored teas are made with a base of regular black tea—again, full of caffeine. While neither black nor green tea has as much caffeine as coffee, if you sometimes have trouble falling asleep, you probably shouldn't be drinking a caffeinated beverage (including sodas) much after 4 p.m. Ditto, I am afraid, chocolate, though I would be lying if I said I observed that rule very strictly! Dr. Michael Breus, aka "the Sleep Doctor," is a leader in the science of sleep, and he recommends these natural beverages, opposite, to help lull you to sleep. They really work!

Banana Tea

V GF

SERVES 1

The magnesium in banana peel helps to calm nerves and is especially helpful for those who toss and turn all night. Dr. Breus suggests sipping a cup of this soothing tea twenty minutes before bedtime for a more restful night's sleep.

1 ripe banana
1 teaspoon honey or a dash of ground cinnamon, to taste

Bring 2 cups water to a boil. Cut off and discard the top and bottom of the banana. Cut the banana in half, leaving the fruit in the peel. Place the banana with the peel in the boiling water, and simmer for 4 to 5 minutes. Remove from the heat and discard the banana. Pour the banana water into a mug. Add honey or cinnamon to taste.

Banana Tea

Dr. Breus's Tart Cherry Smoothie

V V GF

SERVES 1

Sour cherry juice has been proven to be helpful as a sleep aid, making this the perfect midnight snack or pre-bedtime soother.

1 cup tart cherry juice
½ ripe banana
½ cup soy milk (or 4 to 6 ounces soy yogurt plus ½ cup nonfat milk)
5 ice cubes
¼ teaspoon pure vanilla extract

In a blender, combine the cherry juice, banana, soy milk, ice, and vanilla. Blend until smooth.

Tart Cherry Smoothie

Weeknight Warriors

Being a working parent (and a single one at that) sometimes means that compromises are inevitable. For me, though, eating family dinner with Jade is a nonnegotiable, and it's almost always the best part of my day. Sitting down together, talking over the events of our days, introducing her to new flavors—even chatting about proper table etiquette—is a true pleasure that I always make time for.

Which doesn't mean that I'm in the kitchen whipping up cookies when she gets home from school (I wish). Between her after-school activities, my work responsibilities, and a thousand other things, I need an arsenal of weekday workhorses that can either be prepped ahead or made in minutes to ensure we're not still waiting for dinner at nine o'clock.

The recipes in this chapter help take the stress out of weeknight cooking so I can focus my attention on the meal rather than the making. Sometimes I marinate chicken in the morning and refrigerate it all day so it's ready to bake or broil when I get home. If I'm in a real time squeeze, I opt for fish, which cooks in minutes. And I'm a relatively new convert to the slow cooker, but after hearing from so many of my readers how much they rely on this time-saving appliance, I'm happy to be able to provide a few great recipes that make the most of it.

A Chicken in Every Pot

We sure do love our chicken—we're actually eating twice as much today we did 40 years ago! Of course it's not difficult to understand why. A waft of chicken roasting in the oven just smells like home.

Boneless, skinless breasts are the default option for weeknight cooking, but there are so many other ways to serve chicken, even when time is precious. If you haven't tried spatchcocking (which is a fancy word for flattening the bird by removing the backbone and rib cage), it's time to give it a go. The advantages are many: More surface area means more crispy, delicious skin. Your chicken will also cook much faster, and carving is easier because you've already done the work of removing the bones. And appliances like slow cookers and pressure cookers can be a bird's best friend when it comes to cooking against the clock. So broaden your chicken horizons; your dinners will be a lot more varied and a lot more interesting for it.

A note on buying: I'm not one of those people who insists on organic everything, but when it comes to chicken and eggs, the extra cost for organic and cage-free is absolutely worth it. Not only can you be sure you're not consuming hormones, chemicals, and other harmful ingredients, but they also just taste better.

Chicken with Preserved Lemon and Herbs

GF

SERVES 4

Spatchcocking a chicken—that is, removing the backbone and rib cage so it can be opened up flat—allows the bird to cook more quickly and to make better contact with the hot pan, resulting in a crisp skin and juicy meat. It also allows you to roast a whole bird in about forty-five minutes! You can ask the butcher to cut out the backbone for you, but after you've done it once or twice you'll realize it's quite easy to do with poultry shears.

2 garlic cloves, minced
1 tablespoon finely chopped fresh thyme leaves
½ teaspoon crushed red pepper flakes
3 tablespoons minced preserved lemon rind (discard the flesh before chopping)
½ teaspoon dried oregano
1 teaspoon kosher salt
5 tablespoons extra-virgin olive oil
1 (3½-pound) chicken, spatchcocked
½ lemon
½ cup baby arugula
¼ cup fresh basil leaves
¼ cup freshly grated Parmesan cheese

In a food processor, puree the garlic, thyme, red pepper flakes, preserved lemon, oregano, ½ teaspoon of the salt, and 2 tablespoons of the olive oil to form a paste. Loosen the skin from the breast and legs of the chicken by gently working your fingers between the flesh and skin. Rub three quarters of the herb paste under the skin of the chicken, spreading it evenly over all of the parts. Turn the chicken over and rub the remainder of the paste on the flesh side of the chicken. Place the chicken in a resealable plastic bag and allow it to marinate in the refrigerator for at least 6 hours or overnight. Remove from the refrigerator 30 minutes before cooking.

Preheat the oven to 400°F. Heat a large ovenproof skillet over medium-high heat. Add the remaining 3 tablespoons olive oil. Pat the chicken dry with paper towels.

Season the chicken on both sides with the remaining ½ teaspoon salt and add to the hot pan, skin side down. Weight the bird with a brick wrapped in foil or a heavy smaller pan. Sear for 4 to 5 minutes or until golden brown. Remove the weight, flip the chicken so the skin side is up, and transfer the pan to the preheated oven. Cook for 30 minutes or until an instant-read thermometer inserted in the thigh reads 160°F.

Transfer the bird to a platter and immediately squeeze the half lemon over the flesh side of the chicken. Turn the chicken skin side up and allow to rest for 15 minutes; the residual heat will finish cooking the bird. Sprinkle with the arugula, basil leaves, and Parmesan. Drizzle with the pan juices and serve.

Chicken with Preserved Lemon and Herbs

Easy-Peasey Chicken Salad

Easy-Peasey Chicken Salad

GF

SERVES 4

This delicately flavored salad starts with a store-bought rotisserie chicken. It is important to taste the salad before seasoning, as the amount needed will vary depending on how the chicken was prepared.

½ cup plain whole-milk yogurt
2 tablespoons chopped fresh tarragon leaves
¼ cup extra-virgin olive oil
2 teaspoons grated lemon zest
2 tablespoons fresh lemon juice (from 1 lemon)
¾ teaspoon kosher salt
1 (2½-pound) rotisserie chicken, meat pulled off the bones and shredded
¼ cup chopped fresh chives
1 cup thinly sliced sugar snap peas (about ¼ pound)
1 head of Bibb lettuce, leaves separated and washed

In a large bowl, combine the yogurt, tarragon, olive oil, lemon zest and juice, and salt. Whisk well to combine. Add the shredded chicken along with the chives and sliced snap peas. Mix together using a rubber spatula to coat all of the chicken and vegetables evenly.

Allow the salad to sit for at least 15 minutes, or cover and refrigerate for up to 3 days. To serve, place a few leaves of lettuce on each plate and top with the chicken salad.

Yogurt-Marinated Chicken

Yogurt-Marinated Chicken

GF

SERVES 2 TO 4

An abundance of herbs in the marinade makes this dish a pretty emerald green; the yogurt helps to tenderize and keep the chicken moist as it bakes. Marinate the chicken in the morning and it will be ready to pop in the oven when you get home.

1 cup plain whole-milk yogurt
4 scallions, coarsely chopped
1½ cups packed fresh cilantro leaves
½ cup packed fresh mint leaves
¾ teaspoon ground cumin
¼ teaspoon crushed red pepper flakes
1½ teaspoons kosher salt
1 (3- to 4-pound) chicken, cut in 8 pieces
3 tablespoons extra-virgin olive oil

To a blender add the yogurt, scallions, cilantro, mint, cumin, red pepper flakes, and 1 teaspoon of the kosher salt, and blend on high for about 30 seconds or until completely smooth. Place the chicken pieces in a resealable plastic bag and pour the marinade over the chicken. Seal the bag and marinate in the refrigerator for at least 4 hours or up to 12 hours.

Twenty minutes before cooking, remove the chicken from the refrigerator. Preheat the oven to 400°F.

Drizzle a rimmed baking sheet with 1½ tablespoons of the olive oil. Remove the chicken from the bag and arrange it on the baking sheet so the pieces are not touching one another (it should still be coated with the marinade). Drizzle the pieces with the remaining 1½ tablespoons oil and season with the remaining ½ teaspoon salt.

Bake for 45 minutes or until an instant-read thermometer inserted in the thickest part of the chicken reads 160°F. Allow the chicken to rest for 10 minutes before serving.

Pressure Cooker Chicken Thighs with Prunes and Green Olives

GF

SERVES 4 TO 6

For trimming precious minutes off a recipe, nothing beats a pressure cooker. This recipe, from gadget gurus (and all-around great cooks) Bruce Weinstein and Mark Scarbrough, has flavors from across the Mediterranean: prunes and capers, garlic and green olives.

2 tablespoons olive oil
8 bone-in, skin-on chicken thighs, trimmed (about 3 pounds total weight)
4 medium garlic cloves, slivered
½ cup packed pitted green olives
½ cup packed pitted prunes (see Cook's Note)
2 tablespoons capers, rinsed and drained
2 tablespoons loosely packed fresh oregano leaves, minced
2 tablespoons (packed) dark brown sugar
2 tablespoons white wine vinegar
½ cup dry white wine, such as chardonnay
½ teaspoon freshly ground black pepper

Heat the oil in a 6-quart stovetop pressure cooker set over medium heat. Add half the chicken thighs skin side down; cook, turning once, until well browned, about 6 minutes. Transfer to a large bowl and repeat with the remaining thighs.

Add the garlic and cook for 1 minute, stirring all the while. Add the olives, prunes, capers, oregano, brown sugar, and vinegar. Toss until bubbling wildly. Pour in the wine and scrape up any browned bits from the bottom of the pan. Stir in the pepper, then return the chicken to the pan along with any juices in the bowl.

Lock the lid onto the pot. Raise the heat to high and bring the pot to high pressure (15 psi). Once this pressure has been reached, reduce the heat as much as possible while maintaining this pressure. Cook for 12 minutes.

Reduce the pressure. Remove the pot from the heat and let its pressure fall to normal naturally, about 12 minutes. If the pressure hasn't returned to normal within 15 minutes, use the quick-release method to bring it fully back to normal (refer to your owner's manual). Unlock and open the pot. Transfer the thighs, prunes, and garlic to serving plates or a platter; stir the sauce before ladling it on top.

Cook's Note: You can substitute dried apples for the prunes (if so, substitute thyme for the oregano).

Chicken Sausages and Mash

SERVES 4

Chicken sausages are such a great pantry product, providing convenience and lots of flavor with far less fat than their porky cousins. My take on a gastropub classic is perfect for a raw, chilly evening when you need something rib-sticking.

MASH

1 celery root, diced (about 2 cups)
1½ cups heavy cream
Kosher salt
2 pounds Yukon Gold potatoes, peeled and cut into large chunks
6 tablespoons (¾ stick) unsalted butter
2 tablespoons extra-virgin olive oil

BANGERS

2 tablespoons extra-virgin olive oil
4 sweet Italian chicken sausages
1 onion, halved and thinly sliced
1 red bell pepper, cored, seeded, and thinly sliced
⅛ teaspoon crushed red pepper flakes
¼ teaspoon kosher salt
½ cup beer
3 tablespoons finely chopped fresh basil leaves

For the mash: In a small saucepan, combine the celery root and cream. Place the pan over medium heat, season with ½ teaspoon salt, and bring to a simmer, keeping an eye on it so it does not boil over. When the celery root is tender, after about 10 minutes, place the entire mixture in a food processor and puree until smooth.

Meanwhile, place the potatoes in a medium saucepan and cover with cold water. Salt the water well and bring to a boil over medium-high heat. When the potatoes are tender, around 15 minutes, drain well and place in a large bowl with the butter and olive oil. Mash with a potato masher until smooth. Add the celery root puree and ½ teaspoon salt and combine thoroughly. Keep warm.

For the bangers: Heat a medium straight-sided skillet over medium-high heat. Add the olive oil. Using a small paring knife, pierce the skin of the sausages with the tip in 2 or 3 spots per sausage. Add the sausages to the hot pan and brown well on all sides, about 3 minutes per side.

Remove the browned sausages from the pan to a plate, then add the onion and bell pepper to the same pan, stirring up the brown bits from the bottom with a wooden spoon. Season with the red pepper flakes and salt and continue to cook, stirring often, until the onion starts to brown, about 6 minutes. Deglaze with the beer and nestle the sausages back in the mixture. Cover with a lid, reduce the heat to medium low, and allow to cook for 8 to 10 minutes or until the sausage is cooked through.

To serve, place the mash on a platter. Pile the sausages, onions, and peppers on top of the mash and spoon some of the sauce over the entire dish. Garnish with the chopped basil.

Chicken Sausages and Mash

Honey-Brined Roasted Chicken

SERVES 2 TO 4

Wildflower honey has a savory, herbaceous quality that makes it pair well with chicken. In this dish the brine tenderizes the bird, keeps it juicy, and flavors the meat all the way through. Brine the chicken in the morning and it will be ready to toss in the oven by dinnertime.

BRINE

⅓ cup kosher salt
⅓ cup wildflower honey
2 fresh rosemary sprigs
2 garlic cloves, smashed and peeled
1 teaspoon freshly ground black pepper
½ lemon
2 cups ice
1 (3½-pound) chicken, cut into serving pieces

ROAST AND GLAZE

1 onion, thinly sliced
2 tablespoons extra-virgin olive oil
½ teaspoon kosher salt
¾ cup wildflower honey
2 teaspoons soy sauce
2 fresh rosemary sprigs
4 fresh thyme sprigs
2 teaspoons freshly ground black pepper

Honey-Brined Roasted Chicken

TO SERVE

1 bunch of Tuscan kale, ribs removed, leaves chopped
1 teaspoon apple cider vinegar
1 tablespoon extra-virgin olive oil
⅛ teaspoon kosher salt

For the brine: In a medium saucepan, combine 2 cups water, the salt, honey, rosemary, garlic, and pepper. Bring the mixture to a simmer over medium-high heat and stir to dissolve all the salt and honey. Turn off the heat and squeeze in the juice of the half lemon, then add the lemon as well. Allow the mixture to cool slightly.

Place the ice in a large resealable plastic bag or container. Pour the warm brine onto the ice and stir until the ice is fully melted. Add the chicken pieces to the mixture, making sure they are fully submerged. Seal the bag and brine in the refrigerator for at least 6 hours or overnight.

An hour before cooking, remove the chicken from the brine and dry well with paper towels. Place the chicken on a cooling rack over a baking tray and allow it to air dry and come to room temperature for an hour. This will help promote even browning.

Preheat the oven to 425°F.

On a rimmed baking sheet, toss the onion slices with the olive oil and salt. Place the dried chicken pieces on the bed of onions and place in the oven. Bake for 20 minutes.

While the chicken is in the oven, in a small sauté pan over medium heat stir together the honey, ¼ cup water, the soy sauce, rosemary, thyme, and pepper. Bring the mixture to a boil, then reduce the heat to low and simmer for about 8 minutes. Remove from the heat and set aside to cool slightly. Strain the honey mixture into a small bowl.

After the chicken has baked for 20 minutes, pour the honey glaze all over the pieces of chicken and the onions. Return the tray to the oven for another 20 minutes, basting with the thickened glaze every 7 minutes or so.

For serving: Place the chicken on a platter to rest for 5 minutes. Meanwhile, place the glazed onions in a bowl with the kale, vinegar, olive oil, and salt. Serve the kale salad alongside the chicken.

Sweet on Honey

Like beer, coffee, chocolate, and so many other foods these days, honey has made the transition from commercially produced to craft, from golden-hued syrup packaged in bear-shaped bottles to small-batch, even single-origin, nectars. In the United States alone, there are more than 300 unique honeys and something like 125,000 beekeepers.

Compared to sugar, honey is absorbed more slowly by your body, which means you won't get that sugar rush, or the crash. It also tastes sweeter and more complex, so you need less of it. The honeys you find at your local farmers' markets, specialty shops, and high-end grocery stores may range in color from nearly transparent to dark, molasses-like hues. They can be thin and viscous in consistency or thick and creamy; they can taste delicate and floral, nutty and spicy, or full-bodied and bitter, depending on the flowers the bees fed on before returning to their hives. Honey flavors include buckwheat, chestnut, and, one of my favorites, lavender.

Besides tasting better than the supermarket stuff (which, it turns out, may not be real honey after all), artisanal honeys typically contain more antioxidants and have higher anti-inflammatory and antibacterial properties. They may help you sleep better, thanks to the snooze-inducing amino acid tryptophan; and, because the pollen hasn't been filtered out, these purer forms may also relieve seasonal allergies by building up your body's tolerance to local pollens and allergens.

Stuffed Chicken Parmesan

SERVES 4

There are times when nothing but something deep-fried to a crisp golden brown will do, and for those times, this is a real people pleaser. Slice the rolls and fan them on a plate for a pretty presentation, too.

4 boneless, skinless chicken breasts, each cut horizontally into 2 cutlets
1½ teaspoons kosher salt
1 teaspoon freshly ground black pepper
1 cup shredded mozzarella cheese
⅓ cup freshly grated Parmesan cheese, plus ¼ cup for garnish
24 whole fresh basil leaves
1 cup all-purpose flour
3 large eggs, beaten
2 cups fine, dry bread crumbs
1 cup grapeseed oil
1 cup extra-virgin olive oil
2 cups marinara sauce, homemade (see page 121) or store-bought, warmed
¼ cup chopped fresh flat-leaf parsley (optional)

Preheat the oven to 400°F.

Place the chicken cutlets on a board and cover with plastic wrap. Using a meat mallet, lightly pound the cutlets to ¼ inch thick. (You can ask your butcher to split and even pound the chicken breasts for you to save time.) Remove the plastic wrap and season the cutlets evenly using ½ teaspoon of the salt and ½ teaspoon of the pepper. Sprinkle each cutlet with 2 tablespoons mozzarella and 2 teaspoons Parmesan. Top each cutlet with 3 basil leaves. Starting from one long edge, carefully roll each cutlet into a cylinder and secure with a toothpick.

Place the flour, eggs, and bread crumbs in 3 separate shallow bowls. Season both the flour and the bread crumbs with ½ teaspoon salt and ¼ teaspoon pepper each. Working with one rolled cutlet at a time, dip the roll into the flour, then the egg, then the bread crumbs. Dip the breaded rolls back into the egg a second time and into the bread crumbs again to finish. Repeat with the remaining rolls.

Pour the oils into a 10-inch straight-sided sauté pan and heat to 350°F over medium heat. Working in two batches, gently lower 4 rolls into the hot oil and fry for 3 minutes per side or until golden brown and crispy all over. Using a slotted spoon, remove from the oil and drain on a paper towel–lined plate. Transfer the drained rolls to a rimmed baking sheet and bake for approximately 5 minutes or until they register 160°F on an instant-read thermometer. Allow the rolls to rest for 5 minutes.

To serve, place ½ cup of warmed marinara sauce on each plate. Remove the toothpicks from the rolls and halve on an angle. Place 4 pieces on each plate atop the sauce. Top with more grated Parmesan and a sprinkling of chopped parsley if desired. Serve immediately.

Skinny Chicken Parm

Skinny Chicken Parm

GF

SERVES 4

Jonesing for chicken Parm but watching your bottom line, too? This should do the trick. Baked instead of fried and minus the breading, it's much lighter than the traditional version with lots of flavor from fresh herbs, especially rosemary, and just a bit of cheese.

1 tablespoon extra-virgin olive oil
1 teaspoon chopped fresh thyme leaves
1 teaspoon chopped fresh rosemary leaves
1 teaspoon chopped fresh flat-leaf parsley leaves
4 chicken cutlets (about 3 ounces each)
1 teaspoon kosher salt
½ teaspoon freshly ground black pepper
¾ cup marinara sauce, homemade (see page 121) or store-bought
¼ cup shredded mozzarella cheese
8 teaspoons freshly grated Parmesan cheese
1 tablespoon unsalted butter, cut into pieces

Preheat the oven to 500°F.

In a small bowl, stir the oil, thyme, rosemary, and parsley together to blend. Brush both sides of the cutlets with the herb oil and sprinkle with the salt and pepper.

Heat a large heavy ovenproof skillet over high heat. Add the cutlets and cook just until browned, about 1 minute per side. Remove from the heat.

Spoon the marinara sauce over and around the cutlets. Sprinkle 1 tablespoon of the mozzarella over each cutlet, then sprinkle each with 2 teaspoons of the Parmesan. Dot the tops with the butter pieces and bake until the cheese melts and the chicken is cooked through, about 5 minutes. Serve hot.

Slow-Cooker Saffron Rice with Chicken Sausage

GF

SERVES 4 TO 6

This easy rice dish has a Spanish paella vibe. You could even make it with vegetable broth and omit the sausage for a substantial vegetarian entrée or a nice side dish to accompany grilled chicken, fish, or steak.

2 tablespoons extra-virgin olive oil
4 Italian-style chicken sausages, cut into 1-inch pieces
1 cup bomba rice or other short-grain rice
1 small onion, diced
1 celery stalk, diced
3 garlic cloves, minced
16 yellow cherry tomatoes, halved
1 red bell pepper, cored, seeded, and diced
½ cup frozen peas, thawed
½ teaspoon kosher salt
2 tablespoons dry vermouth
2 cups low-sodium chicken broth
¼ teaspoon saffron threads
¼ pound green beans, trimmed and cut into 1-inch pieces
½ teaspoon smoked sweet or hot paprika
2 tablespoons chopped fresh flat-leaf parsley leaves

Heat the olive oil in a medium sauté pan over medium-high heat. Add the sausage and cook until the pieces begin to brown, about 4 minutes.

Transfer the sausage to the slow cooker. Add the rice, onion, celery, garlic, tomatoes, bell pepper, peas, salt, vermouth, chicken broth, saffron (rubbing it between your fingers to break it up a bit), and the green beans. Stir gently to combine all of the ingredients, cover, and cook on low for 4 hours, until the rice and vegetables are tender.

Uncover, sprinkle with the smoked paprika and parsley, and serve.

Slow-Cooker Saffron Rice with Chicken Sausage

Sole with Lemon Caper Sauce

Sole with Lemon Caper Sauce

SERVES 2 TO 4

In Italy this combination of capers, lemon, and herbs is often served with scallops or swordfish. Sole is both lighter and less costly, and because it is so delicate, it cooks in a flash, making this a nearly instant entrée.

- 4 sole fillets
- ½ teaspoon kosher salt
- 2 tablespoons extra-virgin olive oil
- 4 tablespoons (½ stick) unsalted butter, at room temperature
- ⅓ cup all-purpose flour, for dredging
- 1 garlic clove, minced
- ¼ cup capers, rinsed and drained
- ¼ cup fresh lemon juice (from 1 to 2 lemons)
- ½ cup low-sodium chicken broth
- 2 tablespoons chopped fresh flat-leaf parsley leaves
- ½ teaspoon chopped fresh oregano leaves

Using paper towels, pat the sole fillets very dry. Season the fish with the salt. Heat a medium skillet over high heat. Add 1 tablespoon of the olive oil and 1 tablespoon of the butter to the pan. When the butter is melted and the bubbles have subsided, dredge 2 fillets on both sides with the flour. Shake off the excess and add the fish to the pan. Reduce the heat to medium high.

Cook the fish for 2 to 3 minutes on the first side or until they start to brown around the edges. Using a wide spatula, flip the fillets gently and cook for another 30 seconds. Remove the fillets to a plate and cook the remaining fish, adding another tablespoon each of oil and butter to the pan. Keep the fish warm.

Add the garlic and capers to the pan and stir over medium heat for about 15 seconds or until fragrant. Add the lemon juice and chicken broth and stir, scraping up the bits from the bottom of the pan. Simmer for about 2 minutes to reduce the liquid slightly. Finish the sauce by stirring in the remaining 2 tablespoons butter and the parsley and the oregano. Spoon the sauce over the fish and serve.

Pan-Seared Salmon Burgers with Fennel Slaw

SERVES 4

Burgers are a smart way to serve fish to non-fish lovers. The omega-3 fats in salmon naturally provide the richness you crave in a burger, and with super-flavorful ingredients like herbs, fennel, and citrus, you don't need to add tons of fat or salt to make it taste good. I sometimes use smaller, slider-size buns to improve the ratio of filling to bread.

SLAW

1 fennel bulb, cored, shaved into rings on a mandoline or sliced thin
1 orange, cut between the membrane into segments (see Cook's Note, page 149)
2 tablespoons chopped fresh dill
1 tablespoon apple cider vinegar
1 tablespoon extra-virgin olive oil
½ teaspoon kosher salt

BURGERS

¾ pound wild-caught salmon fillet, cut into 1-inch pieces
¼ cup chopped fresh flat-leaf parsley leaves
4 teaspoons capers, rinsed and drained
1 large shallot, chopped
½ teaspoon grated orange zest
1 teaspoon grated lemon zest
2 tablespoons whole-wheat panko bread crumbs
1 egg white
⅓ teaspoon kosher salt
1 tablespoon extra-virgin olive oil

4 (3-inch) whole-wheat buns, for serving

Preheat the broiler.

For the slaw: In a medium bowl, combine the fennel, orange segments, dill, vinegar, olive oil, and salt. Toss gently to mix and set aside to let the flavors mingle while you prepare the burgers.

For the burgers: In a food processor, combine the salmon, parsley, capers, shallot, orange and lemon zests, panko, egg white, and salt. Pulse a few times just to coarsely chop the salmon and mix everything together. Remove from the bowl and divide the mixture in quarters. Gently shape each portion into a patty about ½ inch thick.

Preheat a medium sauté pan over medium-high heat. Add the olive oil, and when it's hot, add the salmon burgers. Cook for approximately 3 minutes per side or until the patties are cooked through and golden on both sides.

Meanwhile, place the split buns under the broiler until toasted, about 4 minutes. Place each patty on a toasted bun and top with some of the fennel slaw.

Fish Facts

Wild-caught fish is the aquatic equivalent of grass-fed or free-range in the meat case, but according to Ed Brown, chef/innovator for Restaurant Associates and author of *The Modern Seafood Cook*, farm-raised is no longer a dirty word when it comes to buying fish. "There's not enough fish supply in the ocean to continue at the rate we're at. We need aquaculture," he told me. He also recommends opting for small fish, like perch, anchovies, and sardines, which are a more sustainable choice than the usual suspects like sea bass or snapper. Small fish have a shorter life cycle, so they are constantly replenishing their populations, and they have less opportunity to accumulate unwanted contaminants like mercury, which is found in higher concentrations in fish like swordfish and tuna.

When buying fish it's important to look for proper signage. It should not only list the species and the price of the fish, but also the origin, and if it's really good, the method of catch. All wild fish caught in the United States is managed by the US Department of Fish and Game. The agency regulates where, when, and how much can be taken to ensure fisheries remain healthy now and in the years to come.

As far as farmed fish are concerned, look for labels from organizations like the Aquaculture Stewardship Council that ensure that it's free of antibiotics and grown under responsible environmental and labor conditions. The Seafood Watch provided by the Monterey Bay Aquarium is a great resource for confirming that the wild-caught fish you're considering isn't on the endangered list.

Pan-Seared
Salmon Burgers
with Fennel Slaw

Pan-Seared Salmon with Year-Round Succotash

Pan-Seared Salmon with Year-Round Succotash

GF

SERVES 4

True succotash can only be made when fresh lima beans and corn are in the marketplace, but it adds so much brightness to the plate that I always want to extend the season. Using edamame and tender baby kale makes this a dish you can make any time, and increases the nutrient quotient at the same time.

SAUCE

½ cup crème fraîche
¼ cup whole-grain mustard
2 teaspoons grated lemon zest
¼ cup fresh lemon juice (from 2 to 3 lemons)
¼ teaspoon kosher salt

SALMON

4 (6-ounce) salmon fillets, wild-caught preferred
½ teaspoon kosher salt
2 tablespoons extra-virgin olive oil

SUCCOTASH

3 tablespoons extra-virgin olive oil
1 small red bell pepper, cored, seeded, and diced (about ¾ cup)
1 large shallot, diced
¾ cup frozen shelled edamame, thawed
1 cup fresh corn kernels, cut from 2 cobs, or 1 cup frozen corn, thawed
½ teaspoon kosher salt
½ cup baby kale, coarsely chopped
2 teaspoons fresh lemon juice (from 1 lemon)
2 tablespoons chopped fresh basil leaves

Preheat the oven to 350°F.

For the sauce: In a medium bowl, whisk together the crème fraîche, mustard, lemon zest and juice, and salt. Cover with plastic wrap and set aside.

For the salmon: Heat a large ovenproof skillet over medium-high heat. Season the salmon on both sides with the salt. Add the oil to the pan, then use tongs to gently place the salmon flesh side down in the pan. Allow the salmon to cook undisturbed for 3 minutes to form an evenly golden crust. Using a spatula, gently flip each fillet. Place the pan in the oven and roast for an additional 5 minutes. Remove from the oven and cover with foil to keep warm.

For the succotash: Heat the olive oil in a medium skillet over medium-high heat. Add the bell pepper and shallot and cook for 4 minutes, stirring often with a wooden spoon. Add the edamame, corn, and salt and continue to cook for 3 minutes. Remove the pan from the heat and stir in the kale, lemon juice, and basil.

To serve, place 2 tablespoons of the sauce in a circle on each serving plate. Top with ½ cup of the succotash and a salmon fillet. Serve with more sauce on the side if desired.

Buyer's Guide

There is really no substitute for good old two-way communication when it comes to buying fish. Not only is a trusted seller the key to getting the best quality fish, he or she can also give you tips for storing and preparing fish and suggest substitutions if you're looking for a specific style of fish.

Read any signs or labels your shop has posted regarding origin—imported or domestic, farmed or wild-caught—and when possible opt for what is local and sustainable (see page 178). Most important, look at the fish carefully; if it is whole it should be colorful and shiny, and have all its scales. The gills should be vibrant red, not brown, pink, or gray. And if in doubt, ask to take a whiff. It should smell briny, like the sea. If you can smell it from two aisles away, or it smells "fishy," think about chicken for dinner instead.

Campfire Salmon in Packets

Campfire Salmon in Packets

GF

SERVES 4 TO 6

The better your salmon, the tastier these packets will be. As the fish cooks, its juices combine with the herbs and vegetables to make a delicious light sauce to serve over rice or couscous.

2 cups cherry tomatoes, halved
2 medium shallots, minced
2 tablespoons capers, rinsed and drained
2 tablespoons plus 2 teaspoons extra-virgin olive oil
2 tablespoons fresh lemon juice (from 1 lemon)
1½ teaspoons kosher salt
¼ teaspoon freshly ground black pepper
4 (5-ounce) skinless salmon fillets
4 fresh thyme sprigs
4 fresh oregano sprigs

Place a grill pan over medium-high heat or preheat a gas or charcoal grill.

In a medium bowl, mix together the tomatoes, shallots, capers, 2 tablespoons of the oil, the lemon juice, ½ teaspoon of the salt, and the pepper. Brush the salmon fillets on both sides with the remaining 2 teaspoons oil and season with the remaining teaspoon salt.

Put each salmon fillet on a piece of aluminum foil large enough to fold over and seal. Wrap the ends of the foil to form a spiral shape. Spoon the tomato mixture over the salmon and top each piece with 1 sprig of thyme and 1 sprig of oregano. Fold the sides of the foil over the fish and tomato mixture, covering completely, sealing the packets closed.

Put the foil packets on the hot grill pan or grill rack and cook until medium, about 10 minutes. Serve in the foil packets or open the packets and serve over your grain of choice.

On the Road Again

Those who know me as a bit of a girly girl are often amused to learn I spent my childhood summer vacations camping, but it's true. For years, my family piled into a motor home and drove from Southern California to places as far away as Alaska, stopping to explore along the way. Some days we hiked in a national park, other times we visited museums. At night we would pull into a campsite and cook dishes like this one over an open fire, eating under the stars with the sound of a stream nearby or small animals rustling through the brush. As a teenager, I will freely confess, I was not a fan. Showering under a trickle of cold water, cooking everything in a couple of banged-up pots and pans, being far from my friends, and—shudder—no dishwasher was not my thing. Only with the benefit of time and distance have I come to realize those were some of the best days we shared as a family.

Now more than ever, finding activities that can drag us away from screens and devices is a good thing. I'm always looking to show Jade you don't need to have an outlet or an electronic device—or even a kitchen—to have fun and eat well.

Food Swaps

Most of us know the basics of eating right: Seek out whole, natural foods—fruits, vegetables, whole grains, lean proteins—while limiting salt, fat, and too-large portion sizes. But those guidelines leave a lot to interpretation. How do you make sure you're eating the best food to satisfy your body and your taste buds?

While it's true that seasonal, unprocessed foods are generally best, certain ingredients just pack in more of the good stuff—health-promoting vitamins, minerals, fiber, and "good" fats. Here are some ways to amp up your nutrition without sacrificing your satisfaction.

Wild-Caught Salmon: Salmon's omega-3 fatty acids are thought to lower blood pressure; they and other nutrients are also believed to have anti-inflammatory properties. Farmed salmon has fewer of these health benefits, so it's worth it to upgrade your steak or fillet to the wild variety.

Almond Butter: Instead of spreading your toast with or dipping your apple slices into peanut butter, try almond butter. The heart-healthy fats in almonds help lower "bad" cholesterol, while their vitamin E works against inflammation.

Quinoa: This easy-to-prepare grain (actually the seed of a spinach-like plant) is packed with protein and filling fiber. Use it instead of rice, couscous, and small pasta in pilafs or cold salads. For breakfast, mix some cooked quinoa into pancake batter or add it to your morning oatmeal.

Extra-Virgin Olive Oil: Olive oil has "good" fats that lower "bad" cholesterol, and extra-virgin olive oil has more disease-fighting antioxidants. Use it as a condiment for your carbs or to add a finishing touch to soup.

Avocados: Yes, avocados are high in calories (one average-size avocado has almost 300 calories), but their fat is the beneficial variety that increases "good" cholesterol while lowering the "bad." They also have lots of fiber. Try mashed avocado as a sandwich spread in lieu of less-nutritious mayonnaise.

Kale and Spinach: Salad is a go-to light lunch for anyone wanting to up their veggie intake while watching calories. But it's important to make those greens earn their keep in your salad bowl. Packed with vital nutrients—including vitamin K important for blood clotting and healthy bones—these darker greens outperform more pallid greens and taste delicious cooked, too.

Fresh Herbs: Bursting with flavor, not to mention helpful antioxidants, fresh herbs are an easy upgrade over the dried variety in salads and in cooked dishes. To prolong their life, stand them in a glass of water—like flowers in a vase—wrapped loosely in a plastic bag and store in the fridge.

Mussels with Fennel and Italian Beer

SERVES 2 TO 4

Mussels are inexpensive, and because most of those you'll find in the market are farmed rather than gathered in the wild, they don't require debearding and scrubbing, making them superfast to prepare—two good reasons to give them a try if you don't make mussels often.

1 tablespoon extra-virgin olive oil
1 small head of fennel, cored and diced small
2 shallots, finely chopped
1 garlic clove, chopped
¼ teaspoon kosher salt
1 pound mussels, washed and beards removed if needed
1 cup Italian beer, such as Peroni
2 tablespoons chopped fresh tarragon leaves
2 tablespoons (¼ stick) unsalted butter, at room temperature
Slices of rustic bread, for serving

Heat a 3½-quart soup pot or Dutch oven over medium-high heat. Add the olive oil and heat for another 30 seconds. Add the fennel and shallots to the hot pan and sweat, stirring often with a wooden spoon, for 2 minutes or until fragrant and beginning to soften. Add the garlic and salt and cook for another 2 minutes.

Add the mussels and stir gently once or twice to coat in the oil. Add the beer and stir one more time. Cover the pot with a tight-fitting lid and cook for about 4 minutes, stirring halfway through, or until the mussels have opened. Discard any unopened mussels. Stir in the tarragon and the butter and serve in shallow bowls with crusty bread to dip in the sauce.

Deconstructed Clams “Casino”

Alex's Shrimp Stir-Fry

Deconstructed Clams "Casino"

SERVES 2

With the old-school version of clams casino you get just a whisper of clam flavor and a lot of soggy bread crumbs. In this updated, deconstructed version the briny flavor of the clams shines through and you get more crunch from the crumb topping. Win-win! This works as a first course for three or four people, too.

2 tablespoon extra-virgin olive oil
2 ounces pancetta, diced fine
1 shallot, minced
2 garlic cloves, minced
2 dozen small Manila clams (1½ to 2 pounds)
½ cup dry white wine
¼ teaspoon dried oregano
2 tablespoons chopped fresh flat-leaf parsley leaves
¼ cup freshly grated Parmesan cheese
10 melba toasts, crushed into bite-size pieces

Heat an 8-inch shallow saucepan over medium-high heat. Add 1 tablespoon of the olive oil and the pancetta and cook, stirring often, until the pancetta is crispy and golden, about 4 minutes. Add the shallot and garlic to the pan and stir for 1 minute. Add the clams and stir to coat them in the flavored oil. Add the wine and oregano. Stir together, reduce the heat to medium, and cover with a lid.

Cook the clams for 4 to 5 minutes, shaking the pan every couple of minutes so they cook evenly. Once all of the clams are open, they are done. Turn off the heat and discard any clams that have not opened.

Pour the clams and the juice into a large serving bowl and sprinkle with the parsley, Parmesan, and crushed melba toasts. Drizzle with the remaining tablespoon of olive oil.

Alex's Shrimp Stir-Fry

GF

SERVES 2 TO 4

Chef Alex Guarnaschelli has become a soul sister to me, and like me, she loves to spend time in the kitchen with her daughter. When the two make dinner together, she says Ava is "definitely attracted to the immediate-gratification aspect of certain recipes. On weeknights we tend to make things that come together quickly, like this shrimp stir-fry." I'm betting your family will go for this, too.

2 tablespoons canola oil
16 medium shrimp, peeled and deveined
½ teaspoon paprika
Kosher salt
2 medium garlic cloves, grated
2 tablespoons dry sherry
1 cup tightly packed spinach leaves
Juice of ½ lemon

Heat a large skillet (or wok) and add the oil. Place the shrimp in a bowl and toss with the paprika, salt to taste, and the garlic. When the oil begins to smoke, shut off the heat and add the shrimp and toss them around with a metal spatula so they are coated with the oil and cook more evenly. Stir in the sherry.

Turn the heat back on and cook for a minute or two, until the shrimp are no longer translucent. Stir in the spinach and lemon juice, and taste for seasoning. Remove from the heat and drain any excess liquid. Serve immediately.

What to Cook When There's Nothing to Cook

Fried rice is a handy recipe to have in your pocket when it feels like the cupboard is bare. As long as you have some leftover or even frozen rice you can always have dinner ready to serve in about twenty minutes.

The beauty of fried rice is that it can be a vehicle for just about any kind of cooked meat, fish, or vegetables—cooked squash or salad greens—even cubes of tofu. Just make sure they are cut small enough to heat through quickly. I like nutty brown rice for a somewhat heartier dish, but you can substitute white rice or even another cooked grain. The only absolute here is that the rice must be day-old and chilled; freshly cooked rice will be too soft and the grains will become gummy when you fry them. Keep everything moving as the rice cooks so that the sauce coats every grain and some crunchy bits develop on the bottom.

Make It at Home Fried Rice

V GF

SERVES 4

This is the basic template for a fast weeknight dinner. I like to add quartered sea scallops to this, but shrimp is nice, too. It's as tasty as takeout but ten times better for you.

2 tablespoons soy sauce
½ teaspoon toasted sesame oil
½ teaspoon rice wine vinegar
1 teaspoon chile sauce, such as sriracha
3 tablespoons vegetable oil
1 bunch of scallions, green and white parts, sliced into thin rounds
2 garlic cloves, chopped fine
2 teaspoons grated peeled fresh ginger (from a 2-inch piece)
⅛ teaspoon kosher salt
3 cups cooked day-old brown rice
1 cup frozen peas, thawed
2 large eggs, beaten

In a small bowl, whisk together the soy sauce, sesame oil, rice wine vinegar, and chile sauce. Set aside. Heat a large skillet over high heat. When the pan is hot, add the oil followed by the scallions, garlic, ginger, and salt. Cook for about 30 seconds or until the mixture is fragrant.

Turn the heat down to medium high and add the rice. Using a wooden spoon or rubber spatula, toss the rice in the oil to coat. Then, spread the rice evenly over the skillet and let it be. Fry for about 2 minutes. Stir the rice and cook for an additional 2 minutes, until the rice is hot all the way through.

Add to the skillet the peas and the soy sauce mixture and stir well. Push the rice off to one side, making a little open space on one side of the skillet. Pour the beaten eggs into the space, and cook for 30 seconds before scrambling gently with a spatula. When soft curds have formed, stir the eggs into the rice and serve.

Make It at Home Fried Rice

Cheese Soufflé

V

SERVES 4

A soufflé on a weeknight? Absolutely! Pantry meals don't get much swankier than this, and no one will ever guess you're just using up all those odds and ends kicking around in your cheese drawer.

2 tablespoons plus 1 teaspoon unsalted butter
1 tablespoon freshly grated Parmesan cheese
2 tablespoons all-purpose flour
1 cup whole milk, at room temperature
1 well-packed cup mixed grated cheeses, such as Gruyère, sharp Cheddar, and Parmesan (strong cheeses work well here)
¼ teaspoon cayenne pepper
½ teaspoon kosher salt
3 eggs, separated, at room temperature
1 egg white
¼ teaspoon cream of tartar

Use 1 teaspoon of the butter to grease the inside of a 1½-quart baking or soufflé dish. Sprinkle with the grated Parmesan and rotate the dish to coat the inside. Store in the refrigerator until ready to use.

In a medium saucepan, melt the remaining 2 tablespoons butter over medium heat. Add the flour and whisk to form a smooth paste. Slowly add the milk, whisking constantly to avoid lumps. Bring to a simmer and remove from the heat. Whisk in the mixed cheeses, cayenne, and salt until smooth.

Meanwhile, whisk the 3 egg yolks in a medium bowl. Whisk in the warm sauce a little at a time to avoid cooking the egg. Whisk constantly until all of the warm mixture is mixed into the egg. Set aside to cool to room temperature.

Preheat the oven to 375°F.

Using a hand mixer, in a clean bowl beat the 4 egg whites and the cream of tartar on high speed until stiff peaks form. They should be opaque and shiny, not dry. Fold one-quarter of the whites into the cheese mixture to lighten slightly. Fold the remaining whites into the cheese mixture in 2 batches, being careful not to overmix and deflate the whites; it's okay if there are a few remaining streaks.

Pour the mixture into the prepared dish and place the dish on a rimmed baking sheet. Bake for 25 to 30 minutes or until puffed and golden. It should be firm but still jiggle slightly. Serve immediately.

Operation Clean Sweep

On the one hand, it's hard to be a spontaneous cook if you don't have a well-stocked pantry and refrigerator. On the other, shelves packed with half-filled jars and forgotten ingredients don't exactly inspire creativity.

As much as I like a clean fridge and organized pantry, I also hate the idea of wasting good food, so I had the brilliant idea of instituting a biweekly ritual I call "operation clean sweep."

Every other Saturday morning, I take inventory of my fridge. Tired veggies and meaty leftovers like chicken carcasses go into a stockpot to simmer. After a quick skim once it reaches a boil, I let the stock simmer, knowing that in a few hours I'll have a nice broth to use for soups, risottos, or just sipping throughout the week. Veggies with a little more life in them get chopped (or a quick steam and ice water bath), then combined with any fresh leafy herbs and greens for a massive salad I can eat all weekend.

If I'm getting to the bottom of a mustard jar, I'll use it to make a week's worth of vinaigrette, adding some chopped shallots, lemon juice or vinegar, plus olive oil to the jar. Sometimes I mix in the last of some creamy yogurt, sour cream, or mayo, making a sturdier dressing that works well on pasta, potato, or chicken salads.

Leftover cheeses can go into a light and fluffy cheese soufflé that's a lot less tricky to make than its reputation would have you think. It will never occur to anyone that you're feeding them leftovers when you bring this golden-brown beauty to the table—they'll be too busy applauding.

Bulk Up

If you're looking to save money on kitchen staples, make a beeline for the bulk-bin aisle, where you can buy everything—flavored granola, loose teas, sushi rice—by the pound, at prices that range from reasonable to rock bottom.

Almost everything that can be bought in bulk will set you back less than its packaged counterpart because the producer is able to pass along what is saved on packaging materials and marketing costs. Buying in bulk is also more cost effective because you don't need to buy a full package of an ingredient when you need only a few tablespoons. And bulk shopping is eco-friendly because you keep all that packaging out of the landfill (extra points if you remember to bring your own bags from home!). Most stores offer an impressive range of rices and other grains, specialty flours and various baking ingredients, heirloom beans and legumes, plus trail mix, fair-trade coffees—even olive oil and freshly ground almond butter. Bulk-bin shopping allows you to experiment with new ingredients without committing to a large quantity. Are you a farro fan? Try swapping it out for freekeh (roasted green wheat), wheat berries, or barley in your favorite recipes. Buy an ounce or two of ground flaxseed meal and blend it into your morning smoothie or bake it into muffins. If you like the new ingredient you can always go back for more. Here are a few pointers to help make the most of your trip down the aisle.

Look for specials. Around the holidays some stores offer even better values on popular baking ingredients such as shelled nuts or dried fruits; if your recipe is flexible, you may be able to substitute a deeply discounted alternative for what is called for.

Shop in well-trafficked stores. High turnover ensures the bin products are replenished regularly. If the bins themselves look dusty, or the scoops seem dingy, try another store.

Label your items. Many grains and legumes resemble one another; avoid confusion with tags noting a container's contents and the purchase date.

Follow your nose. Before you commit, take a big scoop of the grains, beans, or flour you plan to buy and give it a sniff. If it smells rancid or off, put it back in its bin. A complete absence of aroma can also be a sign that the item in question has been hanging around too long. Grains and flours should have clean, nutty aromas.

Don't buy more than you need. This is especially true if it's an unusual ingredient that you won't use often. Most bulk areas provide scales, which can be helpful when buying flours and other baking ingredients, but to be even more accurate, bring your own cup measures from home and scoop out the precise amount called for in your recipe. You don't want to clutter your shelves with odds and ends that may never get used.

Invest in attractive, airtight containers for your bulk purchases. Flimsy plastic bags can rip or split and won't keep grains and other items as fresh as glass jars or heavy-duty canisters will. And a shelf lined with handsome canisters that display their contents will spark your culinary creativity.

Use cold storage. Store oil-rich items like whole-grain flours and nuts in the freezer to keep them fresher longer.

Go big. If there are items you go through very frequently, inquire about true bulk purchases of 10, 15, or 25 pounds for even bigger savings.

Tofu with Broccoli and Sweet Chile Glaze

V GF

SERVES 4

Made for meatless Mondays or anytime you want a lightning-fast entrée with bold, appealing flavors, this dinner can be thrown together almost entirely with pantry items. You can substitute chicken or shrimp for the tofu.

¼ cup sweet chile sauce
2 teaspoons soy sauce
1 tablespoon rice wine vinegar
1 teaspoon dark sesame oil
1 tablespoon vegetable oil
2 garlic cloves, chopped
1 (2-inch) piece of fresh ginger, peeled and chopped
1 shallot, diced
1 head of broccoli, cut into small florets
1 red bell pepper, cored, seeded, and diced
½ teaspoon kosher salt
1 pound firm tofu, cut into 1-inch dice
Cooked rice, for serving

In a small bowl, whisk together the chile sauce, soy sauce, vinegar, sesame oil, and 2 tablespoons water. Set aside.

Place a large skillet over medium-high heat. Add the vegetable oil to the pan and heat for 1 minute, then add the garlic, ginger, and shallot. Cook for 30 seconds or until fragrant. Add the broccoli, bell pepper, and salt and cook, stirring often with a wooden spoon, for 3 to 4 minutes, until the broccoli is almost crisp-tender. Add the tofu and toss gently to combine. Add the glaze and stir once or twice to coat everything evenly. Reduce the heat to medium and simmer for 2 minutes. Serve over rice.

Lamb Chops with Tomato and Feta Salad

GF

SERVES 4

Lamb chops are a busy-night go-to in my house, and this Mediterranean take is as delicious as it is quick to throw together. Use a nice fruity olive oil for the tomato salad.

Lamb Chops with Tomato and Feta Salad

SALAD

2 cups coarsely chopped tomatoes (about 2 large tomatoes)
¼ cup lightly packed torn fresh basil leaves
⅓ teaspoon kosher salt
2 tablespoons extra-virgin olive oil
2 tablespoons crumbled feta cheese

YOGURT SAUCE

½ English cucumber, peeled
¾ cup low-fat plain Greek yogurt
1 teaspoon grated lemon zest
1 tablespoon fresh lemon juice (from 1 lemon)
1 tablespoon extra-virgin olive oil
¾ teaspoon kosher salt

LAMB CHOPS

8 lamb T-bone chops, cut about 1 inch thick
3 garlic cloves, chopped
1 teaspoon chopped fresh rosemary leaves
½ teaspoon kosher salt
¼ teaspoon freshly ground black pepper
2 tablespoons extra-virgin olive oil

Preheat a grill or grill pan to medium-high heat.

For the salad: Combine the tomatoes, basil, salt, olive oil, and feta in a medium bowl. Toss lightly with a rubber spatula. Set aside.

For the yogurt sauce: Grate the cucumber on the large holes of a box grater and place in a fine-mesh strainer. Squeeze the excess liquid from the grated cucumber using your hands and place in a medium bowl. Add the yogurt, lemon zest and juice, olive oil, and salt. Mix well and set aside.

For the lamb chops: Season the lamb chops with the garlic, rosemary, salt, pepper, and olive oil. Grill the chops to desired doneness, about 4 minutes per side for medium rare. Remove from the grill and tent with foil to keep warm.

Serve the chops alongside the marinated tomatoes and with a dollop of the yogurt sauce.

Veal Piccata

SERVES 4

This is a classic for a reason: It couldn't be easier to make—or more of a treat. The piquant sauce gets a double dose of tanginess from lemon juice and capers, and the thin veal scallops cook in mere minutes.

8 veal scallopini, less than ¼ inch thick
½ teaspoon kosher salt
½ teaspoon freshly ground black pepper
All-purpose flour, for dredging
6 tablespoons (¾ stick) unsalted butter
2 tablespoons extra-virgin olive oil
⅔ cup low-sodium chicken broth
⅔ cup fresh lemon juice (from 2 to 3 lemons)
¼ cup capers, rinsed and drained
2 tablespoons chopped fresh flat-leaf parsley leaves

Sprinkle the veal with the salt and pepper. Dredge the veal lightly in the flour, shaking off the excess. In a large sauté pan, melt 2 tablespoons of the butter with the olive oil over medium-high heat. Add half of the veal scallops and cook just until brown, about 3 minutes per side. Using tongs, transfer the scaloppini to a plate. Repeat with the remaining veal. Cover loosely with foil while you make the sauce.

To the same sauté pan, add the broth, lemon juice, and capers. Bring the mixture to a boil over medium-high heat, scraping up the brown bits from the bottom of the pan for extra flavor. Simmer for 2 minutes. Whisk the remaining 4 tablespoons butter into the sauce. Return the veal to the pan just to heat through. Arrange the scaloppini on a platter, pour the sauce on top, and garnish with the parsley.

Veal Piccata

Broccoli Rabe Tacos

V

SERVES 4

In California where I live, Mex-Italian mashups are becoming increasingly common. That's good news for me, since those are pretty much two of my favorite things! Leftovers are a great take-along lunch.

SPREAD

1 (15-ounce) can chickpeas, rinsed and drained
1 garlic clove (optional)
½ teaspoon ground cumin
1 teaspoon grated lemon zest
1 tablespoon fresh lemon juice (from 1 lemon)
⅓ cup extra-virgin olive oil
¾ teaspoon kosher salt

TACOS

2 bunches of broccoli rabe
¼ cup extra-virgin olive oil
¼ teaspoon kosher salt
1 tablespoon Calabrian chile paste or hot sauce
2 tablespoons fresh lemon juice (from 1 lemon)
8 small whole-wheat tortillas
1 cup grated ricotta salata cheese
½ cup roasted peanuts, chopped

For the spread: In a food processor, combine the chickpeas, garlic, if using, cumin, and lemon zest and juice. Pulse to blend. With the machine running, drizzle in the olive oil. Stop to scrape down the sides as needed. Season with the salt and puree until smooth. Set aside.

For the tacos: Bring a large pot of salted water to a boil. Cut off and discard the bottom 2 inches of each broccoli rabe stem. Working in batches, blanch the greens in the boiling water for 1 minute, then transfer to a colander and drain.

Preheat a grill pan over medium-high heat. Toss the parboiled broccoli rabe with 2 tablespoons of the olive oil and the salt. In 2 batches, grill the broccoli rabe for 2 minutes on each side. Remove to a cutting board and chop into 1-inch pieces.

Meanwhile, in a medium bowl, whisk together the chile paste, lemon juice, and the remaining 2 tablespoons olive oil. Add the grilled broccoli rabe and toss to coat well.

Place the tortillas on the grill pan to warm slightly, turning once. Fill each tortilla with some of the bean spread and broccoli rabe. Sprinkle with the ricotta salata and peanuts and serve.

Broccoli Rabe Tacos

Hazelnut Beef with Noodles

SERVES 4 TO 6

Recipes like this one are really making me a convert to slow-cooking. The braised meat gets a pop of flavor from ground hazelnuts and graded parm.

3 pounds chuck roast, cut into 1-inch pieces
4 carrots, peeled and chopped
2 celery stalks, chopped
1 onion, chopped
3 garlic cloves, minced
¼ cup tomato paste
1 bay leaf
2 sprigs of thyme
1 (2-inch) piece of Parmesan cheese rind
½ cup white wine
2 cups beef stock
2 teaspoons kosher salt
½ cup panko bread crumbs
½ cup toasted peeled hazelnuts
1 cup frozen peas, thawed

Cooked egg noodles, for serving
Freshly grated Parmesan cheese, for serving
3 tablespoons chopped Italian parsley, for serving

Place the chuck, carrots, celery, onion, garlic, tomato paste, bay leaf, thyme, Parmesan rind, white wine, beef stock, and salt in a large slow cooker. Cover, turn the slow cooker to high, and cook for 5 hours.

Meanwhile, in a food processor, combine the panko and the hazelnuts and pulse until ground to medium fine. Add the bread crumb mixture for the final 30 minutes of cooking along with the peas. Serve over egg noodles topped with grated Parmesan cheese and chopped parsley.

Hazelnut Beef with Noodles

Skirt Steak with Pistachio Gremolata

GF

SERVES 4 TO 6

Think of this easy green sauce as a secret weapon; its vibrant color and citrus tang wake up the flavors of vegetables and oily fish as well as braised dishes and grilled meats. Be careful when grating the grapefruit zest not to include any of the pith, which can make your sauce bitter.

1½ pounds skirt steak
1½ teaspoons kosher salt
Ground black pepper, to taste
¼ cup roasted pistachios, chopped
1¼ cups packed fresh flat-leaf parsley leaves, chopped
2 teaspoons grated lime zest (from 2 limes)
1 tablespoon fresh lime juice
½ cup extra-virgin olive oil
1 garlic clove, smashed and peeled
1 teaspoon Calabrian chile paste

Season the steak with 1 teaspoon of the salt and a generous amount of black pepper. Set aside at room temperature while you make the gremolata.

In a medium bowl, combine the pistachios, parsley, lime zest and juice, olive oil, garlic clove, chile paste, and the remaining salt. Mix well with a wooden spoon. Allow the mixture to sit at room temperature for at least 30 minutes. You can also refrigerate the gremolata for 24 hours; bring it to room temperature before serving.

Heat a ridged grill pan over medium-high heat until very hot. Grill the steak until deep grill marks develop, 3 to 5 minutes. Turn and grill on the second side another 3 or 4 minutes, then remove to a cutting board to rest for 5 minutes. Slice the steak across the grain and serve with the gremolata.

Skirt Steak with Pistachio Gremolata

Chile-Rubbed Pork Chops with Grilled Pineapple Salsa

GF

SERVES 6

Pork chops are great on the grill, indoors or out, and I like to give them extra punch with a slightly spicy, smoky rub. Pineapple caramelizes beautifully when grilled, adding a deep flavor that pairs nicely with the meat.

SALSA

1 small pineapple, cored and sliced ½ inch thick
½ red onion, peeled and sliced ½ inch thick
Extra-virgin olive oil
1 cucumber, peeled, seeded, and diced
1 small serrano chile, seeded and finely diced
2 tablespoons chopped fresh mint leaves
2 tablespoons chopped fresh cilantro leaves
Grated zest and juice of 1 lime
½ teaspoon kosher salt
¼ teaspoon freshly ground black pepper

PORK CHOPS

6 boneless pork chops
½ red onion
1 tablespoon chili powder
1½ tablespoons (packed) light brown sugar
½ teaspoon cayenne pepper
1 teaspoon smoked paprika
¼ teaspoon ground cumin
2 teaspoons kosher salt
Extra-virgin olive oil

Put a grill pan over medium-high heat or preheat a gas or charcoal grill.

For the salsa: Lightly brush the pineapple and onion slices with oil. Grill the pineapple slices until they have grill marks and are heated through, about 2 minutes per side.

Remove the pineapple slices from the grill, chop into ½-inch dice, and transfer to a medium bowl. Grill the onion slices until tender, about 3 minutes per side. Chop the onion into ½-inch pieces and add to the bowl with the pineapple.

Add the cucumber, chile, mint, cilantro, lime zest and juice, salt, and pepper and toss lightly to combine. Set aside, and keep the grill pan over medium-high heat.

For the pork chops: Rub both sides of the pork chops with the cut side of the onion half. Discard the onion.

In a small bowl, combine the chili powder, brown sugar, cayenne, paprika, cumin, and salt. Sprinkle both sides of the pork generously with the spice mixture and then drizzle with olive oil. Grill the pork chops until cooked to medium, about 7 minutes per side depending on thickness. Remove from the grill, tent loosely with foil, and let rest for 5 minutes.

Serve the pork chops topped with the pineapple salsa.

Chile-Rubbed Pork Chops

Handy Portion Sizes

I've long maintained that watching how *much* you eat is at least as important as *what* you eat; if you keep your portion sizes reasonable (especially of calorie-dense foods), nothing is out of bounds. If you are a close reader of food labels, you know that a "serving" of many foods is far smaller than what often ends up on your plate, especially in restaurants.

Fortunately the perfect tool for measuring portion size is readily within reach: your own hand. Here's how:

Fist: Your closed fist is about the same volume as a cup. This is the size you want for larger portions of vegetables. When it comes to leafy greens, which are low in calories and brimming with nutrients, go ahead: Punch it up by serving yourself two fists' worth!

Palm: The surface of your palm (no fingers included) can help you visualize what 3 ounces of protein look like, the perfect portion for a chicken breast, serving of steak, or fish.

Cupped hand: This is about a half cup—a good portion size for whole grains, such as brown rice, quinoa, oatmeal, and farro, which are great sources of filling fiber and a key nutrient for digestive and overall health.

Index finger: Use the tip of your index finger up to the first knuckle to measure out about a teaspoon of any items you'd like to consume in moderation, such as the sugar or honey you add to your coffee or tea.

Thumb: Your thumb, from tip to first joint, represents around a tablespoon, an ideal serving size for calorie-dense foods like salad dressings, or the nut butter you spread on whole-grain toast.

Lentil Salade Niçoise

V GF

SERVES 4

Meatless entrées don't get more appealing—or more Française—than this.

SALAD

1 pound green lentils (*lentilles du Puy*), picked over and rinsed
1 teaspoon kosher salt
1 cup haricots verts or thin green beans, trimmed and halved
½ pound baby potatoes, quartered
4 large eggs
1 cup grape tomatoes, halved
½ cup Niçoise black olives, pitted and halved
1 cucumber, peeled, seeded, and diced

VINAIGRETTE

⅓ cup fresh lemon juice (from 2 to 3 lemons)
1 tablespoon minced shallot
1 tablespoon chopped fresh thyme leaves
1 tablespoon Dijon mustard
1 teaspoon honey
½ teaspoon kosher salt
¼ teaspoon freshly ground black pepper
⅓ cup grapeseed oil

For the lentils: Place the lentils in a saucepan with enough water to cover by 2 inches. Bring to a boil, then reduce the heat to a simmer and cook for 15 minutes. Add the salt and continue to cook until just tender, 5 to 10 minutes longer. Drain well.

For the vinaigrette: In a small bowl, whisk together the lemon juice, shallot, thyme, mustard, honey, salt, and pepper. Gradually add the oil, whisking until the dressing is thick. Set aside.

Meanwhile, bring a large pot of salted water to a boil over high heat. Add the green beans and blanch for 1 to 2 minutes, until just tender. Use a slotted spoon or skimmer to transfer the green beans to a large bowl of ice water to cool, then transfer again to a medium bowl. Set aside. Add the potatoes to the same pot of boiling water and cook until tender enough to pierce with a knife, 8 to 10 minutes. Drop them into the ice bath to stop any further cooking, then transfer to the bowl with the beans. Gently lower the eggs into the boiling water and cook for exactly 10 minutes. Transfer the eggs to the ice bath to cool for 5 minutes before peeling, then slice into quarters.

In a large salad bowl, combine the lentils, potatoes, and beans with the tomatoes, olives, and cucumbers. Add the vinaigrette and gently toss until all the ingredients are coated. Arrange on a platter and top with the egg.

For the Love of Lentils

Lentils don't receive nearly the respect they should, and I'm on a mission to change that. Consider these selling points: Lentils are a fat-free, high-protein food that are worth their weight in iron, fiber, and other nutrients. Lentils are versatile and inexpensive and can be cast as the leading lady or in a supporting role in many recipes. And because lentils cook quickly and don't require soaking ahead of time, they are much easier than dried beans to work into spontaneous meals and weeknight dinners.

While lentils are especially popular in other cuisines, notably Indian and French, in this country we tend to relegate them almost entirely to cold-weather soups. In France, lentils pop up all year long in warm and cold salads, side dishes, and stews. If you avoid lentils because they are sometimes too earthy or mushy, get ready to meet the humble brown lentil's sophisticated European relation, the Puy lentil, or *lentille du Puy*. Greenish in color, these petite legumes are grown in the volcanic soil of France's Puy region. French green lentils have a nutty, elegant flavor and retain their firm texture and shape when cooked.

Lentils couldn't be easier to cook: Just put them in a pot with water or stock to cover by an inch or so and add a little bit of salt and some aromatics such as thyme sprigs, a clove of garlic, or an onion stuck with cloves. Bring to a boil, then reduce the heat to a simmer and cook for twenty to twenty-five minutes or until tender but still firm and separate. Drain, discarding any aromatics you added to the pot, and serve warm, tossed with a vinaigrette; or cool and refrigerate for up to five days, ready to toss into pastas and grain salads, mix with grilled vegetables to fill a wrap sandwich, or puree into a dip or spread.

Lentil Salad Niçoise

Vegetables & Sides

Is it just me, or do vegetables seem a lot more interesting than meat these days? I'm still unabashedly carnivorous, and in fact I feel better when I do include some meat in my diet . . . just not too much, and not necessarily every day. Vegetables, on the other hand, are what I truly crave, and I never get tired of devising new ways to prepare and serve them. Salads, of course, are a standby, and I serve one with almost every meal. But especially in the cooler months I like to make a cooked vegetable dish the stand*out,* with some simply prepared protein playing a supporting role.

When dining out, I often choose my entrée based on the side dishes that come with it. After all, even the best pan-roasted salmon is just a nice piece of fish; it's when it comes on a bed of farro salad or with an interesting kale or spinach preparation that it calls out to me. The same is true at home. A creative grain or vegetable side can dress up a store-bought rotisserie chicken to make the quickest meal ever. Pull out one of these sides when you need to reinvent last night's grilled steak or pork roast, and no one will know they're getting a rehash.

Corn Fritters with Cherry Tomato Salsita

Corn Fritters with Cherry Tomato Salsita

V

SERVES 6 TO 8

A *salsita*, or "little salsa," is typically a garnish of chopped tomatoes, onions, and cilantro. My aunt Carolyna's version uses halved cherry tomatoes, scallions, and a little balsamic vinegar. Make it first so that you can serve the fritters while they're hot and crisp.

TOMATO SALSITA

6 scallions, finely chopped
2 tablespoons extra-virgin olive oil
1 tablespoon balsamic vinegar
1 pound mixed red and yellow cherry tomatoes, halved
Kosher salt and freshly ground black pepper

CORN FRITTERS

1 large ear of corn
1 large egg
1 cup whole milk
⅔ cup yellow cornmeal
⅔ cup all-purpose flour
1 teaspoon sugar
¼ teaspoon kosher salt
⅛ teaspoon baking soda
Freshly ground black pepper
⅓ cup vegetable oil

For the tomato salsita: In a medium bowl, combine the scallions, oil, vinegar, and tomatoes and stir gently. Season to taste with salt and pepper. Allow the salsita to sit for 15 minutes before serving.

For the fritters: Over a large bowl, carefully cut the corn kernels off the cob. With the back of the knife, scrape the juice from the cob into the bowl. Add the egg and the milk and whisk.

In a separate bowl, combine the cornmeal, flour, sugar, salt, and baking soda. Season with pepper. Slowly stir the dry ingredients into the wet ingredients to gently combine.

Heat the oil in a skillet over medium heat until it reaches 375°F.

Preheat the oven to 200°F.

Spoon in a big tablespoon of batter and repeat 4 or 5 times, depending on the size of your skillet. Do not overcrowd. After 2 minutes, turn the fritters over and allow the other side to lightly brown.

Once both sides are golden brown, remove the fritters from the skillet and transfer to a paper towel–lined plate. Season with salt. Place in the oven to keep warm while you cook the remaining batter. Arrange the fritters on a platter and serve with the tomato salsita.

Smoky Candied Carrots

V V GF

SERVES 4

Use tender young bunch carrots for this, not the peeled nuggets labeled "baby carrots" in the produce section, which are far less tender and flavorful. Smoked brown sugar is a genius way to add slow-cooked flavor to lots of dishes; it's available from thesmokedolive.com.

2 bunches of baby carrots, tops trimmed and carrots washed
¼ cup smoked brown sugar
½ teaspoon kosher salt

Place the carrots in a 10-inch sauté pan with the sugar and salt. Add 1 cup water. Place the pan over high heat and bring to a boil, stirring occasionally with a rubber spatula to dissolve the sugar. Reduce the heat to medium-high and continue to simmer vigorously until the liquid has thickened to a syrup and the carrots are fork-tender, about 12 minutes.

Remove from the heat and allow the carrots to cool for 5 minutes before serving. Toss the carrots to coat them in the smoky syrup and serve.

Smoky Candied Carrots

Roasted Cauliflower with Capers and Almonds

Roasted Cauliflower with Capers and Almonds

V GF

SERVES 4

Quickly roasting cauliflower takes it from bland to brilliant. The capers, almonds, and Parmesan make this side dish a real standout.

1 head of cauliflower, cut into 1-inch florets
2 tablespoons extra-virgin olive oil
½ teaspoon kosher salt
2 tablespoons capers, rinsed, drained, and chopped
⅓ cup fresh flat-leaf parsley leaves, chopped
⅛ teaspoon crushed red pepper flakes
¼ cup toasted sliced almonds (see Cook's Note, page 75)
2 tablespoons freshly grated Parmesan cheese

Preheat the oven to 425°F. On a rimmed baking sheet, toss together the cauliflower, olive oil, and salt. Roast for 15 minutes, stirring halfway through.

In a large bowl, mix together the capers, parsley, red pepper flakes, and almonds. Set aside.

Remove the cauliflower from the oven and sprinkle with the Parmesan. Toss and return to the oven for an additional 5 minutes.

With a spatula, scrape the bottom of the pan to release any of the good, browned cheese that may be sticking. Add the roasted cauliflower to the caper mixture and mix gently. Serve warm.

Citrus-Chile Acorn Squash

V GF

SERVES 4

It's hard to get excited about squash in the dead of winter because it's practically the only game in town when it comes to fresh produce. Not so with this dish. A triple dose of orange—juice, zest, and the bright squash flesh—make it a colorful addition to a winter plate, and it has a nice kick, too.

2 small acorn squash, halved, seeds scooped out, and sliced ¼ inch thick
¼ cup extra-virgin olive oil
¼ cup freshly grated Parmesan cheese
1 teaspoon kosher salt
1 teaspoon grated orange zest
2 tablespoons fresh orange juice (from ½ large orange)
¼ teaspoon Calabrian chile paste or crushed red pepper flakes
¼ cup fresh basil leaves, chopped

Preheat the oven to 475°F. Place the rack in the upper third of the oven and place a rimmed baking sheet in the oven as it heats.

In a large bowl, toss the sliced squash well with the olive oil, cheese, and ¾ teaspoon of the salt. Remove the hot baking sheet from the oven and spread the squash evenly over the hot pan. Return the pan to the oven and bake for 15 to 20 minutes or until the squash is just tender and cooked through.

In the same bowl, whisk together the orange zest and juice, chile paste, and remaining ¼ teaspoon salt. Add the warm squash to the bowl and toss gently, being careful not to break apart the squash too much. Sprinkle with the basil and serve.

Citrus-Chile Acorn Squash

Sweet Potatoes vs. Yams

Sweet potatoes are good for so much more than a marshmallow-topped holiday side dish. Their naturally sweet flesh is loaded with nutrients, beta-carotene in particular, but also vitamin C, potassium, calcium, magnesium, and manganese. They tend to be higher in fiber and lower in calories than regular potatoes—and, of course, they're fat-free. They're also inexpensive, store well, and are readily available to roast, grill, puree, or simply microwave and eat year-round.

Sweets come in a bewildering array of varieties boasting colorful names like Covington (favored in the South for their malty sweet flavor), Creamsicle (cream color on the outside, vibrant orange on the inside), and Okinawan (a Hawaiian variety with purple flesh). Most common are Jewels, Hannahs, Garnets, and Japanese, a white-fleshed potato that cooks up dry and nutty, a bit like like a roasted chestnut.

But you're most likely to find two main types, often confusingly (and incorrectly) labeled as yams. "Firm" sweet potatoes have a thin golden skin with pale yellow flesh; "soft" sweet potatoes have a coppery hue on the outside and orange flesh.

When choosing, look for small-to medium-size potatoes that feel heavy, have smooth, unbruised skins, and are free of sprouts. Store them somewhere cool, and they'll keep for several weeks.

Salt-Roasted Sweet Potatoes

V GF

SERVES 4

This dish is in the sides chapter, but it could easily be the centerpiece of a meatless meal, paired with a salad and some steamed or sautéed vegetables. The potatoes' meaty texture is filling and satisfying.

3 cups kosher salt
Leaves from 4 fresh rosemary sprigs
Leaves from 6 fresh thyme sprigs
4 garlic cloves, unpeeled and gently smashed
4 small sweet potatoes, scrubbed
½ cup low-fat plain Greek yogurt
2 tablespoons extra-virgin olive oil
¼ teaspoon freshly ground black pepper
Grated zest of 1 lemon

Preheat the oven to 400°F.

In a small baking dish or on a rimmed baking sheet, mix together 2 cups of the salt, the rosemary, thyme, and garlic cloves and spread it in an even layer. Nestle the potatoes in the salt, pressing the salt slightly up the sides of each potato. Top with the remaining cup of salt, covering the potatoes as completely as possible. Roast for about 1 hour or until a thin knife or skewer can be inserted with no resistance.

In a small bowl, whisk together the yogurt, olive oil, and pepper. Remove the potatoes from the salt bed, brushing off any salt that may stick to the skin. Slice each potato open lengthwise and gently fluff the flesh with a fork. Top each potato with a dollop of the seasoned yogurt and sprinkle with the zest.

Lemon-Roasted Fennel

V GF

SERVES 4 TO 6

When roasted, fennel's licorice flavor mellows a bit and is a great match for salty Parmesan. This is fast to throw together and adds an elegant note to a weeknight dinner plate or a more formal meal.

4 fennel bulbs, cored, cut horizontally into ⅓-inch-thick slices, fronds reserved
1 teaspoon kosher salt
1 teaspoon grated lemon zest
1 garlic clove, sliced
⅓ cup freshly shredded Parmesan cheese
¼ cup extra-virgin olive oil

Preheat the oven to 375°F. Lightly oil a 13 × 9 × 2-inch baking dish. Arrange the fennel in a single layer in the dish. Sprinkle with salt, lemon zest, and garlic. Top with the Parmesan. Drizzle with the oil.

Bake until golden brown and tender, about 45 minutes. Sprinkle with chopped fennel fronds and serve warm.

Your Friend Fennel

The chameleon-like nature of fennel, which can take center stage in a simple yet elegant gratin or turn demure in a supporting role as a bed for grilled seafood, makes it one of the most versatile veggies I know. Raw, it has a licorice flavor and a celery-like texture that is very refreshing; cooked, it becomes even more alluring, adding a note of sophistication whether braised, broiled, grilled, or boiled and pureed. In Italy, where fennel is known as *finocchio*, the bulbs are baked into flans, dipped raw into bagna cauda, and even fried. To find the most tender specimens you should head to the farmers' market, where you are likely to find smaller, younger bulbs complete with their stalks and fronds, both of which are completely usable. Start cooking with fennel and you'll quickly find it's your secret weapon for amping up the flavor of your favorite tuna salad, fish stews, and roast veggie dishes. Use it whenever you might reach for celery, onions, or leeks in a braise, and don't forget to save the feathery tops to sprinkle on salads and broiled dishes for a touch of color.

Lemon-Roasted Fennel

Braised Swiss Chard with Curried Bread Crumbs

Braised Swiss Chard with Curried Bread Crumbs

SERVES 2 TO 4

This dish works best with coarse, semi-dry crumbs made from one slice of a country loaf. The curried crumbs would be delicious also as a garnish for soup or sautéed zucchini ribbons.

1 bunch of rainbow Swiss chard
1 tablespoon plus 1 teaspoon extra-virgin olive oil
1 slice thick-cut bacon, chopped
1 shallot, sliced into thin rings
1 garlic clove, smashed and peeled
½ teaspoon kosher salt, plus more to taste
3 tablespoons dry vermouth
1 cup halved red seedless grapes
¼ cup bread crumbs
½ teaspoon curry powder

Strip the chard leaves from the stems. Chop the stems into ½-inch pieces and cut the leaves into 1-inch ribbons. Wash well and reserve separately.

Pour 1 tablespoon of the olive oil into a 10-inch straight-sided pan, add the bacon, and place over medium heat. Cook, stirring with a wooden spoon, until the bacon becomes crispy, 3 to 4 minutes. Add the shallot and garlic and cook for another 3 minutes or until the shallot is soft and fragrant. Increase the heat to high and add the chopped chard stems. Cook for 1 minute. Add the chopped chard leaves and the salt and stir until they begin to wilt. Add the vermouth and the grapes. Stir gently, then cover and cook for 2 minutes. Uncover the pan and continue to cook over high heat until most of the liquid has evaporated and just a small amount remains, another 3 minutes. Keep warm.

In a small sauté pan, combine the bread crumbs, curry powder, the remaining 1 teaspoon olive oil, and a pinch of salt. Place over medium heat and cook, stirring often with a rubber spatula, until the bread crumbs are golden brown and fragrant.

Spoon the braised chard into a serving bowl and sprinkle with the bread crumbs.

Crumbs of Wisdom

The next time you discover you've left a loaf of bread on the counter and it's gone stale, don't toss it—crush it! Homemade bread crumbs have a million uses that go way beyond the obvious.

You'll get very different effects depending on how finely you grind them. For breading and binding meatballs, process the crumbs to a uniform size and fine texture. When you want the crumbs to add more of a golden crunch to a braised dish or the top of a casserole, go for a coarser result, with some larger, jagged shards that will crisp up in the oven. For the largest, most irregular crumbs, try this trick: Wrap the stale bread in a kitchen towel or resealable plastic bag and whack away with a rolling pin.

Whichever way you prepare them, make sure your crumbs are completely dry—spread them on a rimmed baking sheet and leave them out overnight if they are still moist—before transferring them to an airtight container where they can be stored for weeks. Alternatively, you can store your crumbs in the freezer for a month or so.

Once you realize how transformative a handful of homemade crumbs can be, you'll find endless uses for them. Sprinkle some toasted bread crumbs on a salad instead of croutons; mix them with parsley and chopped anchovies to stuff artichokes; or blend them with sautéed onions and greens as a filling for a pounded and rolled chicken breast. Sautéed with a little olive oil, garlic, and red pepper flakes, they make a plate of plain pasta or simple steamed vegetables sing. Stir a few cups of coarse bread crumbs into a sweetened egg-and-cream mixture for a silky bread pudding.

Bacon Bourbon Brussels Sprout Skewers

GF

MAKES 10 SKEWERS

Bacon, bourbon, Brussels sprouts—'nuff said? These are so over the top you'll want to serve them with something simple and virtuous, like a roast chicken.

4 tablespoons (½ stick) unsalted butter
⅓ cup dark brown sugar
⅛ teaspoon cayenne pepper
½ teaspoon kosher salt
⅔ cup bourbon
1 pound slab bacon, cut into 1-inch cubes
15 small Brussels sprouts (about ½ pound), trimmed
Vegetable oil cooking spray
10 (8-inch) bamboo skewers

Preheat the oven to 375°F.

In a small saucepan, combine the butter, brown sugar, cayenne, salt, and bourbon over medium heat. Whisk until the butter has melted and the mixture forms a smooth sauce, about 8 minutes. Keep warm over low heat.

Spread the bacon on a small rimmed baking sheet and bake for 8 to 10 minutes, just to begin to render the fat. Set aside.

Bring a large pot of salted water to a boil over high heat. Add the sprouts and simmer for 5 minutes, or until just barely tender and still bright green. Drain well. When cool enough to handle, cut each sprout in half lengthwise.

Preheat a grill pan over medium heat.

Assemble the skewers starting with a Brussels sprout half, then a piece of bacon, another sprout half, and another piece of bacon, and finishing with a sprout half. Brush the glaze lightly over the skewers.

Spray the grill pan with vegetable oil cooking spray. Place the skewers on the pan and grill each side, brushing them with glaze with every turn, until the bacon is beginning to crisp and the Brussels sprouts are starting to char, 1 to 2 minutes per side. Serve warm drizzled with any remaining glaze.

Peas, Pancetta, and Prosecco

GF

SERVES 4

A few tablespoons of prosecco make this stellar side dish light and a little bit decadent.

4 ounces bacon, chopped
2 shallots, minced
1 (10.8-ounce) bag frozen peas, thawed
⅓ cup fresh mint leaves, chopped
½ cup freshly grated Pecorino Romano
¼ teaspoon kosher salt
3 tablespoons prosecco

Place the bacon in a large skillet over medium heat. Cook, stirring often, until the bacon is crispy and the fat has rendered out, about 5 minutes. Drain all but 2 tablespoons of the bacon fat. Add the shallots and cook for about 2 minutes or until soft and fragrant.

Using a wooden spoon, stir in the peas. Cook the peas for 4 minutes or until they are heated through. When the peas are hot, turn up the heat to medium high. Add the chopped mint, pecorino, and salt. Toss gently to combine. Add the prosecco and remove from the heat. Stir until everything is evenly combined and coated in the sauce.

Peas, Pancetta, and Prosecco

Spicy Sesame Green Beans and Kale

Spicy Sesame Green Beans and Kale

V V GF

SERVES 6

There are so many great flavors going on in this simple, ready-in-twenty-minutes dish: garlic, ginger, mushrooms, red pepper flakes, lemon, and sesame oil. Add the textures and tastes of kale and green beans, and you've got one great and very nutritious side.

3 tablespoons extra-virgin olive oil
1 shallot, sliced
10 shiitake mushrooms, stemmed and quartered
2 garlic cloves, sliced
2 tablespoons chopped peeled fresh ginger (from a 1-inch piece)
1½ pounds green beans, trimmed and sliced into 1-inch pieces
2 teaspoons kosher salt
¼ cup dry white wine
½ teaspoon crushed red pepper flakes
1 bunch of kale (½ pound), rinsed, stemmed, and coarsely chopped
1 tablespoon fresh lemon juice (from 1 lemon)
1 tablespoon toasted sesame oil

In a large heavy sauté pan, warm the olive oil over medium-high heat. Add the shallot and cook until translucent, about 3 minutes. Add the mushrooms and sauté until they begin to soften and brown, another 3 minutes. Add the garlic, ginger, green beans, and salt and cook for 2 minutes.

Add the wine and continue cooking until the green beans are almost tender, about 5 minutes. Add the red pepper flakes and kale and continue cooking until the kale has wilted, 3 to 4 minutes. Add the lemon juice and the sesame oil. Toss to coat and serve immediately.

Creamy Polenta

V GF

SERVES 4 TO 6

This recipe produces a creamy polenta that is soft enough to spread on a platter (or plank; see page 232), but will set up around the edges to contain any sauce you ladle on top.

2 cups milk
2 teaspoons kosher salt
1¼ cups medium-grind cornmeal
5 tablespoons unsalted butter
1½ cups freshly grated Parmesan cheese

In a large pot, bring 4 cups water, the milk, and the salt to a boil over medium-high heat. Reduce the heat to medium low and slowly whisk in the cornmeal. Cook, whisking constantly, for about 3 minutes to prevent lumps.

Continue to cook for about 20 minutes, stirring often with a wooden spoon. The mixture should bubble every so often but not boil. After 20 minutes, whisk in the butter and cheese, stirring until melted and fully incorporated.

Spicy Sesame Bok Boy

Caesar-Roasted Broccoli

SERVES 4

Why should romaine lettuce have all the fun? When roasted broccoli gets the Caesar treatment, that weekday workhorse is transformed into an addictively delicious—and far more nutritious—dish than your standard salad.

1 large bunch of broccoli, cut into florets (about 5 cups)
2 tablespoons extra-virgin olive oil
½ teaspoon kosher salt
¾ cup freshly grated Parmesan cheese
1 anchovy, chopped
1 garlic clove, chopped
2 tablespoons mayonnaise
½ teaspoon freshly ground black pepper
2 tablespoons panko, toasted (see Cook's Note)

Preheat the oven to 400°F.

Place the broccoli florets on a rimmed baking sheet. Drizzle with the olive oil, sprinkle with the salt, and toss to coat. Roast the broccoli for 15 minutes, stirring halfway, until just cooked through and beginning to brown.

While the broccoli is roasting, stir together the Parmesan, anchovy, garlic, mayonnaise and black pepper in a medium bowl. Add the hot broccoli directly to the bowl and let it sit for 30 seconds to warm the dressing slightly. Then use a rubber spatula to toss the broccoli in the mixture until coated. Top with the toasted bread crumbs and serve.

Cook's Note: Toast the panko in a small dry skillet over medium heat until golden, about 3 minutes, stirring regularly.

Spicy Sesame Bok Choy

V V GF

SERVES 4

There is a world of green vegetables to explore in any Asian market, and bok choy is a great one to experiment with. Its subtle cabbage flavor is a good foil for a bit of hot pepper action!

¼ teaspoon Gochujang (Korean chile paste)
¼ teaspoon Korean chile powder or crushed red pepper flakes
1 teaspoon sugar
½ teaspoon toasted sesame oil
1 teaspoon rice wine vinegar
⅛ teaspoon kosher salt
2 to 3 heads of baby bok choy
¼ teaspoon toasted sesame seeds

In a medium bowl, whisk together the chile paste, chile powder, sugar, sesame oil, vinegar, 1 teaspoon cold water, and the salt. Pull apart the leaves of the bok choy and wash and dry well. Add to the bowl with the dressing and toss gently to coat. Sprinkle with the sesame seeds and serve immediately.

Caesar-Roasted Broccoli

Know Your Grains

Here are the basics on the grains you're most likely to find in your market (don't forget to check the bulk bins for the best prices). Cook up a batch of two or three over the weekend then use the cooked grains throughout the week as the basis of breakfast bowls, stir-fries, pilafs, salads, and more. Go ahead and mix cooked grains to create visual and textural interest in your dishes, too.

Amaranth: This staple of the ancient Aztecs is a tiny gluten-free powerhouse. It's loaded with vitamin C, calcium, iron, magnesium, and potassium and is a complete source of protein. You can cook it like porridge or polenta, or pop it for a crunchy breakfast cereal (or as an addition to homemade granola).

Brown Rice: This has become a real staple for me, and I eat it on a nearly daily basis. I find it a bit easier to digest than some other grains and it's both filling and tasty, with a nice nutty flavor. Whether long or short grain, basmati or otherwise, white rice is simply brown rice minus the bran and the germ. Brown rice is a bit higher in protein, fiber, vitamins, and minerals, but white rice has a longer shelf life and a less assertive flavor, so choose according to your preference and taste.

Barley: Barley retains its shape and nutty flavor even in soups and stews and stands up to strong-flavored ingredients well. Pearled barley is processed to reduce cooking time, but it can lose nutrition and flavor in this form, so opt for unpearled barley if available.

Buckwheat: Buckwheat is a fruit seed that's naturally gluten-free, high in fiber, and full of immune-boosting minerals like magnesium, manganese, copper, and zinc. Its flavor is strong and earthy.

Wheat: Ancient or heirloom wheat varietals like einkorn, emmer, spelt, and kamut have been getting a lot of buzz lately because they tend to be lower in gluten and higher in protein than modern varietals. Einkorn, emmer, and spelt all fall under the umbrella of farro, the Italian word for "grain with a hull," and they all have a similar nutty flavor that pairs well with salty cheese like feta (and, of course, Parmigiano!). Einkorn is thought to be the oldest and least hybridized version of wheat, while kamut or Khorasan wheat is also known as pharaoh's grain because it was discovered in ancient Egyptian tombs. It's high in fatty acids, as well as selenium, zinc, and magnesium, and may lower blood sugar and cholesterol.

Freekeh: An ancient Middle Eastern grain, freekeh is actually a form of spelt. The spelt is harvested while still green, before it has fully ripened and dried, then smoked to finish the drying process. It has a deeply complex, nutty, smoky flavor that is a fantastic base for risotto-style dishes and warm grain salads.

Grits: Slightly coarser than polenta, grits are a southern breakfast staple, but they're also a blank canvas for an any-time-of-day sweet-and-savory combination (like shrimp and grits, grits and greens, cheesy grits with sausage and pickles). Commercial grits and hominy grits have had the hull and germ removed, so opt for stone-ground grits, which are made from whole-corn kernels.

Millet: This fast-cooking, gluten-free grain is easy to digest and rich in iron, calcium, and B vitamins. It has a sunny, cornlike flavor and can be similar to pilaf or polenta in texture, depending on how much water you use to cook it.

Quinoa: The Incas called *quinoa chisaya* mama, or "mother of all grains," though it is technically a member of the grass family. Still, the seeds can be cooked just like grains—and in about 20 minutes. Naturally gluten-free, quinoa works well with lentils, fava beans, and peas. Also consider kaniwa, quinoa's smaller, sweeter, nuttier cousin, which has more iron, flavonoids, and fiber and doesn't have saponins (which give quinoa a bitter taste if you don't rinse it first).

Sorghum: In the South, sorghum is used as a molasses-like sweetener—but it's also a gluten-free cereal grain that can be cooked like risotto, popped like popcorn, or ground into flour. The spherical grain takes about an hour to cook, and stands up well in soups and stews. It's lighter than farro or barley and a good substitute for couscous.

Teff: Also known as the quinoa of Africa, this tiny grain is the smallest in the world, but it's loaded with protein, fiber, and minerals. Used to make injera, the spongy Ethiopian flatbread, teff is also typically cooked as porridge.

Fiesta Quinoa Salad

SERVES 4 TO 6

Round Swamp Farm in East Hampton, New York, makes some of the best food-to-go on Long Island, and I always stop by when I'm in the area to swap recipes and stories with Lisa Niggles, who came up with this brilliant salsa-fied salad. Its bright, fresh flavors partner perfectly with grilled chicken skewers or fish.

DRESSING

1 tablespoon finely minced garlic
½ cup fresh lime juice (from about 6 limes)
½ cup extra-virgin olive oil
1 rounded tablespoon agave syrup
1 teaspoon kosher salt
½ teaspoon freshly ground black pepper
½ teaspoon crushed red pepper flakes

SALAD

4 cups cooked organic red quinoa
½ cup cored, seeded, and diced red bell pepper
½ cup cored, seeded, and diced yellow bell pepper
1 cup cooked black beans or well-rinsed and drained canned beans
1 cup roasted corn kernels (from about 2 ears)
1 cup chopped fresh cilantro leaves
¼ to ½ cup chopped red onion
1 small jalapeño chile, seeded and finely minced
3 cups loosely packed baby arugula

For the dressing: In a blender or food processor, combine the garlic, lime juice, oil, agave, salt, pepper, and red pepper flakes and process until the mixture is emulsified.

For the salad: In a large bowl, combine the quinoa, red and yellow bell peppers, beans, corn, cilantro, onion, and jalapeño. Add the dressing and toss to coat thoroughly.

Just before serving, add the arugula and toss once more to combine.

Smashed Root Vegetables

Smashed Root Vegetables

V GF

SERVES 4

Don't overpuree this wintery mix; it should be a bit chunky so you can taste the individual veggies in every bite.

1 celery root, peeled and cut into 1-inch pieces (about 2 cups)
3 parsnips, peeled and cut into 1-inch pieces (about 2¼ cups)
2 Yukon Gold potatoes, peeled and cut into 1-inch pieces (about 2 cups)
2 garlic cloves, smashed and peeled
Kosher salt
Zest of 1 small lemon
½ teaspoon chopped fresh thyme leaves
¼ cup extra-virgin olive oil
¼ cup freshly grated Parmesan cheese

Place the celery root, parsnips, potatoes, and garlic into a large pot. Cover with cold water by an inch and add 2 tablespoons salt. Place over high heat and bring to a boil. Reduce the heat to medium and simmer for 10 to 15 minutes or until all of the vegetables are tender. Drain well and return the cooked vegetables to the pot.

Using a wooden spoon, stir the vegetables over medium heat to remove some of the excess moisture, about 4 minutes. Using a large fork or a potato masher, lightly mash the vegetables. Remove the mashed vegetables from the heat and add 1 teaspoon salt, the lemon zest, thyme, olive oil, and cheese. Mix until well combined. Serve hot.

Crispy Zucchini and Potato Pancake

V

SERVES 4 TO 6

Baked as one large pancake to serve in wedges, this blend of shredded potato and zucchini is crunchy outside, tender inside. You can also drop it into a skillet by the spoonful to make small, crisp cakes to top with crème fraîche and salmon or caviar for a very snazzy hors d'oeuvre.

Vegetable oil cooking spray
2 pounds russet potatoes, peeled and grated
2 medium zucchini, grated
2 garlic cloves, minced
½ cup plain bread crumbs
1 teaspoon chopped fresh rosemary leaves
2 large egg whites, lightly beaten
2 teaspoons kosher salt, plus more for seasoning
¼ teaspoon freshly ground black pepper, plus more for seasoning
1 tablespoon vegetable oil
1 tablespoon extra-virgin olive oil
½ cup mascarpone cheese (optional)

Place a rack in the center of the oven and preheat the oven to 450°F. Spray a baking sheet liberally with vegetable oil cooking spray.

Put the grated potatoes in a kitchen towel and the grated zucchini in another. Bring the corners of the towels together and squeeze out the moisture from the vegetables. Transfer the vegetables to a large bowl. Add the garlic, bread crumbs, rosemary, egg whites, salt, and pepper. Mix well until combined.

Heat the vegetable oil in a 12-inch nonstick skillet over medium-high heat. When hot, add the vegetable mixture to the pan and, using a spatula, press it evenly into the pan to form a pancake. Drizzle with the olive oil and cook for about 8 minutes or until the edges begin to brown.

Gently slide the pancake, cooked side down, onto the prepared baking sheet. Bake until the top of the pancake starts to brown and the edges are crispy, 20 to 25 minutes.

In a small bowl, beat the mascarpone, if using, until smooth. Season to taste with salt and pepper.

Cut the large pancake into wedges and arrange on a serving platter. Spoon some of the seasoned mascarpone on each serving.

Crispy Zucchini and Potato Pancake

Weekends & Holidays

Feeding family and friends is the reason I became involved in the food world in the first place, and few things make me happier than putting something delicious in front of an appreciative—or just hungry!—recipient. When the weekends or holidays roll around, though, putting those smiles on people's faces is almost all I think about! The spontaneity of weekday cooking, which can be a bit improvisational and free-form when it's just Jade and me at the table, goes out the window for these more special meals. I even spend a bit of time with a pad and pencil planning and refining my menu before heading out to the store. These are meals I want to get just right.

I think of this as investment cooking, and not just because the raw ingredients might be a little fancier and pricier than your average weeknight recipe; I'm usually investing a fair amount of time, too, either in preparation or long, slow roasting or braising, or all of the above. The payoff, though, is so totally worth it, both in the satisfaction I feel when I see guests gathered at the table, and later on when I use all the delicious leftovers to make entirely new and entirely speedy meals all week long.

Weekends are also the time to get a jump on making gifts from my kitchen for celebrations throughout the year. They're a way to send an important message to anyone I share them with: You mean the world to me.

Roasted Chicken with Potatoes and Leeks

GF

SERVES 4

This is the quintessential Sunday night supper. Period.

1 pound small red potatoes, halved
3 leeks, white parts only, halved lengthwise, washed well, and cut into 1-inch pieces
4 tablespoons extra-virgin olive oil
2½ teaspoons kosher salt
¼ teaspoon crushed red pepper flakes
1 teaspoon chopped fresh thyme leaves, plus 4 whole sprigs
1 teaspoon chopped fresh rosemary, plus 2 whole sprigs
1 lemon, zested and halved
1 (4-pound) chicken, innards removed if included
1 whole head of garlic, cut in half through the equator
¾ cup low-sodium chicken broth

Preheat the oven to 450°F.

In a shallow braising pan or a large ovenproof skillet, toss together the potatoes, leeks, 2 tablespoons of the olive oil, ½ teaspoon of the salt, and the red pepper flakes. Spread evenly over the bottom of the pan.

In a small bowl, mix together the chopped thyme, chopped rosemary, 1 teaspoon lemon zest, the remaining 2 teaspoons salt, and the remaining 2 tablespoons olive oil. Pat the chicken dry with a paper towel. Gently slide your fingers under the skin along the breast, being careful not to tear the skin, and rub one-third of the seasoning mixture under the skin.

Rub the remaining seasoning all over the outside and inside of the bird. Stuff the cavity with the herb sprigs, lemon halves, and garlic. Tie the legs together, crossing the ankles, using butcher's twine.

Place the dressed bird on top of the vegetables and place the pan in the oven. Roast for 55 to 60 minutes, adding the chicken broth to the bottom of the pan for the last 15 minutes of cooking. An instant-read thermometer should read 155°F in the thickest part of the thigh, and the potatoes should be fork-tender. Allow the chicken to rest for 15 minutes before carving and serving with the vegetables and pan sauce.

Making Memories

I am so fortunate to have grown up in a family that loved food and introduced me to cooking from a very young age. Spending time in the kitchen with your little ones is the perfect opportunity to teach them the basic cooking skills that will form the foundation of a lifelong love of cooking. I've always encouraged Jade to pull up a stool next to me when I cook, and she loves to help make dinner, snapping the ends off green beans, measuring out rice, setting the timer, and other tasks. Now that she's a bit older I'm starting to let her use a child-size knife, and she loves to suggest dishes for us to try.

Getting kids involved in the prep work and menu-planning process is also a great way to help them expand their culinary horizons and break them out of the chicken-nugget and pasta-with-Parm rut.

Roasted Chicken with
Potatoes and Leeks

Sunday Pot Roast

Sunday Pot Roast

GF

SERVES 6 TO 8 (OR 4, WITH LEFTOVERS)

My aunt Raffy inspired this homey all-in-one dish made with lots of fragrant herbs. It has a deep, earthy flavor.

3 garlic cloves, peeled and finely chopped
1½ teaspoons chopped fresh thyme leaves
2 teaspoons chopped fresh rosemary leaves
2 teaspoons kosher salt
¼ teaspoon freshly ground black pepper
1 (5-pound) beef chuck roast
1 tablespoon extra-virgin olive oil
1 onion, cut into 8 wedges
1 medium fennel bulb, trimmed, cored, and cut into 8 wedges
1 cup dry red wine
½ cup low-sodium beef broth
1 cup marinara sauce, homemade (see page 121) or store-bought
½ pound small Yukon Gold potatoes (about 8)

Preheat the oven to 300°F.

In a small bowl, mix together the garlic, thyme, rosemary, salt, and pepper. Rub this mixture evenly all over the chuck roast.

In a Dutch oven or heavy stockpot, heat the olive oil over high heat. Reduce to medium high and add the roast, searing the meat on all sides until golden brown all over, about 4 minutes per side. Remove the roast to a plate and add the onion and fennel to the pot. Cook, stirring often, for 3 minutes or until fragrant.

Deglaze the pot with the red wine and the beef broth and simmer for 2 to 3 minutes, scraping up any brown bits that may have stuck to the bottom. Stir in the marinara sauce. Return the roast to the pot, nestling it into the vegetables. Cover with the lid and place in the oven for 2 hours and 30 minutes, turning the meat once about halfway through.

Remove the lid from the pot and scatter the potatoes around the meat. Return the pot to the oven, uncovered, and cook for another 30 minutes or until the potatoes are cooked through and the meat is tender. Allow the pot roast to rest for 30 minutes before serving.

Reheat the braised fennel and potatoes in the pan juices, then arrange on a platter. Slice the pot roast and serve alongside the vegetables. Spoon some of the pan juices over everything before serving.

Cook Once, Eat Three Times

I've often said that I inherited my love of food from my grandfather Dino, but a lot of what I know about entertaining I've learned from my aunt Raffy. She is an amazing host who manages to make putting together a gorgeous spread for twenty look like a walk in the park. And because she is so relaxed and welcoming, everyone who comes to her parties feels instantly at ease—just like family.

The heart of her menu is almost always a one-pot dish, something that can be scaled up or down, and preferably made in advance to be reheated as needed so she can spend the day as she likes. When the weather is cold, she's likely to make a hearty stew or other beefy, rib-sticking dish, like a pot roast. It braises slowly on a bed of vegetables, and its flavor actually improves if made a day ahead of time; on the day of her get-together all she needs to do is slice the meat, puree some of the cooked vegetables and braising liquids to make a quick sauce, and return it all to the oven for a bit to heat through.

The real genius of meals like these, though, is that they provide the basis for additional meals all week long. I don't think of them as "leftovers." Instead, I regard them as an ingredient—precooked and seasoned to perfection—that can add substance and flavor to quick-and-easy weeknight meals. They give me a leg up when I need a next-to-instant sauce for pasta, topping for pizza, or addition to risotto that doesn't come from a package.

Polenta Aplenty

Today we think of polenta as synonymous with cornmeal, but the dish was first made with barley, and later with grains like farro, millet, and buckwheat, as well as peas, chestnuts, and just about anything that could be ground into a coarse meal.

At Sauce restaurant in Manhattan, chef-owner Frank Prisinzano uses polenta as the base for the "plank," which takes its inspiration from northern Italy. There, it's traditional to ladle polenta directly onto a wood table, top it with meat sauce, and eat in communal fashion without plates. Frank's version is only slightly less rustic: It's served on a wooden plank and finished with a drizzle of olive oil and more Parmesan.

When buying polenta, look for medium or medium-coarse cornmeal (steer clear of the finely ground stuff that's like flour in texture). Anything specifically labeled polenta is really just cornmeal in a different (more expensive) package. Instant polenta is par-cooked and is ready to serve in fifteen to twenty minutes. Expect to cook the coarse-ground grains for 40 minutes or longer.

Frank's Bolognese

GF

MAKES ABOUT 3½ CUPS

At Sauce in New York City, chef-owner Frank Prisinzano serves this substantial ragù over a mound of polenta, a fun and rustic presentation for a winter dinner party. It's an easy recipe to scale up, and it freezes well, so consider making a double or triple batch and storing the leftovers in the freezer.

1 tablespoon olive oil
1 pound coarsely ground beef
⅓ cup finely chopped carrot
⅓ cup finely chopped onion
⅓ cup finely chopped celery
¾ teaspoon kosher salt
¾ cup dry white wine
2 cups whole milk
1 cup unsalted beef broth
⅓ cup tomato paste
1 bay leaf
1 fresh sage sprig
Creamy Polenta (see page 219)
½ cup freshly grated Parmesan cheese
Olive oil, for drizzling

Heat the oil in a heavy pot or Dutch oven over high heat. Add the ground beef and cook until all the liquid has evaporated and the meat starts to fry in its own fat.

Add the carrot, onion, celery, and salt to the pot. As the meat is frying, use a flat-bottomed wooden spoon to scrape the pan vigorously so the meat gets golden brown but doesn't burn. When it starts to stick to the pan, reduce the heat to low and deglaze the pan with the white wine, again using your wooden spoon to scrape up all the brown bits from the bottom of the pan.

Add the milk, beef broth, and tomato paste to the pot and stir well to combine. Reduce the heat to low and simmer the Bolognese for 1 hour, until the meat is very soft and the sauce is beginning to thicken. Add the bay leaf and sage and simmer for an additional 30 minutes.

Mound the polenta on a platter or wooden board. Top with the Bolognese and sprinkle with the cheese. Drizzle with the olive oil and serve.

Frank's Bolognese on Creamy Polenta

Raffy's Polpettone Two Ways

SERVES 4 TO 6

One well-seasoned meatloaf mixture takes on a completely different character when braised in milk or marinara, and the loaves lend a layer of depth and complexity to their sauces as they cook.

2 cups diced day-old bread, crust removed
2½ cups milk, at room temperature
2 small shallots, minced
2 garlic cloves, minced
1 large egg, at room temperature
½ cup freshly grated Parmesan cheese
¼ pound thinly sliced prosciutto di Parma, chopped fine
1 pound ground turkey
2 tablespoons chopped fresh flat-leaf parsley leaves
2 tablespoons extra-virgin olive oil
2 tablespoons (¼ stick) unsalted butter
¼ teaspoon kosher salt
1½ cups marinara sauce, homemade (see page 121) or store-bought

In a large bowl, combine the bread with ½ cup of the milk and break it up with your fingers. Mix well and allow the bread to soak for 5 minutes. Add the shallots, garlic, egg, Parmesan, and prosciutto and mix with a wooden spoon to distribute the prosciutto. Add the turkey and parsley and mix well. Divide the mixture equally into 2 oblong-shaped loaves.

Heat 2 medium skillets over medium-high heat. Add 1 tablespoon of the olive oil and 1 tablespoon of the butter to each pan. Place one loaf in each of the pans and cook them on all sides until golden brown all around, 10 to 12 minutes total.

Season the remaining 2 cups milk with the salt and add to one of the skillets. Bring to a simmer over medium-high heat. Add the marinara to the second skillet and bring to a simmer as well. Reduce the heat under both skillets to medium low, cover, and braise the meat loaves for about 25 minutes, carefully turning them about halfway through. They are done when an instant-read thermometer inserted in the center of each loaf registers 160°F. Transfer them to a cutting board and allow to rest for 10 minutes before slicing.

To serve, return the skillet with the milk sauce to medium heat and simmer until reduced by half, stirring occasionally. It will look slightly curdled, which is fine. When somewhat thickened, use an immersion blender to blend the sauce until emulsified and creamy. Transfer to a small pitcher. Reheat the marinara if necessary, using a wooden spoon to scrape up any brown bits from the pan, and transfer to a second pitcher. Serve the polpettone with their respective sauces.

Baby Back Ribs with Spicy Plum BBQ Sauce

GF

MAKES 2 RACKS

2 racks of pork baby back ribs, membrane removed (about 5 pounds total)
2 tablespoons (packed) light brown sugar
2 teaspoons paprika
1 tablespoon kosher salt

SAUCE

1 tablespoon extra-virgin olive oil
1 small onion, diced
1 garlic clove, chopped
1- to 2-inch piece of ginger, peeled and chopped
4 plums (about 1 pound), pitted and chopped
⅛ teaspoon ground allspice
¾ cup apple cider vinegar
½ cup light brown sugar
½ teaspoon kosher salt
1 habanero chile pepper, halved

Preheat the oven to 300°F.

Place the ribs on two sheets of aluminum foil large enough to wrap around them and seal. In a small bowl, mix together the sugar, paprika, and salt. Rub the ribs evenly on all sides with the mixture. Bring the foil up and around the rubbed ribs and crimp closed. Place on a rimmed baking sheet and bake in the preheated oven for about 3 hours or until tender but not falling apart. Remove from the oven and allow them to cool slightly, about 30 minutes.

To make the sauce: Heat a medium saucepan over medium heat. Add the oil, onion, garlic, and ginger to the pan and cook, stirring often with a wooden spoon, until the onions are soft and fragrant, about 4 minutes. Add the plums and allspice and stir to coat with the flavors. Add the vinegar, sugar, salt, and habanero and stir to combine. Bring to a simmer and reduce the heat to low to maintain a gentle simmer. Simmer for about 20 minutes or until the plums are very soft. Remove the habanero. Using an immersion blender, puree the sauce until it is as smooth or as chunky as you like.

Preheat a grill to medium heat. Brush the ribs all over with the sauce. Oil the grill and place the ribs meat side down until lightly charred. Flip the ribs and cook on the other side. Brush both sides with more sauce and continue to cook until the sauce is thick and sticky and golden brown. Serve with more sauce on the side if desired.

Cook's Note: **Alternatively, you can brown the ribs under the broiler on high. Keep brushing the ribs every 4 minutes until the sauce is thick and sticky.**

Baby Back Ribs with Spicy Plum BBQ Sauce

Summer Celebrations

There's so much that's fabulous about the Fourth of July. It's a happy accident of American history that our Founding Fathers declared independence from the British during the summer, giving us a chance to celebrate our nation's freedoms when the weather is at its best for being outside, and produce is nearing its peak. (Can you imagine if we celebrated the Fourth in January?)

When it comes to entertaining, though, it's the perfect time to go old-school with steamed lobsters, an old-fashioned clambake, and all the trimmings.

A fire heats the rocks, and once it has burned down to embers, layers of seaweed and shellfish go on top and then get covered with a tarp or dampened burlap to trap the heat and steam. It's a complicated operation that involves permits and shovels, and while it's impressive, it's also hard to control the cooking times with a great deal of precision.

I prefer to steam the lobsters separately to ensure that they don't overcook for even a minute, and serve them with an herbed aioli. While they steam I cook the clams, sausage, and veggies together in a big pot, adding the ingredients in order from the longest to the quickest cooking, so everything comes out done to perfection. The broth in the pot may be the best part: briny, smoky from the sausage, infused with butter—just the thing to dip the clams in or even hunks of good bread. Pass around a platter of crostini while the shellfish is working, open a crisp white wine, and you have yourself a world-class seafood feast, no beach required.

Stovetop Clambake

GF

SERVES 6

Traditionally, a clambake is cooked in a stone-lined pit dug in the sand. Here's a much easier and superfast way to enjoy this summertime classic any time of the year. Make sure you use the freshest corn you can find, and feel free to substitute spicy andouille sausage for the kielbasa if you like dishes with some heat.

2 tablespoons extra-virgin olive oil
1 medium onion, halved and thinly sliced
1 teaspoon Old Bay seasoning
½ teaspoon kosher salt
2 cups dry white wine
1½ pounds small red bliss potatoes
1 pound smoked kielbasa, sliced into 1-inch pieces
4 ears of corn, shucked and sliced into thirds
2 pounds medium-size clams, such as littleneck or cherrystone, scrubbed well
2 tablespoons (¼ stick) unsalted butter
1 teaspoon smoked salt
2 lemons, cut into wedges

In a large stockpot, heat the oil over medium-high heat. Add the onion, Old Bay, and salt and cook, stirring occasionally, until the onion softens and begins to brown, about 8 minutes. Add ¼ cup of the wine and the potatoes, then cover and cook for 10 minutes.

Layer the sausage over the potatoes, then add the corn, clams, and the remaining 1¾ cups wine. Bring to a simmer, then cover and cook for 15 to 20 minutes, until all the clams have opened.

Using tongs, transfer the clams, corn, potatoes, and sausage to a large platter, discarding any unopened clams. Strain the liquid through a fine-mesh strainer into a bowl; add the butter to the bowl, swirling it until it melts and incorporates into the liquid. Divide the liquid among small bowls for dipping or pour it over the clambake, and sprinkle with the smoked salt. Serve with the lemon wedges.

Stovetop Clambake

Fourth of July Pizza

SERVES 4

Why make a round pizza when this flag-themed rectangle is so much fun—and so much easier to cut into app-sized squares? You'll have bites for veggie lovers, pepperoni fans, and plain cheese folks all from the same pie.

FOR THE SPINACH

2 tablespoons extra-virgin olive oil
2 garlic cloves, smashed and peeled
5 ounces baby spinach, chopped
½ teaspoon kosher salt

TO ASSEMBLE

2 tablespoons flour
1 pound pizza dough (see page 64)
1 tablespoons extra-virgin olive oil
¾ cup pizza sauce
2 cups shredded mozzarella cheese
1 tablespoon ricotta cheese
28 slices pepperoni

Preheat the oven to 500°F. Position a rack in the lower third of the oven.

Heat a medium skillet over medium-high heat. Add the oil and the garlic and cook until fragrant and lightly browned. Add the spinach and the salt and cook, stirring often, until the spinach is wilted, 1 to 2 minutes. Remove from the heat and drain the spinach in a fine mesh strainer. Set aside.

Sprinkle 1 tablespoon of flour on a clean work surface. Place the dough on top and sprinkle it with the remaining tablespoon of flour. Roll the dough out to a 15 × 10-inch rectangle. Drizzle the oil on a rimmed baking sheet and spread it evenly using a pastry brush. Transfer the dough to the prepared baking sheet.

Spread the sauce over the entire crust. Sprinkle with the mozzarella, creating a 5 × 4-inch rectangle in the upper left corner with slightly less cheese. Squeeze the liquid from the spinach and spread the spinach evenly over the upper left corner. Dot small clumps of ricotta cheese over the spinach to form the "stars." Arrange the pepperoni over the remaining surface of the pizza in horizontal rows, slightly overlapping the slices to form the stripes.

Bake for 12 to 15 minutes or until the crust is golden brown and cooked though and the cheese is bubbly.

Steamed Lobster with Lemon-Parsley Aioli

GF

SERVES 4

If you have leftovers from this recipe, make lobster rolls for lunch the next day by mixing together the shellfish and aioli with some chopped celery and serving on hot dog buns.

Kosher salt
4 (1½-pound) lobsters
⅔ cup mayonnaise
2 tablespoons grated lemon zest
¼ cup fresh lemon juice (from 2 lemons)
2 teaspoons Dijon mustard
¼ teaspoon kosher salt
⅔ cup fresh flat-leaf parsley leaves, chopped

In a very large pot, bring 3 inches of well-salted water to a boil. Add the lobsters, cover tightly, and cook for 12 minutes or until they are bright red. Remove the lobsters from the pot (you can let them stand in the sink) and allow to cool slightly.

While the lobsters steam, in a medium bowl whisk together the mayonnaise, lemon zest and juice, mustard, and salt. Fold in the chopped parsley.

Serve the lobsters with a small bowl of the aioli for dipping.

Steamed Lobster with
Lemon-Parsley Aioli

Turkey Breast "Porchetta" with Brown and Wild Rice Dressing

Thanksgiving

People are often surprised to learn that I didn't start celebrating Thanksgiving until I was well into my teens, even though I moved to the United States from Italy when I was seven. To my Italian parents, Thanksgiving was just another Thursday, and dinner was just another meal. To my brothers, sister, and me, the best part of the holiday was getting an extra two days off from school!

All that changed, though, when my aunt Raffy and my grandfather Dino married Americans. Buzz and Martha both loved Thanksgiving, and my grandfather loved having an excuse to gather the extended family together. Slowly but surely we began to incorporate American traditions into our own family celebrations, and now Thanksgiving is one of my favorite times of the year.

My Thanksgiving menus reflect all of this history and cross-cultural influences: American traditional with an Italian accent. I always try to include corn on the menu in some form as a nod to the first Thanksgiving, whether it's a corn soufflé, spicy cornbread, or herbed polenta—the Italian version of mashed potatoes. And because the Thanksgiving table wouldn't be complete without the tangy flavors of cranberry sauce, I top a winter greens salad with dried cranberries and orange segments in a sweet-tart balsamic vinaigrette. The centerpiece is, of course, turkey, but whether rolled and tied in the manner of porchetta or roasted with aromatic herbs, there's always a hint of my Italian heritage at work.

Turkey Breast
"Porchetta"

Turkey Breast "Porchetta"

SERVES 4 TO 6

Carving a turkey in front of your assembled friends and family is rarely a lot of fun. This boned, stuffed, and rolled breast, made in the style of stuffed and roasted pork, is tender on the inside and crispy on the outside. It's also a dream to slice and serve. Note that the turkey breast is seasoned a day before roasting.

1½ teaspoons fennel seeds
2 teaspoon kosher salt
1 teaspoon orange zest
1 (3½-pound) boneless, skinless turkey breast, butterflied
¼ cup panko bread crumbs
¼ teaspoon crushed red pepper flakes
3 tablespoons extra-virgin olive oil
1 small fennel bulb, cored and cut into ¼-inch dice
1 shallot, minced
1 small apple, cored and cut into ⅓-inch dice
1 tablespoon chopped fresh rosemary leaves

The day before roasting: Begin by chopping ½ teaspoon of the fennel seeds. In a small bowl, combine them with 1¼ teaspoons of the salt and the orange zest. Rub both sides of the turkey with the salt mixture. Place the turkey breast in a gallon-size plastic storage bag and refrigerate overnight.

The day of roasting: Preheat the oven to 400°F. Remove the turkey breast from the refrigerator and allow it to come to room temperature for 20 minutes before cooking.

Meanwhile, in a 12-inch ovenproof sauté pan, toast the panko over medium heat, stirring with a rubber spatula until golden brown. Remove to a medium bowl and add the remaining teaspoon fennel seeds, the red pepper flakes, and ¼ teaspoon of the salt. Set aside.

To the same pan over medium-high heat, add 1 tablespoon of the olive oil. Add the diced fennel, shallot, apple, rosemary, and the remaining ½ teaspoon salt. Sauté until the fennel softens, about 5 minutes. Add to the bowl with the panko and toss to combine. Wipe out the pan and reserve to sear the turkey.

Place the butterflied turkey breast, opened, in front of you. Spread the fennel-panko filling evenly over the turkey. Roll up the turkey breast to maintain the shape. Tie with twine in 4 spots about 2 inches apart. Place the sauté pan over medium-high heat and add the remaining 2 tablespoons oil. Place the turkey breast in the hot pan and sear on all sides until golden brown, about 3 minutes per side. Place the pan in the preheated oven and roast for about 40 minutes or until an instant-read thermometer placed in the thickest part of the breast reads 155°F. Allow the porchetta to rest for 15 minute before slicing.

Divide and Conquer

Breaking things up makes them more manageable 99 percent of the time, and it's no different when it comes to tackling one of the most gargantuan tasks on any cook's calendar, the Thanksgiving turkey.

Cooking a whole turkey is unwieldy, it monopolizes the oven for hours, and, worst of all, it often results in breast meat that's dried out and overcooked (or dark meat that is less than completely done). To right this historical wrong, try cooking the breast separately from the legs.

Ask your butcher to portion the turkey for you, or, if you know your way around the anatomy of the bird, tackle it yourself. Cut the leg-and-thigh portions away from the carcass and then separate the drumstick from the thigh for four pieces in total. Next, remove the wings and set aside for another use. Finally, smooth the breast skin over the meat before cutting directly down along either side of the breastbone and along the ribs, freeing both breast fillets.

You can stuff and roll the breast, opposite, or rub it with flavorful seasonings and roast it whole (page 246). Legs and thighs can be roasted, braised or, for the most decadent dish of all, slow cooked in duck fat then pan fried to crisp perfection.

Herb-Roasted Turkey Breast

GF

SERVES 6 TO 8

If you are not a fan of turkey because it is too bland and dry, this is the holiday feast for you. Roasting the breast separately with an unctuous rub of herby duck fat ensures it will be moist and cooked to perfection. The drippings will also make *the* most decadent gravy you've ever tasted.

HERB-ROASTED TURKEY BREAST

½ turkey breast (about 3 pounds)
2 teaspoons finely chopped fresh thyme
2 teaspoons finely chopped fresh rosemary
¼ teaspoon crushed red pepper flakes
2 garlic cloves, finely chopped
3 tablespoons duck fat, warmed gently to a liquid
1 teaspoon kosher salt

DUCK FAT GRAVY

2 tablespoons all-purpose flour
3 tablespoons white wine
1 cup low-sodium chicken broth

For the turkey breast: Remove the turkey from the refrigerator 30 minutes before cooking. Preheat the oven to 400°F.

In a small bowl, mix together the thyme, rosemary, red pepper flakes, garlic, and duck fat. Season the turkey evenly with the salt and rub the herb mixture all over. Heat a medium skillet over medium-high heat. Sear the turkey breast, skin side down, until the skin gets crispy and golden brown, about 4 minutes. Flip the turkey and sear for another 4 minutes.

Transfer the breast to a rimmed baking sheet along with the duck fat from the pan. Roast for 35 to 45 minutes, flipping the breast every 15 minutes and basting with the juices. An instant-read thermometer should read 155°F when done. Transfer to a cutting board to rest for 10 minutes before slicing.

For the gravy: In a small saucepan, warm 4 tablespoons of the turkey drippings over medium heat. Whisk in the flour until a smooth paste forms. Add the wine and whisk until smooth. Slowly whisk in the chicken broth and continue to cook over medium heat, whisking often. Bring to a simmer and cook for 5 minutes. Strain if desired.

Turkey Confit

Turkey Confit

GF

SERVES 4

Duck confit, which is duck legs braised and preserved in duck fat, is popular throughout France. Here's how to use the same technique to produce sensationally crisp, decadent turkey legs. Leftovers are spectacular in stir-fries, grain salads, and risottos.

¼ cup kosher salt
1 tablespoon sugar
½ teaspoon freshly cracked black peppercorns
2 bay leaves, crushed
10 fresh thyme sprigs
Leaves from 2 fresh rosemary sprigs (stems discarded)
2 turkey legs (about 2½ pounds)
2 turkey thighs (about 2½ pounds)
4 (7-ounce) containers of duck fat
1 head of garlic, top third cut off and discarded, unpeeled

In a small bowl, mix together the salt, sugar, pepper, bay leaves, thyme sprigs, and rosemary leaves. Place the turkey legs and thighs in a 9 x 13-inch baking dish. With the tip of a knife, cut 4 slits around each leg and thigh. Sprinkle the salt mixture over all sides of the turkey. Cover with plastic wrap and refrigerate for at least 24 hours or up to 2 days.

Preheat the oven to 250°F. Remove the turkey from the refrigerator 30 minutes before starting to cook. In a large Dutch oven, warm the duck fat and head of garlic over medium heat. Meanwhile, rinse the turkey well to remove the excess salt mixture. Dry very well with paper towels.

Carefully add the turkey to the warmed duck fat. The fat should cover the meat. When you see the first bubble come to the surface of the oil, cover the pan and place in the oven for about 3½ hours or until the meat is extremely tender. Allow to cool to room temperature. Store the confit completely submerged in the fat in the refrigerator until ready to use or for up to a month.

To serve, preheat the oven to 425°F. Remove the turkey from the fat and scrape off as much excess fat as possible. Arrange the turkey on a rimmed baking sheet with 2 tablespoons of the duck fat and place in the oven for about 40 minutes, rotating every 15 minutes to crisp the skin evenly.

Monte Cristo Sandwiches

Monte Cristo Sandwiches

SERVES 4

The effort we all put into hosting the Thanksgiving meal shouldn't stop paying dividends once we've said good-bye to the last guest and returned the good china and silver to their storage places. An overstuffed turkey sandwich is as much a part of the post-Thanksgiving game plan as watching football on TV; this one just happens to be spectacularly good.

½ cup cranberry sauce
1 tablespoon Dijon mustard
½ teaspoon chopped fresh rosemary leaves
8 slices brioche bread
8 thin slices Swiss cheese
6 ounces cooked turkey breast, sliced
4 large eggs, at room temperature
¾ cup heavy cream, at room temperature
⅛ teaspoon kosher salt
2 tablespoons extra-virgin olive oil
3 tablespoons confectioners' sugar

In a small bowl, mix together the cranberry sauce, mustard, and rosemary. Lay out the slices of bread. Divide the mustard mixture evenly over the 8 slices of bread and spread almost to the edges. Divide the cheese slices among the bread. Divide the turkey among 4 of the cheese-topped slices of bread. Cover the turkey-topped halves with the cheese-topped halves to make 4 sandwiches.

In a medium bowl, whisk together the eggs, cream, and salt.

Heat a large skillet over medium heat. Add the oil to the pan and heat for 1 minute. Working with one sandwich at a time, dip both sides of the sandwich in the egg batter and place directly into the hot pan. Repeat with the remaining sandwiches. Cover with a lid and allow to cook for 3 to 4 minutes or until the first side is golden brown.

Remove the lid, flip each sandwich, and continue to cook on the remaining side until golden brown and the cheese is melted, approximately another 4 minutes. Cook in batches if needed. Sprinkle one side of each sandwich with confectioners' sugar and serve warm.

Holiday Stress Reliever

If you've stood at the stove for hours on end, you know what a toll it can take on your back. Aches, pains, strains—it can all add up and make a food-centered holiday less festive. Fortunately, my sister, Eloisa, has just the cure to help get the kinks out, and it takes less than a minute.

It's a yoga stretch called "heart opener" and it's great to use when you've been stuck in one stressful posture for too long—in front of the stove, at your computer, wherever. Here's how you do it:

Standing with your feet hip-distance apart, reach your hands behind you, then, one hand in a fist, clasp them together at the base of your back. Looking straight ahead, lift your clasped hands as high as you can behind you, pulling your shoulder blades together. Hold for five full breaths.

If you want more of a stretch, try bending forward, folding your body over your legs, and letting gravity pull your clasped hands behind and above you, toward the floor. Whether or not you opt for this extra stretch, you'll end up feeling reinvigorated, refreshed, and ready to tackle that next course.

Brown and Wild Rice Dressing

Brown and Wild Rice Dressing with Mushrooms and Brussels Sprouts

GF

SERVES 8 TO 10

Holidays can be a tough time to please everyone, especially if you are trying to accommodate special dietary needs. This colorful, flavorful dressing just happens to be gluten-free, but it's no compromise at all. Be sure to buy plain wild rice, not a pilaf or rice blend.

8 ounces applewood-smoked bacon slices, cut crosswise into ½-inch-wide strips
4½ cups low-sodium chicken broth
3 tablespoons chopped fresh thyme leaves
1¼ cups organic brown rice (I used Lundberg's short-grain gluten-free; about 8.6 ounces)
1¼ cups wild rice (about 7.6 ounces)
6 tablespoons (¾ stick) unsalted butter
2 (10-ounce) bags pearl onions, blanched in boiling water for 2 minutes, then peeled
1½ pounds portobello mushrooms, dark gills scraped away and discarded, mushrooms coarsely chopped (7 to 8 cups of ¾-inch pieces)
1 pound Brussels sprouts, root ends trimmed and discarded, sprouts halved lengthwise, then thinly sliced crosswise (about 4 cups)
Kosher salt and freshly ground black pepper
¾ cup hazelnuts, toasted (see Cook's Note, page 75), husked, and coarsely chopped (optional)

In a large heavy skillet over medium heat, cook the bacon until crisp. Using a slotted spoon, transfer the bacon to paper towels to drain. Discard all but 2 tablespoons of the drippings from the skillet; reserve the skillet with the drippings.

In a large heavy saucepan, combine the broth and 1 tablespoon of the thyme and bring to a boil over medium-high heat. Add the brown rice and return to a boil. Reduce the heat to medium low; cover and simmer for 10 minutes. Add the wild rice and bring to boil. Reduce the heat to medium low; cover and simmer until all the rice is tender (but still slightly chewy), about 40 minutes longer.

Meanwhile, add 1 tablespoon of the butter to the bacon drippings in the reserved skillet and heat over medium-high heat. Add the pearl onions and sauté until golden and tender, 7 to 8 minutes. Using a slotted spoon, transfer the onions to a small bowl and set aside. Add 2 tablespoons of the butter and the mushrooms to the skillet and sauté until the mushrooms are brown and tender, 7 to 8 minutes. Stir the Brussels sprouts into the skillet with the mushrooms and sauté until tender but still bright green, about 5 minutes; sprinkle generously with salt and pepper. Add the rice mixture, remaining 3 tablespoons butter, remaining 2 tablespoons thyme, and reserved pearl onions to the skillet and toss gently to blend. Season to taste with salt and pepper. Transfer the stuffing to a large bowl. Sprinkle with the bacon and hazelnuts, if desired, and serve.

Persimmon-Pumpkin Pie

V

SERVES 8

Pumpkin pie is the obvious choice for Thanksgiving, but why be obvious? Coloring a bit outside the lines is so much more enjoyable. Adding the slightly astringent, floral flavor of persimmon to this pie filling and brushing the crust with a bit of apricot preserves adds brightness, and persimmon slices just look cool.

CRUST

Vegetable oil cooking spray
1⅓ cups all-purpose flour
½ cup confectioners' sugar
¼ teaspoon fine salt
8 tablespoons (1 stick) chilled unsalted butter, diced
3 tablespoons mascarpone cheese, chilled
2 to 3 tablespoons apricot preserves

FILLING

2 ripe Fuyu persimmons, trimmed, peeled, and cut into 1-inch pieces, or 1 cup persimmon pulp from 2 very ripe Hachiya persimmons (each 6 to 7 ounces; see Cook's Note)
1 cup canned pumpkin puree (not pumpkin pie filling)
½ cup granulated sugar
⅓ cup mascarpone cheese, at room temperature
⅓ cup heavy cream, at room temperature
¼ teaspoon fine salt
1 teaspoon ground cinnamon
1 tablespoon cornstarch
3 large eggs, at room temperature

Confectioners' sugar, for dusting

For the crust: Preheat the oven to 350°F. Lightly spray a 9-inch glass or ceramic pie dish with vegetable oil spray. In a food processor, blend the flour, confectioners' sugar, and salt until combined. Add the butter and mascarpone cheese and blend until moist clumps form.

Gather the dough into a ball. Drop 2-inch pieces of dough over the bottom and sides of the pie dish. Using moist fingertips, press the dough together to form a smooth crust. Using the tines of a fork, prick the dough all over.

Bake the crust until the edges are browned and the center of the crust is pale golden, about 25 minutes. Transfer the crust to a work surface. Brush the bottom and sides of the crust with apricot preserves. Place on a wire rack to cool.

For the filling: In a food processor, combine the persimmon pieces or pulp and the pumpkin. Blend until smooth. Add the sugar, mascarpone cheese, cream, salt, cinnamon, cornstarch, and eggs. Blend until smooth. Pour the filling into the cooked crust.

Bake until slits or cracks appear around the edges and the center is set, about 35 minutes. Cool the pie on a wire rack. (If making one day ahead, bake and cool to room temperature. Cover loosely with plastic wrap and refrigerate.) Just before serving, dust the top of the pie with confectioners' sugar. Cut into wedges and serve.

Cook's Note: To remove the pulp from Hachiya persimmons, cut off the top of the fruit with a knife and scoop out the pulp with a spoon.

Persimmon-Pumpkin Pie

Spiced Apple Walnut Cake with Cream Cheese Icing

V

SERVES 10 TO 12

This cake keeps well for several days thanks to the apples and oil, which add moisture and prevent it from becoming dry as it sits. Serve a slice with hot cider for an afternoon pick-me-up.

Butter, for greasing the pan
All-purpose flour, for dusting

CAKE
3 medium green apples, such as Granny Smith, peeled, cored, and diced into ¼- to ½-inch pieces
1½ cups pure maple syrup
3 large eggs, at room temperature
¾ cup (packed) light brown sugar
¾ cup vegetable oil
1 tablespoon pure vanilla extract
3 cups all-purpose flour
1½ teaspoons baking powder
1½ teaspoons baking soda
1 tablespoon ground cinnamon
½ teaspoon ground nutmeg
½ teaspoon ground ginger
½ teaspoon fine sea salt
1 cup chopped walnuts

ICING
1 cup confectioners' sugar
¼ cup heavy cream
4 ounces cream cheese, at room temperature
2 teaspoons pure vanilla extract

For the cake: Place a rack in the center of the oven and preheat the oven to 350°F. Liberally butter and flour a 10-inch fluted tube or Bundt pan. Set aside.

In a large bowl, mix together the apples, maple syrup, eggs, brown sugar, oil, and vanilla. In a separate medium bowl, whisk together the flour, baking powder, baking soda, cinnamon, nutmeg, ginger, and salt. In batches, mix the dry ingredients into the apple mixture. Stir in the walnuts.

Pour the mixture into the prepared pan. Bake until a cake tester or skewer inserted into the cake comes out clean, 55 to 60 minutes. Cool for 15 minutes and invert onto a wire rack to cool completely, about 1 hour.

For the icing: In a food processor, combine the confectioners' sugar, cream, cream cheese, 3 tablespoons water, and the vanilla. Process until smooth, adding more water, 1 teaspoon at a time, until the icing is pourable. Spoon the icing over the cake and allow to set for 20 minutes before slicing.

Holiday Entertaining

Holidays and the entertaining associated with them just inevitably seem to add up to stress, no matter how well-intentioned you are. Here are some FAQs and strategies for keeping it all manageable.

Do you have any time-saving tips when preparing for a big holiday feast?

It's all about organization. I always make lists about what needs to be done and when. The more time you spend planning ahead, even making some of the dishes ahead, the fewer extra trips to the store, last-minute emergencies, and pre-party meltdowns there will be, and that ultimately saves time. Do a little bit each day so you can complete each task efficiently. Make and roll out your piecrusts in advance. Set the table and lay out all your platters a day or two ahead. Blanch the vegetables and refrigerate in plastic bags.

I'm helpless at arranging centerpieces; any ideas for a festive holiday table?

I love to incorporate ingredients I am cooking with into my centerpieces . . . like baby pumpkins, herbs, pomegranates, and persimmons mixed with leaves, pinecones, and branches from my yard. Fill a few vases with kumquats and tealights or cordless string lights, to add unexpected sparkle.

I'm always worried about inviting guests who don't know one another. Is there anything I can do to make sure people are mingling? How do you feel about assigned seating?

A well-stocked little bar cart that lets people assemble their own cocktails is always a good conversation starter. I also love making and serving infused vodkas—fennel, tangerine, or cranberry. As for assigned seating, I'm for it. People are sometimes anxious about sitting in the right place. The question that always comes up is, do you split up the couples or not? Here's a fun solution: From a deck of cards, pull out one card for every guest, starting with the ace and continuing in ascending order. Then shuffle them and let everyone pick one. The ace sits at the head of the table, with number two to her left, and so on. It's a random way of seating guests.

Rosemary Garlic–Rubbed Beef Tenderloin with Red Wine–Rosemary Butter

GF

SERVES 6 TO 8

When I want to serve my guests something special and elegant, but I still have my eye on the clock, I turn to beef tenderloin, which cooks in just thirty minutes. What makes this version special is the red wine–rosemary compound butter; melt a little bit onto each slice of beef.

RED WINE–ROSEMARY BUTTER

½ cup dry red wine
1 fresh rosemary sprig
8 tablespoons (1 stick) unsalted butter, at room temperature
½ teaspoon kosher salt

BEEF TENDERLOIN

3 tablespoons olive oil
3 garlic cloves, minced
1 tablespoon finely chopped fresh rosemary leaves
1 tablespoon kosher salt
½ teaspoon freshly ground black pepper
1 (3-pound) center-cut beef tenderloin, trimmed and tied

For the butter: Place the wine and rosemary sprig in a small saucepan over medium heat. Bring the wine to a boil and then simmer until the wine has reduced to a syrup and measures approximately 2 tablespoons, about 20 minutes. Allow the wine to cool to room temperature and discard the herb sprig. Place the butter and salt in a food processor and pulse to combine. Add the wine and process the butter until smooth, about 1 minute.

Scrape the butter into a line on a large sheet of parchment paper. Fold the parchment over the butter and drag a clean spatula down along the line of butter to push it into a log. Twist both ends of the parchment to seal the ends and refrigerate the butter until ready to use, at least 1 hour.

For the tenderloin: Place an oven rack in the center of the oven and preheat the oven to 400°F.

In a small bowl, combine 2 tablespoons of the oil with the garlic, rosemary, salt, and pepper and rub all over the tenderloin. Heat the remaining tablespoon of oil in a large skillet over medium-high heat. Sear the tenderloin on all sides until browned, about 3 minutes per side.

Transfer the skillet to the oven and roast for 30 to 35 minutes or until an instant-read thermometer inserted into the thickest part of the meat reads 125°F, for medium rare. Remove from the oven and transfer the meat to a cutting board. Cover the roast loosely with foil and let it rest for 20 minutes.

To serve, slice the meat into ¼-inch-thick slices and arrange on a platter. Slice the butter into ⅛-inch-thick rounds and arrange across the warm meat slices.

Rosemary Garlic-Rubbed Beef Tenderloin

Noodle Paella

Noodle Paella

SERVES 6

A seafood stew like this one is a typical offering for Christmas Eve dinner in Italian households everywhere. This variation on a traditional Spanish paella features whole-wheat pasta, giving it a wholesome Italian spin.

3 tablespoons extra-virgin olive oil
1 medium fennel bulb, cored and chopped
1 medium red bell pepper, cored, seeded, and diced
1 small onion, chopped
6 large garlic cloves, thinly sliced
Kosher salt and freshly ground black pepper
3 (8-ounce) bottles clam juice
1 (15-ounce) can diced tomatoes in juice
3 bay leaves
1 teaspoon smoked paprika
¼ teaspoon crumbled saffron threads
¼ teaspoon crushed red pepper flakes
8 ounces whole-wheat spaghetti, broken into 1-inch pieces
10 small littleneck clams, scrubbed
10 mussels, scrubbed and debearded
12 large shrimp, peeled and deveined
8 ounces halibut, cut into 1-inch cubes
⅓ cup chopped fresh flat-leaf parsley leaves

In a 5-quart saucepan or Dutch oven, heat the oil over medium-high heat. Add the fennel, bell pepper, onion, and garlic to the pan. Season with ¼ teaspoon each of salt and black pepper. Cook until the vegetables are just tender, about 5 minutes.

Add the clam juice, the tomatoes with juices, bay leaves, paprika, saffron, and red pepper flakes. Bring the mixture to a simmer.

Add the spaghetti and cook, uncovered and stirring occasionally, until almost tender, about 9 minutes.

Add another ¼ teaspoon each of salt and black pepper. Add the clams, mussels, shrimp, and halibut. Cover and cook until the clams and mussels open and the shrimp are pink and cooked through, 5 to 6 minutes. Discard the bay leaves and any unopened clams or mussels. Season with salt and pepper to taste. Mix in the parsley and serve.

Me and my brother Dino waiting for Santa

Buon Natale

In Italian families Christmas Eve is celebrated with the Feast of Seven Fishes, an observance that was originally intended as a form of fasting before the holiday, but is now an excuse to serve fish, shellfish, and other creatures of the sea in a variety of delicious ways. I still carry on this tradition, though with fewer courses, a salad, and, of course, a dessert or two. No matter what, dessert is always the Italian classic, struffoli.

Struffoli (page 258) is a mixture of cooked dough balls and nuts bound with a flavored honey syrup that's then formed into a towering cone or ring and decorated with candies and other goodies. While popular all over Italy, struffoli is made differently from region to region. In the northern part of the country, hazelnuts, a local product, are used. Italians from the south, where hazelnuts were more expensive, added little bits of cooked dough to the mixture as a way to extend the pricey nuts. For as long as I can remember I've gotten together with my aunt Raffy to make struffoli for our Christmas Eve dinner, and now I'm teaching Jade. I usually throw in a couple of extra desserts as well, since struffoli is more centerpiece than delicacy in my book!

Struffoli

V

MAKES 1

You can build the struffoli in a mound or ring; in Naples, where my family is from, an inverted glass is used as a base in order to form a tall pyramid. The glass is removed before the struffoli is served.

DOUGH

- 2 cups all-purpose flour, plus extra for dusting and dredging
- 2 teaspoons grated lemon zest
- 2 teaspoons grated orange zest
- 3 tablespoons sugar
- ½ teaspoon fine sea salt
- ¼ teaspoon baking powder
- 4 tablespoons (½ stick) unsalted butter, cut into ½-inch pieces, at room temperature
- 3 large eggs
- 1 tablespoon white wine
- 1 teaspoon pure vanilla extract
- Canola oil, for frying

ASSEMBLY

- 1 cup honey
- ½ cup sugar
- 1 tablespoon fresh lemon juice (from 1 lemon)
- 1½ cups skinned hazelnuts, toasted (see Cook's Note)
- Vegetable oil cooking spray
- Sugar sprinkles, candied almonds, or dragées, for decoration
- Confectioners' sugar, for dusting (optional)

For the dough: In a food processor, pulse together the flour, lemon zest, orange zest, sugar, salt, and baking powder. Add the butter and pulse until the mixture resembles coarse meal. Add the eggs, wine, and vanilla. Pulse until the mixture forms a ball. Wrap the dough in plastic wrap and refrigerate for 30 minutes.

Cut the dough into 4 equal-size pieces. On a lightly floured surface, roll out each piece of dough until ¼ inch thick. Cut each piece of dough into ½-inch-wide strips. Cut each strip of pastry into ½-inch pieces. Roll each piece of dough into a small ball about the size of a hazelnut. Lightly dredge the dough balls in flour, shaking off any excess.

In a large heavy saucepan, pour enough oil to fill the pan about a third of the way. Heat over medium until a deep-fry thermometer inserted in the oil reaches 375°F. (If you don't have a thermometer, a cube of bread will brown in about 3 minutes at the desired temperature.) In batches, fry the dough until lightly golden, 2 to 3 minutes.

Transfer the dough balls to a paper towel–lined plate to drain. (The remaining rested and quartered dough can also be rolled on a floured work surface into ½-inch-thick logs and cut into equal-size ½-inch pieces. The dough pieces can then be rolled into small balls and fried as above.)

For assembly: In a large saucepan, combine the honey, sugar, and lemon juice over medium heat. Bring to a boil and cook, stirring occasionally, until the sugar is dissolved, about 3 minutes. Remove the pan from the heat. Add the fried dough and hazelnuts and stir until coated in the honey mixture. Allow the mixture to cool in the pan for 2 minutes.

Spray the outside of a small, straight-sided water glass with vegetable oil spray and place in the center of a round platter. Using a large spoon or damp hands, arrange the struffoli and hazelnuts around the glass to form a wreath or pyramid shape. Drizzle any remaining honey mixture over the struffoli. Allow to set for 2 hours (can be made 1 day in advance).

Decorate with sprinkles and candied almonds, and dust with confectioners' sugar, if using. Remove the glass from the center of the platter and serve.

Cook's Note: To toast the hazelnuts, preheat the oven to 350°F. Arrange the nuts in a single layer on a rimmed baking sheet. Bake until lightly toasted, 8 to 10 minutes. Cool completely before using. (Use this method also to toast walnuts, pecans, and almonds. The nuts are ready when you can just smell their aroma; do not leave the kitchen while they are in the oven, because they can easily burn!)

Struffoli

Oysters with Prosecco Mignonette

GF

SERVES 4

Opening raw oysters takes a bit of finesse and elbow grease, but if you're not up for the job, most fishmongers will shuck them for you; just purchase them right before you plan to serve and transport them carefully, as oysters can spoil quickly once opened.

¼ cup fresh lemon juice (from 2 lemons)
1 teaspoon pink or black peppercorns, crushed
2 teaspoons minced shallot
¼ cup cold prosecco
Pinch of coarse salt
24 fresh oysters on the half shell

In a small bowl, combine the lemon juice, peppercorns, and shallot. Allow to sit in the fridge for about an hour to let the flavors marry. Just before serving, stir the prosecco into the mignonette sauce. Season with a pinch of salt.

Arrange a half-dozen oysters on each of four serving plates. Spoon some of the mignonette onto each oyster or pass the sauce separately.

Oysters with Prosecco Mignonette

Blini

V

MAKES 50

While traditional Russian blini call for yeast, these small buckwheat pancakes use baking powder and eggs for quick leavening. Each one should be no more than two inches in diameter. Keep a batch of blini in your freezer and a bottle of Champagne in the refrigerator. For easy, last-minute entertaining, pick up some caviar, smoked salmon, or smoked trout and crème fraîche. Kids love blini with scrambled eggs on top. Reheat frozen blini in a 350°F oven for 8 to 10 minutes.

⅓ cup buckwheat flour
½ cup all-purpose flour
1 teaspoon baking powder
¼ teaspoon kosher salt
2 large eggs, at room temperature
⅔ cup milk, at room temperature
Vegetable oil cooking spray

In a medium bowl, whisk together the buckwheat flour, all-purpose flour, baking powder, and salt.

In a separate small bowl, whisk the eggs with the milk. Pour into the flour mixture and gently mix until there are just a few lumps remaining. Do not overmix.

Heat a medium sauté pan over medium heat. Lightly spray the pan with vegetable oil spray. Spoon the batter into the skillet by teaspoonfuls and spread to a small round with the back of the spoon. When bubbles rise to the surface of the pancake, flip gently and cook for about 1 minute longer on the other side, just to cook through.

Remove to a wire rack to cool and continue with the remaining batter. Serve warm or at room temperature.

Go with the Roe

Caviar is one of those magical ingredients that can transform a dish or an occasion; just a strategic teaspoon or two elevates a dish to celebratory status. To learn what to buy, I went to the source: Russ & Daughters on Manhattan's Lower East Side. Co-owner (and fourth-generation Russ descendant) Joshua Russ Tupper schooled me on the finer points of caviar, particularly American caviar. I was familiar with the three primary imported grades: sevruga, osetra, and beluga (which can no longer be legally imported to the United States as it comes from a threatened fish species). The differences in size and color of the roe are part of what determines its cost, with larger eggs being most prized.

Josh explained that one variety is the American *Acipenser transmontanus,* or white sturgeon. *Transmontanus*, with its rich brown color, is the best suited to eating just as is: Similar in flavor to osetra caviar, the large eggs are full of fresh salinity but not at all "fishy." Since it's also the most costly, make sure to serve it as simply as possible to let its flavor take center stage.

Paddlefish and hackleback are two more affordable wild American varieties that come from species whose harvesting is being monitored to control overfishing. The small gray eggs of paddlefish have a slightly stronger flavor that goes well with soft scrambled eggs. Hackleback roe is similar in size to the paddlefish, but the flavor is more delicate. It's delicious on a canapé or dolloped onto pasta. Most affordable is trout roe, a beautiful bright orange roe similar to salmon roe but a bit sweeter and more refined. Use as a garnish on hors d'oeuvres.

Champagne and
Caviar Linguine

Champagne and Caviar Linguine

SERVES 4 TO 6

Fresh pasta festooned with a spoonful of caviar has off-the-charts wow factor. It's just right for New Year's Eve.

Kosher salt
¼ cup extra-virgin olive oil
2 large shallots, minced
1 cup Champagne
1 pound fresh linguine
¾ cup crème fraîche
¼ cup chopped fresh chives
3 tablespoons capers, rinsed and drained
1 (50-gram) tin of good-quality caviar

Bring a large pot of salted water to a boil.

Heat a large sauté pan over medium-high heat. Add 2 tablespoons of the olive oil, the shallots, and 1 teaspoon salt. Reduce the heat to medium and cook the shallots for 3 to 4 minutes or until they are soft and translucent. Add the Champagne and bring it to a simmer. Let it simmer for 5 minutes.

Meanwhile, add the pasta to the boiling water and cook for 3 to 4 minutes. Drain the pasta, reserving ½ cup of the cooking liquid.

Whisk the crème fraîche into the Champagne mixture. Add the cooked pasta, chives, and capers and toss gently. Cook for an additional 3 minutes, mixing often and adding a splash of pasta water if the mixture gets too dry. Serve with a dollop of caviar on top of each portion.

Treats & Sweets

It's no secret that I have a huge sweet tooth. After all, I did originally go to cooking school to become a pastry chef! So I'd no sooner leave out a section on the sweet stuff in a book about being happy in the kitchen than I would skip over salads or pasta. All of these are the foods that give me joy to eat *and* make, and that I love to serve to friends and family.

But make no mistake: I consider the recipes in this treats chapter not something I eat every day or in large portions. As they say, the heart wants what the heart wants. I've learned the hard way that it's almost always better to submit to temptation and eat a real brownie (of a reasonable size) than try to fool yourself into being satisfied with a fat-free, artificially sweetened, or otherwise ersatz substitute. You'll end up indulging anyway, and you'll already have eaten all that other fake, processed junk food. So go ahead, enjoy. You deserve it . . . and so do I!

TREVOR

Key Lime Panna Cotta

Key Lime Panna Cotta

V

SERVES 4 TO 6

So much lighter and more delicate than the pie that inspired it, this dessert looks especially pretty in a stemmed glass.

1 cup whole milk
1 tablespoon unflavored powdered gelatin (from 1 packet)
2 cups heavy cream
⅓ cup sugar
Pinch of salt
1 tablespoon freshly grated Key lime zest plus 3 tablespoons fresh Key lime juice (from 6 Key limes)
1 Key lime, sliced into wheels, for garnish
¼ cup graham cracker crumbs

Place the milk in a small bowl. Sprinkle the gelatin over. Let stand for 3 to 5 minutes to soften the gelatin.

Pour the milk mixture into a heavy saucepan and stir over medium heat just until the gelatin dissolves but the milk does not boil, about 5 minutes.

Add the cream, sugar, and salt. Stir until the sugar dissolves, 5 to 7 minutes. Remove from the heat. Slowly stir in the lime juice. Strain the mixture into a large measuring cup, then add the lime zest. Pour into 4 to 6 stemmed glasses so that they are half full. Cool slightly. Refrigerate until set, at least 6 hours.

To serve, garnish each glass with a Key lime wheel and sprinkle the tops with graham cracker crumbs.

Limoncello Parfaits

V GF

SERVES 6

Six ingredients and five minutes are all it takes to make this light and elegant pudding. Scoop the mixture into pretty glasses, sprinkle with crumbled meringue cookies, and you're done.

1 cup mascarpone cheese, at room temperature
2 cups heavy cream
¼ cup confectioners' sugar
3 tablespoons limoncello
1¼ cups lemon curd, homemade (see page 269) or store-bought
12 store-bought mini meringue cookies, crushed

In the bowl of an electric mixer, combine the mascarpone, cream, confectioners' sugar, and limoncello. Whip until the mixture has formed soft peaks, about 2 minutes. Remove the bowl from the mixer and use a spatula or wooden spoon to gently incorporate the curd into the mixture.

Fill 4-ounce glasses with the lemon mixture and top with the crumbled meringue cookies.

Limoncello Parfaits

Citrus Primer

Winter is when most citrus fruits are at their sweetest—and when you'll find your grocery store produce aisle bursting with options from heirloom navel oranges and sweet limes to Meyer lemons and satsumas. It's the perfect time to brush up on your citrus know-how.

Buying Choose fruit that feels heavy for its size and has bright, glossy skin that doesn't look faded or dry. Citrus should also be pretty firm, with the exception of Meyer lemons, which have thinner skins and are a bit more yielding to the touch. Smell the fruit; it should have a distinctive aroma.

Storing Most of the citrus you find in stores is waxed to give it a longer shelf life. At home, citrus can be stored on the counter for a few days, and will keep for at least a week and up to a month in the refrigerator.

Prepping If you're planning to use the zest or the peel, make sure to wash the fruit well to get rid of as much wax as possible. Some citrus fruits—notably Buddha's hand lemons and citron—are primarily used for their zest and/or skin. If you will be using both the zest and juice of a fruit, zest it first, then squeeze.

If you want beautiful segments for desserts, fruit salads, or pan sauces, your best bet is supreming, a technique that involves cutting away all the peel and pith of the fruit, then slicing along the membranes to free the perfect, pith-free wedges. Be sure to squeeze the leftover membranes, as they will hold quite a bit of juice.

Lemon Angel Food Cupcakes

Lemon Angel Food Cupcakes with Lemon Curd and Mascarpone Glaze

V

MAKES 24 CUPCAKES

LEMON CURD (MAKES ABOUT ¾ CUP)

3 egg yolks, at room temperature
Zest of 2 large lemons
¼ cup fresh lemon juice (from 2 large lemons)
⅓ cup granulated sugar
⅛ teaspoon fine salt
4 tablespoons (½ stick) unsalted butter, cut into ½-inch cubes

CUPCAKES

1 (1-pound) box angel food cake mix
Zest of 2 large lemons
¼ cup fresh lemon juice (from 2 large lemons)

MASCARPONE GLAZE

2 cups confectioners' sugar
6 tablespoons mascarpone cheese, at room temperature
2 tablespoons milk, chilled
½ teaspoon pure vanilla extract
Silver or pastel dragées, Jordan almonds, or yellow sanding sugar, to decorate

For the curd: In a medium saucepan, whisk together the yolks, lemon zest and juice, granulated sugar, and salt. Place the saucepan over medium-low heat, stirring constantly with a wooden spoon or spatula, making sure to scrape the sides and bottom of the pan. Cook until the mixture is thick enough to coat the back of the spoon or spatula, 3 to 5 minutes. Remove from the heat and add the butter, one piece at a time, stirring until the consistency of the curd is smooth. Transfer the curd to a heat-proof bowl and cover the surface of the curd with plastic wrap to prevent a skin from forming. Refrigerate the curd until firm and chilled, about 1 hour.

For the cupcakes: Place 2 racks in the upper and lower thirds of the oven and preheat the oven to 350°F. Line two 12-cup muffin tins with paper liners. In the bowl of an electric mixer, combine the cake mix, 1 cup water, and the lemon zest and juice. Beat the mixture on low speed for 30 seconds to incorporate the ingredients, then increase the speed to medium for 1 minute until the mixture is light and fluffy. Use a scoop or spoon to fill the muffin cups three-quarters full. Bake until the cupcakes are golden brown and the cracks on top feel dry, 12 to 15 minutes. Cool the cupcakes completely before filling and frosting, about 30 minutes.

For the glaze: In a medium bowl, whisk together the confectioners' sugar, mascarpone, milk, and vanilla until smooth and shiny.

To fill the cupcakes, use a small spoon to push a shallow hole in the center of each cupcake. Fill the center with 1 teaspoon of the lemon curd. Drizzle the cupcake with some of the glaze to cover the top. Sprinkle with the decoration of your choice. Allow the cupcakes to set in the refrigerator for at least 30 minutes.

Pumpkin Ginger Chocolate Muffins

V

MAKES 16 MUFFINS

These muffins have a few things going for them aside from the decadent chocolate topping: beta-carotene- and nutrient-rich pumpkin plus good-for-you olive oil and whole-grain flour. Kefir is a thick fermented milk beverage similar to yogurt or buttermilk.

Vegetable oil cooking spray (optional)
3¼ cups white whole-wheat flour
1 cup coconut sugar
3 teaspoons pumpkin pie spice
2 teaspoons baking soda
1 teaspoon baking powder
½ teaspoon kosher salt
3 large eggs, at room temperature
2 cups canned pumpkin puree (not pumpkin pie filling)
½ cup extra-virgin olive oil
¼ cup kefir
1 teaspoon pure vanilla extract
½ cup chopped candied ginger
8 ounces bittersweet chocolate, finely chopped
3 tablespoons pumpkin seeds

Preheat the oven to 350°F. Spray two 12-cup muffin tins with vegetable oil spray or use paper liners. Set aside.

In a large bowl, whisk together the flour, coconut sugar, pumpkin pie spice, baking soda, baking powder, and salt. In a separate medium bowl, whisk together the eggs, pumpkin, olive oil, kefir, and vanilla until blended. Pour the wet ingredients into the dry and use a rubber spatula to mix together just until combined. Fold in the chopped ginger.

Fill the muffin cups about three-quarters full. Bake until a toothpick inserted in the center comes out with only a few moist crumbs, about 20 minutes. Allow the muffins to cool in the tins for 15 minutes. Remove from the muffin cups and cool completely on a wire rack.

Meanwhile, melt the chocolate in a bowl in the microwave in 10-second intervals on high, stirring with a rubber spatula in between. When it is about 80 percent melted and looking shiny, remove the chocolate from the microwave and stir until completely smooth. Dip the top of each muffin in the melted chocolate, allowing the excess to drip off. Sprinkle with the pumpkin seeds and let stand for 15 minutes to set.

Pumpkin Ginger
Chocolate Muffins

Mini Almond Butter and Strawberry Muffins

Mini Almond Butter and Strawberry Muffins

V

MAKES 24 MUFFINS

These cute little muffins take just fifteen minutes to put together, using ingredients you're likely to have on hand. Jade thinks they're perfect for playdates and so do I.

1 cup all-purpose flour
½ teaspoon kosher salt
½ teaspoon baking soda
¼ teaspoon baking powder
1 cup sugar
1 cup crunchy almond butter
½ cup vegetable oil
2 large eggs, at room temperature
2 teaspoons pure vanilla extract
½ cup strawberry jam or jelly

Place a rack in the center of the oven and preheat the oven to 325°F. Line 24 mini muffin cups with paper liners.

In a medium bowl, whisk together the flour, salt, baking soda, and baking powder. In a large bowl, whisk the sugar, almond butter, oil, eggs, and vanilla until blended. In 2 batches, add the dry ingredients to the batter and stir just until blended.

Fill the muffin cups halfway with batter. Spoon ½ teaspoon jam on top of each muffin and then spoon the remaining batter on top to cover the jam.

Bake until the tops are golden brown, 25 to 30 minutes. Transfer the muffin tins to a rack to cool. Once cool, remove the muffins from the tins and spoon ½ teaspoon jam on top of each muffin.

Where the Pros Shop

For well-priced cooking equipment, hit up a restaurant supply store. You can find warehouse-like stores that cater to restaurateurs, bakers, and other food-service professionals who need equipment that will stand up to hard use in just about any mid- to large-size city. Don't be intimidated by the industrial-size mixers and ranges displayed at the front of the store. If you venture inside, you'll find plenty of items for a home kitchen, often at very nice prices.

- Don't expect fancy packaging. What these items lack in shelf appeal they make up for in functionality and value. Fifty precut sheets of parchment paper is a great buy at $7.50; who cares if the roll comes in a plain plastic bag?
- Focus on fundamentals. Sturdy sheet pans, metal prep bowls, baking pans, and tools like whisks, ladles, and kitchen spoons are generally well priced and will last forever; a heavy-gauge stainless-steel sauté pan will run you between $40 and $60. Be sure to check if your pan comes with a lid; often these are sold separately.
- Be realistic. Unless you routinely cook for a crowd, don't assume bigger is better. Buy pieces you can use comfortably. Resist fancy gadgets that serve a single purpose. Do you really need a $200 stainless-steel French-fry cutter or a $99 rotary citrus zester?
- Join forces. Many of the most deeply discounted items are sold in bulk, so bring along a friend or two and go in together on your purchases to save big. Glassware, for example, may be sold in cases of three-dozen units. Six hundred cupcake liners for less than $4 is undeniably a steal, but unless you are planning to be on bake-sale duty weekly for the next ten years, you're better off sharing.
- Think creatively. Many professional items can be put to alternative uses. A roll of bakery string can add a whimsical touch to your holiday gift wrapping, or silicone baking and chocolate molds can shape butter or even guest soaps.
- Skip the name brands. While many restaurant suppliers carry name brands, their prices are not likely to be significantly lower than you can find elsewhere if you keep an eye out for sales. Look for the less-well-known names that deliver excellent value without the benefit of big marketing budgets.

Ricotta and Chocolate Hazelnut Calzones

V

SERVES 6

When you break open one of these golden brown pockets the molten cheesy, chocolate-y, berry filling oozes out in a completely seductive way. Store-bought pizza dough means they're a cinch to make.

¾ cup whole-milk ricotta cheese
¼ cup mascarpone cheese
1 large egg yolk plus 1 large egg, lightly beaten, for egg wash
2 tablespoons confectioners' sugar, plus more for dusting
8 ounces frozen strawberries, thawed
2 tablespoons granulated sugar
⅔ cup chocolate-hazelnut spread (Nutella recommended), at room temperature
3 tablespoons heavy cream, at room temperature
6 (2-ounce) pieces of pizza dough, homemade (see page 64) or store-bought, cold

In a food processor, blend the ricotta, mascarpone, egg yolk, and confectioners' sugar until smooth and creamy. Transfer the ricotta mixture to a small bowl, then cover and refrigerate for 30 minutes. Meanwhile, in a clean food processor blend the strawberries and 1 tablespoon of the granulated sugar until smooth. Transfer the strawberry sauce to a small bowl and set aside. Whisk the chocolate-hazelnut spread and cream in a medium bowl to blend. Set aside.

Position a rack in the center of the oven and preheat the oven to 450°F. Line a large heavy baking sheet with parchment paper. Roll out each piece of pizza dough into a 7-inch round. Spoon the ricotta mixture atop the center of the lower half of each dough circle. Spoon the chocolate-hazelnut mixture atop the cheese mixture.

Brush the lower edges of the dough with the egg wash. Fold the plain dough halves over the filling, forming half circles. Pinch the edges of the dough firmly together to seal. Using a pastry wheel, trim the edges. Transfer the calzones to the prepared baking sheet, spacing evenly.

Ricotta and Chocolate Hazelnut Calzones

Brush the tops of the calzones with more egg wash, and bake until they puff and become golden brown, about 10 minutes. Transfer the baking sheet to a rack and cool for 15 minutes. Transfer the calzones to plates and dust with the confectioners' sugar. Drizzle the strawberry sauce around the calzones and serve.

Lemon Ricotta Cookies with Lemon Glaze

Lemon Ricotta Cookies with Lemon Glaze

V

MAKES 44 COOKIES

I've published this recipe before, but it's become such a signature for me that I couldn't imagine not including it here. More cakey than crispy, these ladylike little tea cakes are moist and tender with a bit of crunch from the glaze. We serve thousands at my restaurant every week and I send a dozen to my nearest and dearest at the holidays.

COOKIES

2½ cups all-purpose flour
1 teaspoon baking powder
1 teaspoon kosher salt
8 tablespoons (1 stick) unsalted butter, at room temperature
2 cups granulated sugar
2 large eggs
1 (15-ounce) container whole-milk ricotta cheese
Zest of 1 lemon
3 tablespoons fresh lemon juice (from 1 to 2 lemons)

GLAZE

1½ cups confectioners' sugar
Zest of 1 lemon
3 tablespoons fresh lemon juice (from 1 to 2 lemons)

For the cookies: Preheat the oven to 375°F. Line 2 baking sheets with parchment paper.

In a medium bowl, combine the flour, baking powder, and salt. Set aside.

In a large bowl, using an electric mixer, beat the butter and granulated sugar until light and fluffy, about 3 minutes. Add the eggs, 1 at a time, beating until incorporated. Add the ricotta cheese and lemon zest and juice and beat to combine. Stir in the dry ingredients.

Spoon the dough onto the prepared baking sheets using 2 tablespoons for each cookie. Bake until slightly golden at the edges, about 15 minutes. Remove from the oven and let the cookies rest on the baking sheets for 20 minutes.

While they cool, in a small bowl combine the confectioners' sugar with the lemon zest and juice and stir until smooth. Spoon about ½ teaspoon of the glaze onto each cooled cookie and use the back of the spoon to spread it to the edges. Let the glaze harden for about 2 hours. Store the cookies in an airtight container.

Holiday Cookie Exchange

If you love Christmas cookies as much as I do, but you don't want to spend three weeks in the kitchen like a Keebler elf, think about hosting a cookie exchange. It's a great excuse to get together before the holidays *and* a smart way to get a jump on your holiday baking with a lot less stress and cleanup. Here's how to throw your own cookie swap.

Draw up your guest list. It's fun to invite baking hobbyists, as well as people from different backgrounds, and encourage everyone to make their specialty. Want to sample Italian anise cookies, Mexican wedding cakes, or Japanese green tea wafers? Cast your net wide!

Send out your invitations, including instructions on how many cookies to make. A full batch is an ample amount and will ensure that there's plenty to choose from. If you don't want guests to show up with store-bought wares, here's where to let your guests know your expectations. Check RSVPs for duplicate recipes. If you have three people planning to make spritz cookies, now's the time to ask two of them to change it up. Ask your guests for copies of (or links to) their recipes. Once you've collected them all, print them up in a little booklet to distribute to all guests.

Stock up on festive cookie tins that guests can use to store their stash. Even though your guests will transport their own cookies in a container, giving everyone a tin of the same size is an easy way to make sure everyone gets the same amount of cookies to take home, and it's also a nice party favor that they can reuse next year.

A day or two beforehand, bake your own cookies.

The day of the party, set up your space: Top your table with a cloth and move the furniture to give guests plenty of room to mingle. If you're serving drinks and food, arrange them on a separate surface to encourage flow. Ask each guest to tell a little something about his or her cookies—any family stories associated with them, any challenges they encountered while making them, or any secret ingredients.

Chocolate Amaretti Cookies

V GF

MAKES 24 COOKIES

Some almond paste in the batter and a sprinkle of sugar and a few almond slivers on top turn classic chocolate cookies into something special.

1 (7-ounce) package almond paste (make sure yours is gluten-free)
1 cup sugar
⅓ cup unsweetened cocoa powder
⅛ teaspoon fine salt
2 large egg whites
½ teaspoon pure vanilla extract
1 cup almond slivers, for decorating
¼ cup white sanding sugar, for decorating

Place 2 racks in the upper and lower thirds of the oven and preheat the oven to 375°F. Line 2 baking sheets with parchment paper.

Break the almond paste into small pieces and place in the bowl of a food processer. Add the sugar, cocoa powder, and salt and process until the almond paste is very finely chopped and incorporated with the salt and sugar. Add the egg whites and vanilla, and process until a smooth dough forms, about 30 seconds. Using a small scoop or spoon, dollop 1 tablespoon of the batter for each cookie onto the baking sheets, leaving 2 inches between each cookie. Top each cookie with a few almond slivers and sprinkle with the sanding sugar.

Bake until the cookies have risen and cracked slightly but are still soft in the center, 13 to 14 minutes, rotating the baking sheets halfway through. Allow the cookies to cool completely on the baking sheets. Store the cookies in an airtight container.

Orange Cream Butter Cookies

V

MAKES 4 DOZEN COOKIES

Tender and delicate, with just a hint of orange flavor, these cookies are like a baked Creamsicle. You can bake one log of dough now and keep the other in the freezer for impromptu guests or to serve with ice cream or tea.

1 cup (8 ounces) unsalted butter, preferably high-fat European type, at room temperature
½ cup confectioners' sugar
¼ cup granulated sugar
½ teaspoon kosher salt
1 egg, at room temperature
Seeds from 1 vanilla bean (see page 141)
1½ teaspoons grated orange zest
2 cups all-purpose flour
1 egg, beaten, for egg wash (optional)
2 tablespoons vanilla sugar or regular granulated sugar, for sprinkling (optional)

In a large bowl using a hand mixer, beat the butter on medium speed for 1 minute, until light and fluffy. Add the confectioners' sugar, granulated sugar, and salt and continue to beat on medium speed for an additional 2 minutes until pale and creamy. Add the egg, vanilla seeds, and orange zest and mix on low to combine. Add the flour and beat on low speed until the flour is just incorporated. (Alternatively, when you see just a bit of unincorporated flour, switch to a rubber spatula to finish combining. Do not overmix.)

Divide the dough in half. Place half of the dough in the center of an 18-inch-long piece of plastic wrap. Using a spatula, mold the mixture into a log, about 7 inches long and 1½ inches wide. Roll up the log in the plastic and twist the ends together to seal. Repeat with the remaining dough. Refrigerate for at least 3 hours or until firm.

Preheat the oven to 350°F. Line a baking sheet with parchment paper.
Remove the plastic wrap from one log of dough and slice into ¼-inch rounds. Arrange the cookies on the baking sheet with 1 inch between them. Brush with the egg wash and sprinkle with the sugar, if using.

Bake the cookies until just beginning to brown around the edges, 15 to 20 minutes. Cool for 5 minutes on the baking sheet before removing to a wire rack to cool completely. Repeat with the remaining dough log.

Butter Is Back

You know how much I love olive oil—I use it for basically everything!—but even *I* have to admit that some things just taste better with butter. And because studies now suggest that saturated fat may not increase the risk of heart disease after all, butter is most definitely having its moment. The dairy sections are bursting with all kinds of high-fat European-style butters.

More fat—82% to 86% compared to 80% in American-style versions—and less water make these butters richer and better for spreading; and if you've ever made pie dough from scratch, you know that low water content is key when it comes to getting that perfectly flaky layered crust. European-style butters also tend to be cultured (though not all are), which gives them a higher acidity and a nuttier, tangier flavor than their uncultured counterparts.

In butter-centric recipes where the flavor and texture really count, splurge on the good stuff.

Espresso–Peanut Butter Brownies

V

MAKES 24 BROWNIES

I don't often rely on mixes, but if starting with a mix gets you to bake when otherwise you wouldn't, well, I'm all for that. A little espresso powder and peanut butter chips make these brownies taste like they're made from scratch. My favorite part: the pinch of coarse salt flakes sprinkled over the top.

Vegetable oil cooking spray
⅓ cup vegetable oil
1 large egg
2 tablespoons espresso powder
1 (17.6-ounce) box brownie mix
¾ cup peanut butter chips
¼ teaspoon coarse flaked salt

Preheat the oven to 350°F. Spray an 8 x 8-inch baking pan with vegetable oil spray. In a large bowl, whisk ⅓ cup water, the oil, egg, and espresso powder to blend. Add the brownie mix and stir until well blended, then stir in the peanut butter chips.

Transfer the batter to the prepared baking pan. Sprinkle the salt evenly over the top. Bake until a toothpick inserted into the center of the brownies comes out with a few moist crumbs attached, 35 to 40 minutes. Cool completely.

Cut into 24 squares. Arrange the brownies on a platter and serve.

Espresso–Peanut Butter "Better" Brownies

V

MAKES 9 TO 12 BROWNIES

Much as I love my original take on this recipe, this one is nearly as luscious and a lot less likely to make my blood sugar ricochet all over the place. Black beans make the brownies moist and dense.

Vegetable oil cooking spray
1 (15-ounce) can black beans, rinsed well and drained
3 tablespoons unsweetened cocoa powder
½ cup rolled oats
¼ teaspoon kosher salt
½ cup (packed) light brown sugar
2 teaspoons pure vanilla extract
½ teaspoon baking powder
1 tablespoon espresso powder
1 large egg plus 1 yolk, at room temperature
¼ cup coconut oil, warmed so it is liquid
¾ cup peanut butter chips

Preheat the oven to 350°F. Spray an 8 x 8-inch pan with vegetable oil spray. Cut a piece of parchment to cover the bottom of the pan and adhere it to the bottom with the help of the cooking spray. Set aside.

In a food processor, place the black beans, cocoa powder, oats, salt, brown sugar, vanilla, baking powder, espresso powder, egg, and egg yolk. Puree to combine. With the motor running, drizzle in the coconut oil and puree until smooth, about 30 seconds. Sprinkle half the chips on the bottom of the prepared pan. Spread the batter over the chips. Sprinkle the remaining chips over the top.

Bake for 20 to 25 minutes, or until a toothpick inserted in the center comes out with just a few moist crumbs. Allow the brownies to cool to room temperature.

Espresso–Peanut Butter "Better" Brownies

Prosecco Float

V GF

SERVES 4

Lighter than a sundae but with a definite kick, this is an elegant and indulgent way to use up a partial bottle of bubbly.

8 fresh raspberries
1 pint dark chocolate gelato
4 tablespoons orange liqueur, such as Cointreau
2 teaspoons agave syrup
Approximately 16 ounces chilled prosecco

Drop a raspberry in the bottom of a champagne flute or a tall, narrow glass. Drop 3 small scoops of gelato on top and pour a tablespoon of the liqueur and ½ teaspoon of the agave into each glass. Add another raspberry, fill with prosecco, and serve immediately.

Prosecco Float

Cupcake Shake

V

SERVES 6

I call this one the consolation prize, a dessert so decadent and so over-the-top sweet that it is only to be deployed in case of emergency. Or when you just really, really need a pick-me-up. Your call. It contains hazelnut liqueur, so this one is for grown-ups only.

MASCARPONE WHIPPED CREAM
½ cup mascarpone cheese, at room temperature
1 cup heavy cream
3 tablespoons confectioners' sugar
1 teaspoon pure vanilla extract

GARNISH
6 homemade or store-bought mini cupcakes, unfrosted
Sprinkles

CUPCAKE SHAKE
1 quart vanilla ice cream, softened
¾ cup whole milk
½ cup Frangelico
3 tablespoons unsweetened cocoa powder
6 homemade or store-bought mini chocolate cupcakes, unfrosted

For the whipped cream: In the bowl of an electric mixer, combine the mascarpone, cream, confectioners' sugar, and vanilla. Whip until soft peaks form, about 2 minutes.

For the garnish: Transfer ¼ cup of the whipped cream into a piping bag and frost 6 of the cupcakes. Decorate the tops with some of the sprinkles. Place the frosted cupcakes in the freezer, and chill the rest of the whipped cream in the refrigerator while you make the shake.

For the shake: In a blender, combine the ice cream, milk, Frangelico, and cocoa and blend until smooth. Add the 6 unfrosted cupcakes and pulse a few times to incorporate, then puree until the cupcakes are mixed well throughout the shake.

Pour the milkshake into 6 glasses and top with a dollop of the reserved whipped cream and some sprinkles. Push a straw through each frosted mini cupcake and insert the straws into the shakes.

Cupcake Shake

Get on Board

If you don't consider yourself a great baker, or just don't have the time to make a dessert, consider one of two no-cook options to round out your menu. Serving a cheese plate before or in lieu of a dessert course has become commonplace in many restaurants, and if you don't have much of a sweet tooth—or just love cheese!—it might be a fun alternative to explore at your next dinner party. Arrange four or four cheeses on a large platter or wooden board, add some fresh fruit, crostini, or crackers, and pass it around. Try to select a variety of textures, ages, and types; one fresh goat cheese, an aged sheep or cow's milk cheese, a triple crème and a bleu cheese, for instance, make a nice combo. Look for unusual cheeses that are new to you and have fun comparing them as you polish off the last of the wine left from the entrée course.

If the meal just doesn't feel complete without a bit of something sweet (and I can totally relate to that sentiment), there's another easy, no-cook alternative. Recently, restaurants have been getting as geeky about chocolate as they are about wine and cheese, offering a variety of artisanal chocolates in their unadorned states. At Hearth Restaurant in New York, for example, Chef Marco Canora presents a dark chocolate tasting board with a selection of five single-origin bittersweet chocolates to sample. Trying them side-by-side makes it quite easy to pick up on the winey, fruity, or caramel notes of each, and you may be surprised to find which characteristics you like best in your chocolate. Why not give it a try?

Chocolate Cake Tiramisu with Chocolate Zabaglione

V

SERVES 6

If you like chocolate as much I like chocolate, which is to say it's what makes dessert worth eating, this double-chocolate tiramisu cake will knock your socks off. No one but you will ever suspect it starts with a boxed cake mix; they'll be too busy drooling over the flashy chocolate zabaglione sauce and sultry mascarpone filling.

6 large egg yolks, at room temperature
5 tablespoons sugar
½ cup imported sweet Marsala
½ cup plus ⅓ cup heavy cream, chilled
⅛ teaspoon kosher salt
⅔ cup (4 ounces) dark chocolate morsels or semisweet chocolate chips
⅓ cup mascarpone cheese, at room temperature
1 box chocolate cake mix, such as Betty Crocker Super Moist Dark Chocolate, baked according to package instructions
1 (3.5-ounce) bar bittersweet chocolate (such as Lindt), for chocolate curls (optional)

In a medium stainless-steel bowl, whisk the egg yolks and sugar until blended. Whisk in the Marsala, ½ cup of the cream, and the salt. Place the bowl over a large saucepan of simmering water (do not let the bottom of the bowl touch the water). Whisk constantly until the sauce is thick and a thermometer inserted into the sabayon registers 160°F to 170°F, about 15 minutes.

Remove the bowl from over the water. Add the chocolate morsels and whisk until they are melted and the sabayon is smooth and blended. (The sabayon can be made 1 hour ahead. Let stand at room temperature. Whisk before continuing.)

In another medium bowl, whisk the remaining ⅓ cup cream and the mascarpone until peaks form. Dice the cake into small cubes. Place about ½ cup of the cake cubes into each of six 1½- to 2-cup old-fashioned glasses or water goblets. Spoon 2 heaping tablespoons sabayon over the cake. Top with a spoonful of the mascarpone cream. Repeat the layering with cake, sabayon, and mascarpone cream.

To make the chocolate curls, if desired, stand the chocolate bar in a large measuring cup. Microwave on 50% power in 10-second intervals just until the chocolate feels a bit warm. Stand the chocolate bar upright and run a vegetable peeler down one narrow edge, creating chocolate curls. Sprinkle the curls over each tiramisu and serve.

Chocolate Cake Tiramisu with Chocolate Zabaglione

Pine Nut Ice Cream with Banana Caramel Sauce

V GF

SERVES 4

Bananas Foster takes a trip to Italy in this sexy, simple dessert. Make the sauce just before serving; otherwise, it might separate if you reheat it.

- 1 quart premium vanilla ice cream, such as Häagen-Dazs
- ¾ cup toasted pine nuts (see Cook's Note, page 75)
- ½ teaspoon kosher salt
- 5 tablespoons unsalted butter
- ⅓ cup (packed) light brown sugar
- ¼ cup bourbon
- 1 ripe banana, diced

Empty the ice cream into a mixing bowl and allow it to sit at room temperature for about 8 minutes. When it's soft enough to stir with a wooden spoon or rubber spatula, sprinkle in the pine nuts and ¼ teaspoon of the salt. Working quickly, fold the pine nuts into the softened ice cream. Cover the bowl with plastic wrap and put it in the freezer to firm up.

To make the sauce, in a medium saucepan combine the butter, brown sugar, bourbon, and the remaining ¼ teaspoon salt. Bring to a simmer over medium heat, stirring often, until the sugar is completely melted and the mixture has a caramel-sauce consistency, about 4 minutes. Reduce the heat to low, stir in the banana pieces, and cook for an additional 3 minutes to just soften them. Remove the pan from the heat and let the sauce sit at room temperature for about 5 minutes to cool slightly.

To serve, place 2 scoops of the ice cream in each of 4 bowls or sundae glasses. Drizzle the sauce over each and serve immediately.

Double-Cocoa Hot Chocolate

V V GF

SERVES 2 TO 4

Whip this up in a blender in seconds; it's so rich you may want to serve it in espresso cups.

1 tablespoon cocoa nibs
2 cups unsweetened almond milk
1 (1.75-ounce) bar dark chocolate (70% cacao), broken into pieces
2 tablespoons agave syrup
Small pinch of kosher salt

In a blender, combine the cocoa nibs and 1 tablespoon of the almond milk. Blend on high for 30 seconds to break up the nibs. Add the chocolate, agave, and salt to the blender.

In a microwave or in a small saucepan, heat the rest of the almond milk until almost simmering; do not boil. Pour over the chocolate mixture in the blender, cover, and allow it to sit for 30 seconds.

With the vent removed to allow steam to escape, hold a towel over the top of the blender and blend on low speed. Increase the speed to high once it gets going, and blend for 30 seconds. Pour into mugs and serve.

Cuckoo for Cocoa

There really is no comparison between powdered cocoa from a packet and the real deal made with chocolate and whole milk (or almond milk). In my book it's far better to have a small portion of something rich and delicious than a big watery cup of low-fat, artificially sweetened stuff. And I'm not the only one. Upscale spots from coast to coast are upping the ante when it comes to hot cocoa, spiking their blends with everything from herbs and brownie batter to all manner of spirits and even dried mushrooms, which have immune-supporting properties.

Most of the time, though, the only benefit we're expecting from our cocoa is a winter-beating warmth that helps thaw frozen fingers and toes, and a bracing hit of real chocolate flavor. This recipe delivers all that and more. It is decadent enough to stand in for dessert, and indulgent enough to chase away the blahs on even the snowiest day.

Double-Cocoa Hot Chocolate

Rose Eton Mess Semifreddo

Rose Eton Mess Semifreddo

V GF

SERVES 6 TO 8

Eton mess is a meringue-based confection that originated in England; semifreddo is a frozen Italian dessert. When the two collide with a bright berry swirl, the result is as lovely as it is light.

BERRY SWIRL

1 cup strawberries, hulled and sliced
2 tablespoons sugar
1 teaspoon rose water

SEMIFREDDO

Vegetable oil cooking spray
1 cup coarsely crushed pink meringue cookies
1 cup heavy cream, chilled
¾ cup mascarpone cheese, chilled
5 egg yolks, at room temperature
¾ cup sugar
3 tablespoons rose water
¼ teaspoon kosher salt

GARNISH (OPTIONAL)

1 cup strawberries, hulled and sliced
2 tablespoons sugar
1 teaspoon rose water

For the berry swirl: In a medium bowl, toss together the strawberries, sugar, and rose water. Allow the mixture to sit for 10 minutes at room temperature to draw out the juices. Add the mixture to a blender and puree until smooth. Set aside.

For the semifreddo: Spray an 8 x 3-inch loaf pan with vegetable oil spray and line it with plastic wrap, avoiding any creases. Make sure to leave some wrap hanging over the long sides; leaving the short ends uncovered will be just fine. Sprinkle the crushed meringue cookies evenly over the bottom of the pan. Set aside.

To a medium bowl, add the cream and mascarpone. Using a hand mixer, beat on medium speed until incorporated and beginning to thicken. Raise the speed to high and continue to beat just until stiff peaks form. Do not overbeat. Keep in the refrigerator until ready to use.

In a separate large bowl, combine the egg yolks, sugar, rose water, and salt. Whisk together to incorporate. Place the bowl over a saucepan of simmering water so that it fits comfortably on top but doesn't touch the water. Beat on medium speed with the hand mixer for about 5 minutes or until light in color and no longer gritty when rubbed between your fingers (the sugar should be fully dissolved and the mixture quite warm to the touch).

Remove the bowl from the water bath and place on a towel on the counter. Continue to beat at medium-high speed for an additional 5 minutes or until cool, thick, and pale. Using a large rubber spatula, gently fold the whipped cream mixture into the egg mixture, being careful not to deflate the batter.

Pour the strawberry sauce into the bowl. With about 3 large strokes of a rubber spatula, fold the sauce into the pale mixture to create swirls. Pour the swirled mixture over the meringue cookies in the loaf pan. Cover with the overlapping plastic wrap and place in the freezer. Freeze for at least 8 hours or overnight.

For the garnish: If desired, about 10 minutes before serving the semifreddo, toss together the strawberries, sugar, and rose water in a medium bowl. Allow the mixture to sit at room temperature to draw out the juices.

Remove the semifreddo from the freezer and let it sit at room temperature for about 4 minutes before serving. Slice the semifreddo, and garnish with the macerated strawberries if desired.

White Chocolate and Hazelnut Tartlets

V

MAKES 12 TARTLETS

If the occasion calls for something ladylike and pretty, you've come to the right place. I like to garnish these with pansies, but any edible flower, such as nasturtiums or rose petals, adds a lovely touch.

8 (17 x 13-inch) frozen phyllo pastry sheets, thawed
8 tablespoons (1 stick) unsalted butter, melted
6 ounces good-quality white chocolate, chopped
1½ cups heavy cream
½ cup hazelnuts, toasted (see Cook's Note, page 75), skinned, and finely chopped
¼ cup chocolate-hazelnut spread, such as Nutella (optional)
1 (3-ounce) bar bittersweet chocolate, grated, for garnish
Edible flowers, for garnish

Preheat the oven to 375°F. Lay 1 phyllo sheet on a work surface. Brush the phyllo with melted butter. Top with another phyllo sheet. Repeat with more butter and 2 more phyllo sheets. Cut the stacked phyllo sheets into six 5-inch squares.

Press the phyllo stacks into the cups of a 12-cup muffin tin, allowing the edges to ruffle and extend above the rims. Repeat with the remaining 4 phyllo sheets and melted butter to make 12 phyllo cups. Bake until the phyllo cups are golden brown, about 9 minutes. Place the muffin tin on a cooling rack to cool completely.

Meanwhile, in a small heavy saucepan, stir the white chocolate and ¼ cup of the cream over low heat until the chocolate is melted and smooth. Pour into a large bowl and cool to barely lukewarm. Stir in the hazelnuts. Using an electric mixer, beat the remaining 1¼ cups cream in another large bowl to medium-firm peaks. Fold the cream into the white chocolate mixture in 2 batches. Cover and refrigerate until cold, about 1 hour.

Spoon 2 teaspoons of the chocolate-hazelnut spread into each phyllo cup if desired. Spoon the white chocolate mousse into the cooled phyllo cups, mounding slightly. Arrange the mousse-filled phyllo cups on plates. Sprinkle the bittersweet chocolate over the mousse, garnish with edible flowers, and serve.

Cook's Note: **The unfilled phyllo cups can be made 2 days ahead. Store them in an airtight container at room temperature. The white chocolate mousse can be made up to 8 hours ahead. Keep it refrigerated. The filled phyllo cups can be assembled up to 1 hour ahead. Cover and refrigerate them.**

White Chocolate
and Hazelnut Tartlets

Lavender Honey Cake

V

SERVES 8

The honey's light citrus notes followed by a slight floral element work really well with the lavender and lemon.

Butter, for the cake pan

LAVENDER SYRUP

2 tablespoons dried lavender
⅓ cup sugar

CAKE

1 cup all-purpose flour
¾ cup semolina flour
1½ teaspoons baking powder
1 teaspoon baking soda
¼ teaspoon kosher salt
1 teaspoon dried lavender, chopped
1 tablespoon grated lemon zest
1 tablespoon fresh lemon juice (from 1 lemon)
1 teaspoon pure vanilla extract
½ cup coconut oil
½ cup orange blossom honey
2 eggs, at room temperature
⅓ cup lavender syrup

VANILLA CREAM

1 cup heavy cream
1 vanilla bean, seeds scraped out and pod reserved for another use
1 tablespoon orange blossom honey

Preheat the oven to 350°F. Butter an 8-inch round baking pan. Cut a circle of parchment to line the bottom of the pan and butter the parchment. Set aside.

For the syrup: In a small saucepan, combine ⅔ cup water and the lavender and sugar. Bring to a simmer over medium-high heat. Reduce the heat to medium and simmer for about 4 minutes or until reduced by half. Turn off the heat and steep for 3 minutes. Strain and allow the syrup to cool to room temperature.

For the cake: In a large bowl, whisk together the all-purpose flour, semolina flour, baking powder, baking soda, salt, and lavender. In a separate medium bowl, whisk together the lemon zest and juice, vanilla, coconut oil, honey, eggs, and cooled lavender syrup.

Add the wet ingredients to the dry and mix together using a rubber spatula until just combined. Pour into the prepared pan and bake for 30 to 35 minutes or until a toothpick inserted in the middle comes out clean.

For the vanilla cream: In a large bowl, place the cream, vanilla seeds, and honey. Using a handheld mixer, beat on high for about 3 minutes or until soft peaks form. Serve each slice of cake with a dollop of the vanilla cream.

Lavender Honey Cake

Gifts from Your Kitchen

Is it me or does Christmas seem to come earlier every year? One minute I'm helping Jade pick out a Halloween costume and the next thing I know holiday tunes are blaring on the radio.

Of course even if you are as organized as I try to be (and believe me, I'm far from perfect), last-minute gift-giving situations always seem to arise. And since I'd much rather spend my time baking cookies and making ornaments for the tree with Jade or writing holiday cards than battling the crowds at the mall, I've learned to create a stash of homemade, one-size-fits-all gifts that work for all those "oops, I need a little something" moments. A hostess present for the impromptu neighborhood open house we're invited to, a little something for Jade's favorite ballet teacher or the assistant who handed me a much-needed Americano on the last leg of a long book tour—all of these people deserve acknowledgment with something that not only says I remember them but that I made an effort in return.

That's why whenever I can, I love to share something homemade. In a world where time truly is at a premium, showing someone that you invested not just dollars but effort and personal attention is a special gesture, one that is universally acknowledged and appreciated. Whether it's for Christmas gifts, to celebrate a birthday, or to welcome a new neighbor, these are some of my favorites to make and give.

Chocolate Dessert Salami

V

SERVES 6 TO 8

This visual culinary pun looks like a cured salami, but is made with chocolate chips, toasted nuts, and crushed biscotti. Confectioners' sugar gives it an "aged" look.

½ cup (2½ ounces) slivered almonds
½ cup (2½ ounces) chopped walnuts
2 (5-inch-long) plain biscotti, coarsely crushed
6 tablespoons (¾ stick) unsalted butter, cut into ½-inch pieces, at room temperature
1 (12-ounce) bag semisweet chocolate chips
¼ cup brewed coffee, at room temperature
1 teaspoon grated orange zest
½ cup confectioners' sugar

Place an oven rack in the center of the oven. Preheat the oven to 350°F. Arrange the almonds, walnuts, and crushed biscotti in a single layer on a rimmed baking sheet. Bake until the nuts are lightly toasted, 6 to 8 minutes. Cool completely.

Place the butter and chocolate in a medium bowl and set over a pan of barely simmering water (the bottom of the bowl should not touch the water). Stir until the chocolate has melted and the mixture is smooth, about 6 minutes. Stir in the coffee until smooth. Add the almonds, walnuts, biscotti, and orange zest and stir until combined. Cover the bowl and refrigerate for 1½ to 2 hours or until firm but moldable.

Place half of the mixture in the center of an 18-inch-long piece of plastic wrap. Mold the mixture into a log about 7 inches long and 2 inches wide. Roll up the log in the plastic and twist the ends together to seal. Roll on a work surface a few times to make the log evenly round. Repeat with the remaining chocolate mixture. Refrigerate for 1 hour or until firm.

Place the confectioners' sugar on a plate. Remove the plastic wrap and roll each log in the sugar until coated. Using a pastry brush, brush away the excess sugar. If desired, wrap in parchment paper and tie at each end. To serve, use a serrated knife to slice into ½-inch-thick slices.

Chocolate Dessert Salami

Cranberry-Pomegranate Chutney

V V GF

MAKES 4 TO 6 (6-OUNCE) JARS

This condiment goes well with Thanksgiving turkey, Easter ham, or Fourth of July grilled sausages.

2 teaspoons extra-virgin olive oil
1 medium shallot, minced
2 teaspoons grated peeled fresh ginger
½ teaspoon ground cardamom
¼ teaspoon ground cloves
¼ teaspoon fine sea salt
2 cups pomegranate juice
½ cup agave syrup
¼ cup apple cider vinegar
2 tablespoons pomegranate molasses
2 (12-ounce) bags fresh cranberries
1 cup fresh pomegranate seeds (arils)

Heat the oil in a large saucepan over medium-high heat. Add the shallot, ginger, cardamom, cloves, and salt and sauté for 2 to 3 minutes, until the shallot is soft and fragrant. Add the pomegranate juice, agave, vinegar, pomegranate molasses, and cranberries and bring to a boil.

Reduce the heat to medium and simmer until the cranberries have burst and the chutney has thickened, 15 to 20 minutes. Add the pomegranate seeds and cool the chutney to room temperature before transferring it to jars or a storage container. Refrigerate the chutney until ready to use.

Old-Fashioned Buttercrunch

V GF

MAKES ABOUT 2 POUNDS

I haven't found a better or more reliable version of this addictive treat than this one from cookbook author Nick Malgieri. Just follow the directions to the letter and you will be golden.

BUTTERCRUNCH

½ pound (2 sticks) unsalted butter, plus more for the pan
1½ cups sugar
3 tablespoons light corn syrup
1 cup chopped toasted almonds (see Cook's Note, page 258)

TOPPING

1 pound semisweet chocolate
1 cup chopped toasted almonds (see Cook's Note, page 258)

For the buttercrunch: Butter an 11 x 17-inch or 12 x 18-inch jelly roll pan and set aside.

In a medium saucepan, melt the butter. Remove from the heat and stir in the sugar, corn syrup, and 3 tablespoons water. Return to the heat and cook, stirring occasionally, until the mixture reaches 300°F on a candy thermometer. Remove from the heat, stir in the almonds, and pour out onto the buttered pan to cool and harden.

For the topping: Melt the chocolate in a double boiler over simmering water or in the microwave, heating at 50% power in 30-second increments and stirring after each until almost but not fully melted. Stir until smooth. Spread the chocolate on one side of the buttercrunch and sprinkle with half the chopped nuts. Allow to set, flip the slab, and repeat the coating on the other side. Cool the buttercrunch until completely set, then break it into irregular pieces and store in a tin.

Moscow Mule Kit

V V GF

SERVES 6

Here's a novel gift idea for someone who likes to entertain. Fill a decorative bottle with mint-flavored vodka and another with ginger simple syrup and present it to your favorite mixologist with a set of copper mugs and a handwritten copy of the recipe below.

1½ cups ice
1½ cups Mint-Flavored Vodka (recipe follows)
1½ cups Ginger Simple Syrup (recipe follows)
2 cups sparkling water
Fresh mint sprigs, for garnish
Lime slices, for garnish
Lemon slices, for garnish

For each cocktail: Fill a cocktail shaker with ¼ cup of the ice. Add ¼ cup of the mint-flavored vodka, ¼ cup of the ginger syrup, and ⅓ cup of the sparkling water. Shake and pour into a tall glass or flute. Garnish with fresh mint sprigs, lemon slices, and lime slices just before serving.

MINT-FLAVORED VODKA

MAKES 3 CUPS

2 large bunches of fresh mint
1 (750-ml) bottle vodka

Place the mint in a 2-quart pitcher. Pour the vodka over the mint and cover with plastic wrap. Allow the mixture to stand at room temperature for at least 3 days. Remove the mint and discard. Store in the freezer indefinitely.

GINGER SIMPLE SYRUP

MAKES 1½ CUPS

1 cup sugar
1 (3-inch) piece of fresh ginger, peeled and chopped

In a small saucepan, combine the sugar, 1 cup water, and the ginger over medium heat. Bring to a boil, reduce the heat, and simmer for 5 minutes, stirring occasionally, until the sugar has dissolved. Remove the pan from the heat and allow the syrup to cool, about 20 minutes. Strain the syrup and pour into a jar with a tight-fitting lid. It will keep for up to 2 weeks in the refrigerator.

Moscow Mule Kit

TREVOR

Smoky Fennel Salt

V V GF

MAKES ½ CUP

A jar of this seasoned salt makes grilled salmon or other fish sparkle. You can use fennel pollen or fennels seeds, but know that fennel pollen is much more intense.

2 teaspoons fennel pollen or fennel seeds
1 teaspoon smoked paprika
½ cup flaked salt, such as fleur de sel

Using a mortar and pestle or a small spice grinder, grind the fennel and paprika together. In a small bowl, stir the ground mixture into the salt. Store in an airtight container.

Citrus Lavender Hand Scrub

MAKES ABOUT 1 CUP

⅓ cup olive oil
1 tablespoon dried lavender
1 cup kosher salt
2 teaspoons grated lemon zest
1 tablespoon fresh lemon juice (from 1 lemon)

In a small saucepan over low heat, combine the olive oil and lavender and heat for about 5 minutes to warm the oil. Turn off the heat and allow the infused oil to cool to room temperature.

In a small bowl, combine the salt and the lemon zest and juice. Pour in the infused oil and stir to incorporate. Transfer the scrub to a glass jar or container with an airtight lid to store.

Peanut Butter Dog Bone Treats

MAKES 12 (5-INCH) TREATS OR 24 (3-INCH) TREATS

These nutty bones will earn you the everlasting devotion of canine companions.

Vegetable oil cooking spray
2 cups whole-wheat flour, plus more for dusting
½ cup rolled oats
1 tablespoon baking powder
1 cup creamy peanut butter, at room temperature
1 cup low-sodium chicken broth
¼ cup freshly grated Parmesan cheese

SPECIAL EQUIPMENT
1 (3- or 5-inch) bone-shaped cookie cutter

Place an oven rack in the center of the oven. Preheat the oven to 375°F. Spray a heavy baking sheet with vegetable oil spray or line with a silicone baking mat. Set aside.

In a large bowl, combine the flour, oats, and baking powder. Stir in the peanut butter and broth until the mixture forms a crumbly dough. Press the dough together to form a ball.

On a lightly floured work surface, knead the dough for 30 seconds until smooth. Roll out the dough into a 10-inch circle about ½ inch thick. Using the cookie cutter, cut out bone shapes and place on the prepared baking sheet (any scraps of dough can be formed into a ball and rerolled). Sprinkle with the Parmesan cheese.

Bake until golden, about 20 minutes or until firm and dry. Transfer to a wire rack and cool completely. Store in an airtight container for up to 1 week.

Acknowledgments

As always, the book in your hands reflects the efforts and contributions of many people. I am especially indebted to the intrepid band of visionaries who have been involved in the creation and publication of my digital magazine, *Giada Weekly*; it has been an amazing experience that brings new surprises, challenges, and, most of all, fun and excitement every single week as the new issue goes online. Profound thanks to:

Maya Mavjee, David Drake, and Ranjana Armstrong, who have supported my vision from the beginning;

Pam Krauss, Geraldine Campbell, Lindsey Galey, Nina Caldas, Derek Gullino, Amy Boorstein, Sally Franklin, Emily Pollack, Anna Mintz, Neil Spitkovsky, Kevin Jan, Amy Sly, Ian Dingman, Sonia Persad, Alex Martinez, and Kelli Tokos, who go above and beyond, week after week;

The talented photographers who have brought our stories to life: Ray Kachatorian, Lauren Volo, Tara Donne, Pernille Loof, Megan Fawn Schlow, and Quentin Bacon;

All those who contributed their wisdom and recipes to this collection, including my incomparable aunts Raffy and Carolyna, my mother, Veronica, my sister, Eloisa, as well as Alex Guarnaschelli, Mark Bittman, Frank Prisinzano, Bruce Weinstein and Mark Scarborough, Tara Maxey, Marco Canora, Ed Brown, Josh Tupper, and Dr. Michael Breus;

The exceptional members of "team Giada," who are with me every step of the way as I tackle new frontiers: Julie Morgan, Sam Saboura, Lish Steiling, Ashley Reed, and Natasha Wynnyk;

And, as ever, thanks to Eric Greenspan, Jon Rosen, and Suzanne Gluck, for sage counsel and friendship in equal measures.

Photography Credits

Mia Ardito: 172

Quentin Bacon: 85

Tara Donne: vi (bottom row middle), 5 (bottom row right), 27, 29, 30,59, 66 (bottom row right), 67, 86-87, 109, 126, 130-131, 146-147, 149, 155-156, 165 (bottom row right), 170, 189, 217, 224, 243, 246-247, 249, 255, 267, 274

Ray Kachatorian: 47, 61, 64, 94-95, 290-291, 312

Pernille Loof: 18, 32, 165 (top row right), 177, 185-186

Andrew Purcell: 160-161, 242, 244, 250, 269, 277

Jack Rigollet: vi (top row left), 12, 41, 46 (top left), 49, 81-82, 88, 98-99, 108 (bottom row right), 200, 206, 208, 218, 267, 272, 280

Megan Fawn Schlow: ii, vi (bottom row right), 58, 63, 80, 180, 227 (bottom row right) 234, 248, 252-253, 294-296, 300

Lauren Volo: vi (top row right, middle row left, middle row right, bottom row left), viii, 6-11, 13-14, 17, 19-22, 24-26, 28, 33, 36-39, 42-43, 45, 46 (bottom row right), 48, 50-54, 56, 62, 65, 66 (top left), 68, 71 (top row right, middle row left, bottom row left), 72-79, 83-84, 85, 89-93, 108 (top row right), 100-101, 104-107, 112-115, 117, 119-121, 123-128, 133-137, 139-140, 143, 150-154, 157-159, 162-163, 167-169, 171-176, 179, 182-184, 187, 191, 193-199, 201, 203, 207, 209-215, 220-221, 225, 229-230, 232-233, 235-241, 256, 259, 261-263, 266, 268, 270 271, 275-276, 278-79, 281, 283-286, 288, 293, 297-299, 301

Index

be good to yourself